LEN DEIGHTON was born in London in 1929. At seventeen he became a photographer attached to the RAF Special Investigations Branch. After his discharge in 1949 he did a variety of jobs and in 1952 won a scholarship to the Royal College of Art (of which he is now an elected Senior Fellow). While in New York City working as a magazine illustrator, he wrote his first novel, *The Ipcress File*. Published in 1962, it was a spectacular success and was made into a film starring Michael Caine as the English spy Harry Palmer.

Harry Palmer starred in several further Deighton novels: *Horse Under Water*, *Funeral in Berlin*, *Billion Dollar Brain*, *Spy Story* and *Twinkle, Twinkle, Little Spy*. In addition, Deighton wrote three trilogies featuring the character Bernard Samson: *Game*, *Set* and *Match*; *Hook*, *Line* and *Sinker,* and *Faith*, *Hope* and *Charity*, exploring treachery at the heart of post-war espionage. *Game*, *Set* and *Match* was made into a BBC series.

During his long and varied career, Deighton has been a historian, novelist, illustrator and cookery expert. His popular cookery strips were featured weekly in the *Observer* as 'Len Deighton's Cook Strip' and compiled into book format for the first time in 1965. Deighton left Britain in 1969 and now resides in Southern California.

Praise for *Action Cook Book*:

'Len Deighton's *Action Cook Book* is not a good cookbook. It is a shockingly good cookbook'   *Village Voice*

'How does one go about achieving some Harry Palmer style? Details first. Remember, Palmer is a gourmet, so get hold of the Len Deighton *Action Cook Book*'   *GQ* magazine

'[Len Deighton's cookbooks] have attracted cult following for their brilliant design as much as for their comprehensive approach to cooking … his democratising, demystifying approach couldn't be more appropriate'
Guardian

'Cooking as I'd never seen it: fun, cheeky, male and promising the awesome prospect of sex … The taut clarity of Deighton's writing, his encyclopaedic knowledge and attention to detail … The prose reads like Dashiell Hammett channelling Brillat-Savarin'
Waitrose Food Illustrated

'They showed the idiot novice male how to dice an onion without it falling apart; how to fine-cut parsley by rocking the blade rather than chopping it; how to sauté mushrooms without them yielding the water that would turn them into a gelatinous glop'
SIMON SCHAMA

ACTION COOK BOOK

Len Deighton's Guide to Eating

HARPER PERENNIAL

London, New York, Toronto, Sydney and New Delhi

Harper Perennial
An imprint of HarperCollins*Publishers*
77–85 Fulham Palace Road,
Hammersmith
London W6 8JB

www.harperperennial.co.uk
Visit our authors' blog at www.fifthestate.co.uk

This Harper Perennial edition published 2009

9 8 7 6 5 4 3 2 1

First published in hardback by Jonathan Cape in 1995

... Douglas asserts the moral right to
be ... as the author of this work

A ... record for this book is available from the British Library

ISBN 978-0-00-730587-2

CONTENTS

INTRODUCTION

I am delighted to have *Action Cook Book* republished. Now I can have a fresh new copy to replace the dog-eared old one that is on a shelf in our kitchen. Of all the books I have written none of them is dearer to me or more personal than this one. Although the 'cook strips' ran in the *Observer* newspaper for many years they were not created for publication; they were just my notes.

I grew up with an interest in food and cooking. My mother had been a professional chef and, during my six years as a student, I had enjoyed vacation jobs in the kitchens of some top restaurants. I had acquired a small library of cookery books, including some of the classic ones, and I didn't want to see them become stained or gravy-spattered. It was for this reason that I never took them into the kitchen. Having carefully noted the details of each recipe, I pinned these up over the stove. I was an art student and it was inevitable that the notes included little diagrams and drawings. During a dinner party, Ray Hawkey, a graphics specialist who was at the time radically changing newspaper design, came into the kitchen and spotted the fluttering collection of recipe notes. He suggested that they could be published if they were more carefully drawn and my scribbled lettering replaced by that of a lettering expert. It was Ray who added the grid and generally supervised the improvements. Through Ray I found a lettering artist who was creative and resourceful. It was not an easy task for him, and I soon found that it was best to let him do the lettering first, and then fit my drawings into the spaces. This is why some of the pots, pans and basins are of unorthodox shapes.

The next hurdle was to convince the Features Editor of the *Observer* that he would get a reliable and continuous supply of the strips. I was not a journalist and had very little previous contact with newspaper people, who seemed to suspect that all artists were unreliable drunkards. To build up a credible supply of cook strips I retrieved old notes from where they had been stuffed behind the flour bin on the top shelf. For this reason the early recipes were mostly the ones that I liked best and had cooked regularly. And this is why *Action Cook Book* remains so personal.

But as the first set of notes was used, I became more systematic in selecting recipes and I devoted a lot of time to testing them in my cramped kitchen. I was dismayed to find how many well-established recipes simply didn't work. They had been copied from cookbook to cookbook by writers and journalists who were too busy to put them to the test. I turned to cooks I admired, whether they were experienced professionals or accomplished amateurs; French, German or British. I was delighted to find that almost all of them were prepared to share their skills and secrets. My mother was a superb cook but never consulted recipes nor wrote them. The steak and kidney pudding and the English trifle are samples of my mother's recipes and they remain favourites of mine. The Christmas pudding won the BBC Cookery Club prize when a Mrs Dashfield reintroduced the old idea of using soft breadcrumbs to lighten the texture and make a pudding which even foreigners enjoy. At the time this was a radical innovation but now almost all recipes use breadcrumbs. I remember that Mrs Dashfield expressed regret that I'd put the rum butter recipe into the same cook strip as she thought it did not go with the pudding. Mrs Dashfield was a purist.

Publication of the cook strips in the *Observer* did influence cooking, mostly by advocating better ingredients instead of the inferior wartime substitutes that were still widely used. For instance, the reputation of bread and butter pudding had sunk out of sight; it was the last resort of cost-conscious school meals and factory canteens. Tom Maschler – who later published *Action Cook Book* – first declined this pudding when I brought it to the table at a party. I was gratified later to watch him scraping the tin for his third helping, and hear him explain that at his school they had not included cream, eggs or real vanilla in the recipe. Crème caramel and many other traditional English milk puddings, restored to the glory they'd enjoyed a generation earlier, were always dinner party successes.

Although my interest in food preparation has always been grounded in the discipline of French cooking, these recipes do not reflect that. These are my old favourites. A fisherman in Portugal taught me how to cook squid. In the London suburb of Hampstead I watched a Viennese grandmother produce a superb cheesecake using a recipe from her childhood. (She made a Sachertorte too but I never attempted that.) While working as a waiter in Piccadilly, I learned from a Hungarian cook that making strudel dough was not a daunting task or even a very lengthy one. It was a French publisher who introduced me to cooking fish in red wine and, although it was a well-established method, I had more correspondence about that than about anything else. Not all of my readers were appalled but many were.

Ris de veau, tripe, brains, tongue and the rich fragrant stew that only oxtail produces were all dishes my mother had shown me how to cook, for during the war these were available in addition to the meat ration.

I've always been enormously fond of eels and scallops. The huge cassoulet had been the subject of passionate disagreements between neighbours when I was in rural France. Mutton? Salt pork? The *confit d'oie*? Even the beans were disputed. Each one I served was substantially different. And still is.

Cooking, together with all other aspects of food, has always been a very important part of my family life. When my children were of pre-school age we taught them to make a loaf of bread. This meant learning about using weights and liquid measures and about the necessary temperatures for yeast and for baking. After the loaf of bread was eaten I challenged them to do the whole process again, this time after converting to metric measures. Recently one of my sons said that of all the things they learnt when young, nothing had been more interesting or more useful than learning to cook.

My entire family shares my great interest in food. I very much hope you will enjoy these dishes – cooking them, serving them and eating them – as much as I have done.

Len Deighton

In addition to ° F, temperatures are also listed in 'Regulo' (eg. 'Regulo 3'). This is a trademark for a type of temperature control on some gas ovens.

READ THIS FIRST

I have assumed little or no knowledge on the part of my reader; on the other hand I have learnt enough while doing the research for this book to claim that even the serious student of good food (only some of whom are cooks) will learn enough to justify reading it. Throughout this **ACTION COOK BOOK** I have given the classic recipes for the dishes without substitutes or short cuts except where I have stated otherwise. All I have cut out is the smoke-screen of mystique and witch-doctory; professional cooks have no time for that and neither, I suggest, have you. Everywhere I have suggested that the reader ask the shop to prepare food for cooking, e.g. fish, lobster, poultry, etc. This does not mean that the cook should not know how to do it; it means that watching an expert do it is the best way to learn. Things that I can't get your local shopkeeper to show you (like making a roux) I have described. If you can find an expert at making pastry or a sauce, have them show you. If you can find an expert at all other aspects of cooking – who needs a book?

ALL YOU NEED TO KNOW ABOUT NUTRITION

With advice from Dr V. Radclyffe

Nutrition is something no cook can ignore. Here the subject is reduced to a few words but only by over-simplifying. In each group which I have mentioned, I have selected only the good sources and ignored the hundreds of foods with lesser amounts of nutrients. If a food is omitted from this list it does not mean that it is not necessary to a normal diet. These are the good sources of body-building foods. Remember them, buy them and eat them.

Protein. This is essential every day for the normal action of the body (movement, respiration, etc.). Animal protein is the best (beef, veal, etc.), but vegetable protein is also good in dried peas, lentils, haricot beans and nuts (especially peanuts). Fish protein is as rich as meat. Two other good sources are dried egg, dried skim milk.

You could live on meat alone, but you would need 17 lb. per day. So, instead, we turn to the high-energy foods (i.e. carbohydrates and fats); but neither of these are body-building foods.

Calcium. This is a builder of bones and teeth. It is vital during the first six months of life and remains important throughout life for replacement. Cheese (Cheddar-type) and whitebait (surprisingly) are the two finest sources. Next come sardines and the soft cheeses and condensed milk, with fresh milk, watercress and tinned salmon at about one-third of the value per ounce that Cheddar cheese gives.

Iron. This is important for haemoglobin (the red in red blood-cells). The best way to get iron is to cook in iron cooking utensils.* Once a week you should have a portion of undercooked liver. If you don't like it, get to like it – you need it. The sausage called 'black pudding' and any sort of kidney is a good source, so are cocoa and lentils. Curry powder is chock-a-block with it (21 mgs. per oz.), but an ounce of curry powder goes a long way, so it won't give you so much per serving.

Vitamins. There is no need to take vitamin pills if you are eating well, for the body adjusts its intake to the correct proportions for health.

---

* *Strange but true.*

Vitamin A. Important for cell-growth, especially cells of eye, mouth and intestines. It aids the retina in vision. Best sources are undoubtedly fish-liver oils (which are sold in chemists'). Sheep and beef liver also contain Vitamin A, but only one per cent of the amount the best fish liver does (measured ounce for ounce). If your diet is Western and adequate, you are getting enough.

Vitamin B. A large complex, covering many groups of chemicals. It is vital for the working of all muscles and nerves, and is needed in large quantities when convalescing from influenza, colds, pneumonia. If you eat much starch and sugar, you use Vitamin B to convert these foods into energy. Therefore, you need even more Vitamin B. Eat liver, lean meat, peas, whole-grain bread or flour, and lentils.

Vitamin C. This is needed daily because it cannot be stored. It is important in forming the connective tissue between cells. Gums, joints and muscles weaken when there is a deficiency of it. The best sources in order of descending value are: blackcurrants, or blackcurrant juice, brussels sprouts, cabbage, watercress (and other green vegetables) and citrus fruits. Remember Vitamin C is washed away by water and destroyed by heat.

Vitamin D. Important in the formation of bone and therefore growth. It also keeps the bone hard in normal wear and tear. We make it in our skin in sunlight (but we destroy some Vitamin B), and therefore need more Vitamin-D-rich foods in winter. They are the fish-liver oils (especially tuna and halibut), with cod-liver oil also a source. Certain whole fish are also rich sources, namely herring, sardine, pilchard and salmon. There are two other sources, but they are comparatively poor (about one-sixtieth of the poorest of the above foods); they are egg yolk, and the type of margarine that has added vitamin.

Carbohydrates and Fats. The eating of these is proportionate to the sophisticated wealth (but not health) of a person. If you care enough to read this book, you are probably sophisticated and wealthy and already cutting down on these foods.

Our civilization has developed a craving for starches. Starch gives a fast lift, because it is the upper intestine where the enzymes act upon starches and give a rise in blood sugar with its allaying of appetite within twenty minutes. The digestive enzymes that act upon protein do it when the middle intestine is reached, thus it is slower in allaying appetite.

Salt is a mineral ($NaCl$) of which the sodium (Na) is the part the body needs. Sodium occurs naturally, by permeation through the land-mass, in any fish, vegetable or food that is produced within 200 miles of the sea. Therefore only people living in the centre of a huge land-mass need salt, and in these regions one finds salt-traders bringing this life-giving food. Most people in the world use salt only as a luxury.

Salt is one of the most important elements in complex actions in the blood, and although it is true that if you lose sodium you lose weight, salt-restriction must not be used in slimming diets. Any chemist will sell you KCl (potassium chloride) as a salt-substitute, but this is a dangerous expedient, for the body cannot distinguish between K and Na, and will excrete Na, creating a sodium lack and a potassium build-up, which can lead to serious disorders. Use 'salt-free salts' only under medical supervision, if at all. Cooks preparing salt-free food should step up herb and spice content to help cloak the blandness of such a diet.

If you want to lose weight. Starch foods are cheap foods. It is very expensive to eat a non-fattening diet. If you want to lose weight, remember these four points:

1 *Eat plenty of meat, fish and eggs, and you will find that (owing to specific dynamic action) you will be less hungry.*

2 *When eating ask: 'Am I hungry?' When you are not, stop eating.*

3 *It is hard, hard to remove fat once it has formed.*

On a good diet (i.e. not too quick) it is the fourth and fifth weeks which show the true loss of fat. The loss during the first two weeks is mostly fluid and is only too easily picked up again.

4 *Eat two good protein meals a day. Do not have tasters or snacks. Don't cheat.*

Construct your diet around things you don't like. Don't cut out things you are very fond of and tell yourself it's only for a few weeks – it's far better to guide your eating habits into more sensible patterns. The things you must not eat should be left unbought, otherwise they provide a constant temptation. Lastly, remember that most of the world have a diet problem of a different sort: they are hungry.

WHO NEEDS A REFRIGERATOR?

Refrigeration doesn't destroy bacteria. A small refrigerator from which cold air escapes when the door is opened subjects the contents to a fluctuating temperature – one of the quickest ways to turn food bad. Keeping the door closed, however, makes the air inside go stale. The greatest benefit a refrigerator can bestow is a supply of ice. Most refrigerators in common use provide six or eight cubes, then take three hours to make another set. In America there is an ice-making machine; until Britain discovers it, it is a good idea to order a few pounds of ice cubes from an ice company, so that guests can have more than half a cube each in their glass. Crushed ice as a bed under a large plate of oysters, or in a bucket with a couple of bottles of Chablis, will work more efficiently than an overcrowded fridge and be appetizing on the table.

If buying a refrigerator for the first time, note that an absorption type uses over twice as much electricity and has a less efficient freezer than the compression type. On the other hand the former are silent, and the latter will need repairs and replacements now and again. Look at the cubic capacity (ignore the size of shelf space – it doesn't mean a thing), and ask about ice-making capacity and speed. Your refrigerator should be in the coolest, most draughty place in the kitchen. Heat will rise from it, so don't have it in the bottom of the larder.

DEFROSTING: This is necessary when the ice on the freezing compartment is about a quarter of an inch thick – probably about once a week.

1 Remove food.
2 Disconnect supply.
3 Empty freezer of ice and frozen food.
4 Place a tray of boiling water inside refrigerator.
5 Wait. Let all ice melt, don't prod it.
6 Wipe shelves and inside with a damp rag (with a trace of vinegar).
7 Switch on, replace food.

AUTOMATIC DEFROSTING: This switches current off when a certain temperature is reached, and then switches on again. I am not convinced that this is a good way to treat food, even though it is much easier than normal defrosting as above.

WHEN YOU GO AWAY: Empty, switch off, leave door open.

Frozen Food. Frozen-food fanatics (I am not one) should choose their refrigerator with particular care. Frozen food in the retailer's cabinet is kept at 0° F. If it rises even a little above this, it must be eaten within 24 hours. Few refrigerators have a compartment as cold as this, even if you turn the main control to below normal. (You shouldn't do this as it will affect the main compartment.) Ask for a demonstration that involves a thermometer.

No matter what fancy-looking doors it may have the only real combined refrigerator/deep freeze is one that has one separate unit for each compartment. Check on this before buying. If you find a refrigerator that passes the 0° F. test, you still must get the frozen food home before it begins to thaw. Wrapping it in plenty of newspaper will insulate it.

Using Frozen Food. You do not have to store frozen food at 0° F. providing that it is used within a day or so. Many frozen vegetables are pre-cooked before freezing. These are best cooked by popping the whole solid block into a saucepan in which there is already a trace of boiling water. Put a well-fitting lid on, give it a few minutes over a medium flame. I have found that the directions on the frozen-food products often suggest too long a cooking time. Overcooked vegetables are awful; overcooked frozen vegetables are hell.

Frozen fruit should not be thawed too early or it will lose colour very quickly. Serve fresh dessert fruits still a little icy. Poultry and fish should be gently thawed before cooking. Among the most useful frozen foods are the sea foods (scampi, shrimps and whitebait), and frozen puff pastry is very nearly as good as home-made.

USING THE REFRIGERATOR

Food will dry out in the refrigerator. Aluminium foil, plastic boxes or polythene bags will keep separate items more moist, but they must not be placed to block the easy flow of air or the air will go stale. Liquids should be kept covered because they evaporate and the freezing unit then frosts up more quickly. That's why nothing hot must go in the refrigerator. One bad piece of food will contaminate all the others, and fish or other strong smells will make cream, butter, etc.

taste, unless kept covered. Minced meat should be spread out, not piled up, or air particles trapped inside will go stale. Meat (cooked or raw) should have at least an hour at room temperature before use, and ideally, raw meat should not be refrigerated between purchase and cooking. Cooked food is best kept refrigerated.

HANGING. Although all meat, all fish and birds undergo a similar change when 'hung', it is usual in Western cookery to hang only beef, game and mutton. The item should be put not in a refrigerator but in a cool draughty place where air circulates freely, while the bacteria in the flesh break it down and tenderize it, making it far more flavourful. Hang your meat before cooking it; two days will improve it enormously. Frozen chickens are frozen very soon after being killed. They should never be eaten immediately after thawing. Leave them a day or so. Hung meat often develops a faint musty smell, but this is not the smell of putrefaction, which is a stink so powerful it will force you out of the kitchen. If you are sniffing anxiously at a range of three inches, it's good to eat – you couldn't get that near to bad meat.

Milk and cream must be kept covered. Eggs do not need refrigeration. If you do keep them in the refrigerator, give them an hour at room temperature before use. Batter mixture and any sort of uncooked pastry will be better for a couple of hours of refrigeration. Flaky or puff pastry can be put into the cold for half an hour between rollings. White and rosé wines should be cold, but not so cold as to be tasteless. Cooling in an ice bucket is better than in the refrigerator, and in any case, don't put wine near the freezer nor store it in the refrigerator. Lager can be left in the refrigerator, so can light ale, which responds to chilling very well. If your beer pours out cloudy, however, it is too cold. Among other drinks which improve with chilling, tomato juice and fresh orange juice rank high. Avocado pears and salad vegetables can be served cold. Cucumber is better if not put into the cold. Lettuce should be torn gently apart (cutting turns it brown), the leaves washed and then dried with a cloth (moisture dilutes the dressing) before popping into the cold. Cheese is better stored in a cool place than in a refrigerator. Camembert-type cheese can be irreparably spoiled by refrigeration. Bread can be kept cold if in plenty of foil, but it's better to use it as you buy it. Don't refrigerate cereals, cakes, or dry foods like salt, sugar, flour or dried fruit.

Ice cream bought in a shop will melt in the domestic refrigerator. Ice cream can be made in the freezer, but tiny daggers of ice will form in it unless it is stirred from time to time.

THE SECRET WEAPON IN THE KITCHEN: THE BLENDER

The Blender is a set of whirling knives in a heat-proof glass goblet. It will not: beat egg white, whip cream, crush ice, grind raw meat or extract juice, and is not used for cake- or sponge-making. It will, however, grind dry ingredients to dust (if left long enough), or it will grind even more efficiently food particles that are in liquid. If this doesn't sound very useful, let me elaborate.

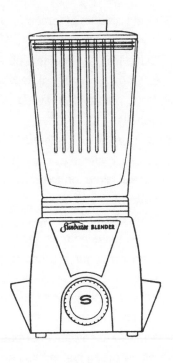

This wonderful machine will

1 Grind dry rice into rice flour.
2 Make sugar into powdered sugar for dusting over fruit pie.
3 Chop nuts, etc. (make your own ground almonds).
4 Grind coffee.
5 Grind cornflakes or cracker-style biscuits for base or tops for cheesecake, pies, cakes, etc.
6 Make fresh, soft breadpieces into wonderful absorbent breadcrumbs for dressings and stuffings (I know no other way to do this).
7 Mix hot drinks (sprinkle Horlicks, cocoa on to boiling milk to which sugar has been added).
8 Whisk the skin on boiled milk back into the milk.
9 Froth milk for coffee (for people who like it like that).

10 Make mayonnaise (put all ingredients except oil into goblet, switch on. Pour oil in gently, add capers etc. if you wish).

11 Make vinaigrette dressing (beware: it will emulsify if you aren't quick).

12 Make bindings for terrines, pâtés, hamburgers, meat loaf, etc. (put egg + piece of raw onion + garlic + salt + pepper + herbs, etc., into blender. Mix. Add to meat mixture).

13 Rescue lumpy sauces (pour hot lumpy sauce into goblet, flick switch to remove lumps. N.B. Too long will make sauce go thin. It seems to reduce thickening power of the flour).

14 Make any kind of milk shake or malted milk (fruit + ice cream + milk).

15 Make potato pancakes (pieces of raw potato + egg + seasoning + flour + enough milk to moisten. Flatten into thin pancakes. Fry golden).

16 Grate chunks of lemon or orange rind (no pith now).

17 Make fruit or vegetable purées for infants (save a lot of money here) or for vegetable soups.

18 Chop parsley (remove stalks first; don't overfill goblet).

19 Make sandwich spreads (use sardines + lemon juice + butter + raw onion + parsley. Blend and spread direct on to bread. Use cream cheese + butter + mustard + onion in the same way. You'll think of hundreds more).

20 Make sauces for ice cream. Try plenty of almonds + brown sugar + apricot brandy + a little cream.

21 Make anchovy sauce (for fish or pasta). Blend lots of olive oil + garlic + tin of anchovy fillets + parsley + stoned olives.

22 Make orange sauce for basting a duck. Blend a whole orange, skin, pips and all; but chop it before

you put it in. Don't serve this, just use it in the cooking.

23 Make Pots de Crème. Really sensational as a short cut. You must try this. Put a bar of plain chocolate + 2 tablespoons sugar + a splash of vanilla + an egg + pinch of salt, into blender; when it's blended pour in 6 oz. of almost boiling milk. When it's mixed, pour into tiny pots (demi-tasse cups) and chill for at least three hours.

24 Cream spinach with egg and cream – reheat gently.

25 Sieve flour. Did you ever wonder why recipe books tell you to sieve flour? When was the last time you found any solid particles in it? You never did. The object of sieving flour is to aerate it. A blender does this in three seconds; you need never sieve flour again.

Are you convinced that this is the most useful tool in the kitchen? If not, let me tell you one last thing. After you use it, pour water in, flick the switch and the blender will clean itself.

BLENDER SOUPS

Vichyssoise: Fry the white parts of 3 leeks and a medium-size onion very gently in butter – they must not brown. (Pressure) cook after adding two chopped potatoes and a pint of some sort of white stock. Blend; chill; add cream just before serving.

Potato Soup: As Vichyssoise, but no leek; lots of potato. Use this Vichyssoise recipe to make similar soups from: skinned tomato (or sieve after), celery, asparagus, spinach, peas, carrots or mushrooms. Or indeed from combinations of them. Potato can be used to make any of them thick (as it did the Vichyssoise) and a few larger pieces can be added as a garnish after blending. These can all be served chilled, but in this case, go easy on the butter. Yoghourt can be substituted for the cream, so can sour cream.

Borscht: To one good-sized cooked beetroot, put ¾ pint any stock (a tin of bouillon is O.K.), also 2 tablespoons sour cream, 2 tablespoons lemon juice, generous salt, a piece of lemon peel and a sprinkle of pepper (paprika is good). Blend this; you will probably have to do it in two batches. Serve it hot or iced, but either way, lash the top with sour cream.

Cucumber Soup is just cucumber (cooked soft) blended with white stock (you can use clear chicken soup), sour cream and seasoning.

Watercress Soup: Cook flour and butter in equal quantities for three minutes; add bouillon + watercress; blend; serve.

BLENDER SAVOURIES

Savoury Mousse, otherwise a marathon, is simple with a blender. The basis can be cooked ham, crab, lobster, poultry or fish (tinned if necessary). It is blended with a third of its volume of a good white sauce (made by cooking equal quantities of butter and flour together over a low flame – it must not brown – and adding stock or milk or cream). The mixture is then put into a mould and chilled. Experts argue about adding some gelatine. If you do so, dissolve it according to directions on packet, making it a little weaker than instructed, and blend into mousse mixture before chilling.

Quenelles: There is one recipe where the blender really takes the stage, that is in making quenelles, which are something between a soufflé and a dumpling. Without a blender this recipe requires hours of pounding in a mortar. With a blender, merely select the flavour you want: veal, fish, chicken, game, etc., and proceed: Measure 15 oz. (by bulk, *see* Measuring section, page 30) of soft breadcrumbs (easy to make in a dry blender). Now put 5 oz. milk in with the breadcrumbs, let it whizz a moment, then tip it out; put it to one side. Don't bother to clean the blender; put into it half a pound of the raw ingredients you have chosen (if it's to be fish, use salmon, whiting, sole, pike, trout or brill – remove skin and bone, of course). Add two teaspoons of salt and a dash of pepper and nutmeg. Whizz the blender until it is all a smooth paste, then add 3 oz. of soft (not melted) butter, one whole egg and two extra yolks, and the milk-and-breadcrumb mixture. When it is all quite smooth, the quenelle mixture is made. Drop spoonfuls of it into just simmering water for ten minutes. Lift out gently. Taste the first one and adjust seasoning.

Here is a simpler (and a little less authentic) **Quenelles de Poisson.** Use one pound of white fish fillets (that saves the boning and skinning), cut them into small pieces and put them into the blender along with a chunk of onion, a teaspoon of salt, a pinch of pepper and four eggs. Whizz the blender until all this is quite smooth, then add 4 oz. of double cream. If your blender is small, you may have to do it in two stages.

Have a tin of fancy cream soup on the simmer (lobster bisque or cream of mushroom), having diluted it with milk. Drop the quenelles gently into the simmering soup. This mixture is a little sloppier than the previous one, but the quenelles get firmer as they cook. Don't boil the soup; just keep it very hot.

Sauce Normande: For a sauce to go with the quenelles, try this: it is not quite the Sauce Normande it pretends to be, but it will pass in a crowd. Make a strong white stock of a suitable kind (i.e. for fish quenelles use plenty of white fish, include the heads – *see* Rich Stock grid). Reduce it to ¾ pint to make it strong. When it is ready, add this to a roux (which is equal amounts – say 1 oz. – of butter and flour cooked over a low flame without going brown for three or four minutes). When you add the fish stock a little at a time to the roux, it will thicken. Stir it and watch that it doesn't go lumpy (if it does go lumpy you can give it a second or so in the blender, but it is much better not to have to). Let it have a quarter of an hour over a low flame; you must not go away and leave it, but you can

be mixing an egg yolk into 3 oz. of cream. Add this to the sauce, stirring it well in. If it boils, it will curdle and nothing can save you. If it doesn't curdle pour it over the quenelles and serve. If it does curdle, pour it over the quenelles and serve them by candlelight.

Croquettes are distant relations of quenelles, but croquettes are made from *cooked* meat or fish. I will give a general style of recipe, but there are a great many variations. For the best croquettes do not use leftover fish – cook it specially in a good fish stock (just a little lemon juice, salt and pepper, and a bay leaf is better than plain water). Remove the flesh, mash carefully (avoid the bones). Blend it. Add to this a Béchamel sauce (which is a roux into which boiling milk has been poured a little at a time while it thickens to a good creamy white sauce). Make some Duchesse potato (*see* page 249). Mix the fish, the Béchamel and the potato together – the fish should predominate. Dip in egg (and breadcrumbs if you like). Shallow-fry. Variations on croquettes are at your discretion. Anchovy and chopped onion are good additions.

Remember that white fish needs a colourful vegetable or garnish.

Real Horseradish Sauce. Horseradish pieces (2 oz.) + 1 teaspoon sugar + ½ teaspoon salt + ½ teaspoon mustard + tablespoon vinegar + 3 tablespoons milk. Blend. Mix generous cream into it. Serve.

To prepare **Steak au Poivre** for 6–8 people, blend briefly about 5 dessertspoons whole peppercorns. Press on to steaks. Fry them to your taste. Remove steaks, déglacer pan.

BLENDER SWEETS

Egg Custard is especially simple with a blender. Blend sugar, hot milk, cream and eggs (at least 3 eggs per pint of milk). Bake 45 mins. in a water-jacket at Regulo 2 (325° F.). Egg custard as a sauce has the same ingredients, but is made over a low flame, stirring all the time. For further instructions, *see* the Crème Caramel pages 276–7.

Various Desserts. *Fruit Fool* is made by putting almost any soft fruit with sugar and thick cream in the blender; chill; serve. The Fruit Fool recipe will give you *ice cream* if you put it in the freezing compartment. Instead of soft fruit, use chocolate or very strong coffee to make coffee or chocolate ice cream.

MEASURING

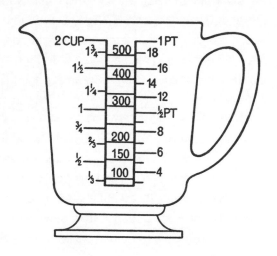

The greatest source of confusion in cookery measurements is the American cup. Most English measurements are in weight, but now and again we hear of the English cup. In each case **'a cup'** is half a pint, but the English pint is 20 oz. and the American pint is 16 oz.

Buy any sort of measure that is marked in ounces. A 10-oz. measure is a convenient size for the average kitchen. Once you have a measure of this sort, the American recipes are easy to understand.

Here are five items showing what one English pound equals in American cups:

Butter	1 lb. = 2 cups
Flour	1 lb. = 4½ cups
Sugar	1 lb. = 2+ cups
	(brown moist sugar 2½ cups)
Raw Rice	1 lb. = 2 cups
Crumbs	1 lb. = 4 cups

Another baffling word in recipes is **gill**. In standard recipe use it means a quarter of a British pint.

French recipes use **litres**. One litre is 1¾ British pints. A demi-litre is half a litre. A deci-litre is a tenth of a litre.

French recipes measure weight in **grammes**.

100 grammes = 3½ oz.
1 litre = 500 grammes = 1 lb. 1½ oz.
1 kilogramme = 1,000 grammes = 2 lb. 3 oz.

BUYING FOOD

Buying food can be confusing. Spinach, for instance, will shrink to almost nothing, while rice can be around the house for days because of miscalculation.

Meat. Buy 8 oz. per head if there is bone in it, and 6 oz. per head if it is without bone. Very lean meat in a rich sauce (e.g. Beef Strogonoff) can have less. Allow 12 oz. per head of the gross weight of chicken, and 4 oz. per head for any liver dish. Fish, as an entrée 6 oz., as a main course 8 oz.

Root Vegetables like carrots and potatoes should be calculated at 6 oz. per head. Double this amount for peas, and for spinach allow 14 oz. per head.

Dried Vegetables (beans, lentils, peas, rice). Allow 2 oz. per head, and the same for pasta, unless it is to be the main course, in which case double it.

Soup. Allowing 8 oz. of soup per person should leave a dribble for some greedy guest to get a second helping.

Dried Fruit. One pound of dried fruit is equal to four pounds of fresh.

SALT

Add half a teaspoon salt to half a pound of meat or to one pint of soup or sauce. For dough put half a teaspoon salt to one pound of flour. Always adjust seasoning before serving.

HEAT

The following figures are most important, especially to cooks using a thermostat control.

Water:	Fast boil 212° F. (Salt water boils at 224° F.)
	Simmer 205° F.
	Slow simmer 180–190° F.
Milk:	Boils at 196° F.

Burning Temperature

Butter	278° F.
Beef Suet	356° F.
Lard	392° F.
Veg. Oil	480–520° F.
Olive Oil	554° F.

Keep temperature below this level when cooking in these fats.

UTENSILS

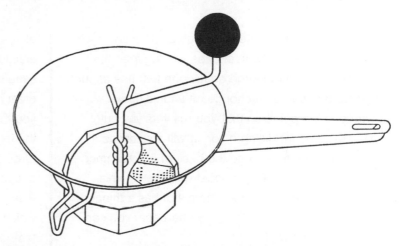

My kitchen is full of useless junk – gadgets that looked like a good idea at the time. Here is my list of the items that I still use, in the hope that it will save your money and temper. When you decide what you need, buy the very best quality there is. Sometimes you will do best to go to the shops that sell to the catering trade, where the equipment may lack bright colours and fancy decoration but will be of better and more enduring quality.

Stainless-steel knives are not much good to any cook. Buy three good-quality steel ones varying from the tiny vegetable knife to the large heavy one that has enough weight to be used as a chopper; it should curve upwards to the point, so that you roll it as you cut.

Use this one for dicing onion. It will also divide a chicken into pieces. Or use the back of it to hammer at a steak or escalope. Buy at least one filleting knife which looks exactly like the others, but has a thinner and more flexible blade. Buy any sharpener you can use, and use it often.

A really good bread knife is most useful. Get one with a saw edge – use it for all sorts of kitchen jobs – it slices tomatoes particularly well.

You probably have a peeler. I find that stainless-steel ones are best, although difficult to get. It is extraordinary how hard the catering shops try to force inefficient stainless-steel knives on the customer, while all the other kitchen gadgets that would benefit from stainless steel are both hard to find and ridiculously expensive. For instance, a stainless-steel strainer is a great help. The conical ones are called 'Chinois' and give you the greatest area of strainer for size – this speeds the job. A French Moulin, which is a strainer with a turning device to force things along, is a wonderful gadget. Two less necessary gadgets are poultry shears – very powerful scissors – and a roasting thermometer which you leave in the meat so that it registers the temperature at the centre of the meat. This is a dead certain way of timing the joint. Two very large serving plates are useful. You can put all the vegetables on one plate, or surround the roast meat with the vegetables. Junk shops are full of these huge plates – buy one.

Get one really good tin-opener. The sort that fix to the wall are best. Whatever sort of purist you are, you are going to open a lot of tins over the next decade. Fix another light in the kitchen – I bet it needs more light.

We all know that saucepans should be thick and heavy and all that jazz, but let me suggest that you buy those with two little metal handles instead of one long burnable plastic one. These saucepans can be put in the oven, which for my money is well worth the penalty that the handles get hot. So the next thing you need is half a dozen thick oven cloths. Those like gloves are very good. You know what I think about blenders: they are wonderful – save up to buy one. Refrigerators are far less important in my opinion and by no means a necessity for the work that many kitchens do.

The butcher will give you a handful of short skewers if you ask him. Use them to hold the joint together; a roasted piece of beef will taste better if you remove it from the bone only just before you cook it. Rolling it and jabbing the skewers in is easy, and you won't have that huge piece of fat inside that the craftier butchers insert. Better still, and even easier, cook the joint still on the bone. Certain joints lend themselves to stuffing, e.g. shoulder of lamb, breast of lamb, leg of lamb or pork. In these cases secure the flap over the stuffing with the skewers. Many experts still use needle and thread, but this is tedious work. These skewers will rust. Dry them carefully after washing. Long (12-in.) skewers are great for kebab: simple, yet most impressive. The authentic ones are flat in section, most of the ones on sale in England are like a piece of wire. They will do. The kebab skewer conducts heat through the centre of the meat, etc., while the outside is being grilled. For this reason wooden skewers are no good for kebab. In the same way potatoes roasted in their jackets will cook more quickly with a couple of short skewers (or nails) run into them (remove before serving).

For maximum efficiency, have two scales: one to weigh small amounts under one pound, the other one for joints of meat. You can do without the latter one if you make a note of the weight of the meat before leaving the butcher's shop. It is important to be able to measure volume as well as weight. A simple transparent plastic measure will do as long as you remember this:

An American pint is 16 oz.
A British one is 20 oz.
A standard cup is half a pint.
Measure therefore according to the nationality of the recipe (*see* Measuring section).

A double boiler is one of the most used kitchen items. It gives a gentle all-round heat by surrounding the cooking vessel with a jacket of hot but not boiling water. It can be simply improvised by putting a basin in a saucepan. On a larger scale a water-container into which saucepans are placed on the stove is called a bain-marie. Mostly seen in restaurants, it keeps sauces at a gentle heat without spoiling. The same principle is applied, inside the oven, for terrines and Crème Caramel (*see* page 276). In using a water-jacket prevent the base of the inner container from resting flat on the bottom of the water-container. If it does, the contact will conduct heat directly and make the water-jacket useless.

A heat diffuser is another way of spreading the heat under a pan. It is very useful, for even the best-organized cooks sometimes face the problem of keeping something warm without spoiling it. If you are brave enough to put earthenware pots on the gas (manufacturers swear they will endure it), you probably already use a mat. Earthenware pots come in all shapes and sizes, both English and French. One really huge one is worth having – cassoulet for less than a dozen is not worth the bother. Make sure the lid fits well.

A cast-iron casserole with a heavy lid is another useful utensil for slow cooking inside the oven, or on top. A marmite is a tall narrow pot designed to present a small surface of liquid and therefore a low rate of evaporation. This is used for long cooking of stocks. A marmite can be made of anything, but the one I like best is a stainless-steel model.

Stoves have now begun to improve dramatically with the import of the transatlantic models. I particularly like the built-in oven units. They can be installed at eye-level, and the interior light and glass door become really useful. The Moffat has a built-in meat thermometer which makes meat cooking a simple and precise science, for the timer rings when the centre of the meat is done. With the built-in oven comes the table-top counter unit, a stainless-steel platform containing four cooking rings which can be gas or electric. This means you can have an electric oven with gas rings, which I personally think is the best of both worlds.

A flour dredger – a thing like a huge pepper pot – makes flouring meat or fish very simple.

An egg whisk is an essential thing. Have whatever kind you like best. There is a device called a Horlicks mixer (a plunger in a straight-sided glass) which beats egg whites better than anything else I know.

A wire rack for cooling is useful.

Have at least one terrine. It can be used for a small stew.

Tins: A pie dish, flan tin, loaf tin (great for pork pies) and a cake tin.

One really good ladle (stainless steel if possible). The decorated porcelain ones are fine for the table, but too fragile for the cook.

A mandoline is a slicing device. Buy it if you do enough slicing, or would do enough if you had it.

A big, kitchen-size pepper mill is a basic necessity. If you can afford another for the table, do so.

A wire basket (panier à salade) gets a lot of the moisture off lettuce, but the leaves should still be dabbed dry or the water will dilute the dressing. Use the basket (plastic ones are no good) to dry out celery leaves, save them to put into stew, etc.

A wooden spoon doesn't get hot, nor does it scratch the pan. Use it when making scrambled egg to prove this. The best kind have a square corner on the bowl to get into the corners.

A really thick, good-quality chopping board will last for ever. Keep it wiped down and clean, and you will be able to use it for bread. Whisk it away after the main course and it reappears with cheese on. Or you can buy three.

Buy a good omelette pan. Keep it clean, use it just for

omelettes. It must be made from heavy-gauge metal. Warm it before use.

Any really large dish or bowl will do for the salad – you don't have to have a wooden one which is very expensive. Keep it only for salad and serve a salad as frequently as possible.

I have half a dozen old china plates which, because they are old and ugly, never get smashed. I use them to serve meals that demand very hot plates. Roast meat, for instance, is more easily carved if you rest it out of the oven, but in a warm place, for 15 minutes before serving. If you do this, a really hot plate will prevent the meat from being distinctly cool by the time the poor old carver gets around to serving himself.

A soufflé dish is something for which there is no substitute. Best buy one small one (say five inches across), big enough for two portions, and one really large one for entertaining. Tiny dishes for individual servings of egg dishes, etc., are rather luxurious. The bowls (with or without lids) in which items like onion soup with grilled cheese floating on it are served individually, are posh.

Plenty of tinfoil (it must be used rather lavishly or not at all), for wrapping joints, poultry, etc., or making papillotes (envelopes in which to wrap fish or chops – more correctly papillotes are made from greased paper). Tinfoil can also be placed over dishes in the oven that are getting a little too much heat.

Greaseproof paper should also be kept on hand.

A tin for small cakes is also useful for tiny Yorkshire puddings.

A large chopper – use side for tenderizing.

Nowadays an electric mixer is no longer considered an extravagance. If you have one it must be kept permanently in the place where it operates, for no one ever gets machines out of cupboards and sets them up. The large Kenwood mixer will peel potatoes, grind meat, knead dough, slice paper-thin vegetables and grate cheese – mine is used every day.

THE AUTOMATIC COOKER AND THE PRESSURE COOKER

These are both luxury utensils, but they will bring not just a saving in time but a gain in precision to your cooking. These two devices, plus a gas ring, can give you an infinite variety of cookery. With them you can steam, boil, stew, poach, braise, fry, roast and even bake. In this short note I only tell you what I use them for, but you may find all sorts of additional advantages. They will be of equal use to the gas-ring gourmet and to the cook with a vast stainless-steel kitchen.

The device which the Sunbeam company call their Automatic Cooker is often described as an electric frying pan. I prefer to call it a thermostat-controlled casserole. While gas rings are unbeatable for quick adjustment of heat, electric thermostats and simmer-stats can be adjusted to keep the heat just right under a stew or braise. On page 32 you will see the burning points of various fats. Cooking in butter? Set the control to just below 278° without risk of disaster. Similarly use the boiling point of water to poach a fish gently so that the convection doesn't smash it into flakes. Heat milk, but never boil it over by setting below its boiling point.

Escoffier once wrote, 'Of all the various culinary operations, braisings are the most expensive and the most difficult.' To braise a good-quality piece of meat, set it upon a bed of lightly fried vegetables in which onion predominates. Put the lid on the cooker and set the control to a fraction above the boiling point of water, then the moisture that comes out of the meat turns to steam and leaves a glazed layer over the meat. The cook must spoon just a little moisture over the meat as often as possible (say every 15 minutes), using good stock. This will result in a real braise and is much better than swamping the meat with liquid and letting it diminish by evaporation. Many vegetables (e.g. celery, leek, turnip, etc.) are suitable for braising.

Use this same basic idea but add more liquid to produce stews and casseroles that cook at exact gentle heat.

The Pressure Cooker will not only cut cooking times to about one-third, but will also cook certain foods particularly well. Read your instruction book, remembering that only when you hear hissing is the food cooking. Time from that moment on.

For things that spoil if overcooked, deliberately

undercook, then finish them off by using the cooker as though it were an ordinary saucepan. In this way you can keep an eye on the contents towards the end of the cooking time. Don't wander out of earshot during pressure-cooking time. If the cooker goes silent, it is either because the heat isn't high enough or because it has burnt dry. Either way it needs attention. When cooking time is up, reduce pressure by cooling. Either put the cooker under running cold water, or stand it aside and let it cool gently. The former method is quick, but will throw the food inside about violently. Choose accordingly. Always before beginning check escape vent and washer (a dirty washer will let pressure escape).

The pressure cooker is at its best when neither overcooking nor violent movement of air will affect the result, e.g. for steak pudding, tomato soup, stock, soups of all kinds, stews, removing marrow from bones, cooking salt beef (brisket needs about 25 minutes to the pound), steamed puddings (rolypoly, etc.). Other highly successful pressure-cooker uses: cooking dried fruits, steamed egg custard (cover it well). The most successful vegetables to pressure-cook are the ones that will end up mashed, e.g. potatoes, swedes, turnips. Green vegetables are so quick to cook that it is not worth pressure-cooking them.

FRUIT AND VEGETABLE NOTEBOOK

Here are some items from my own notebook. It is by no means complete, because no notebook of this sort ever can be. Use these observations as a basis for notes of your own. You obviously won't buy items that are shrivelled, decaying, discoloured or limp. Most fruit and vegetables suffer severely from delay in transit; go for the freshest you can get.

Lettuce, chicory and cabbage have more nutriment in the outer leaves than inside. Don't trim too much away. Keep skins on potatoes wherever possible; mashed potatoes will be more flavourful if you cook the potatoes in their jackets, remove skins after cooking. Anyway, what's wrong with putting the mashed potato back into the jackets again and serving it in them?

Water used in the cooking process will capture much of the nutriment. Therefore, use little or no water, or use the water in soup, gravy or sauce. Vegetable water will go bad quickly; it should be used in the same meal for which the vegetable was cooked. Don't add it to stock unless the stock is brought to the boil every day.

Mashing or creaming is good for root vegetables (potatoes, turnips, swedes or carrots, etc.) and there are many ways of serving them. Butter is most usual, but try a little cream, or poach some cut-up marrow bones (ask the butcher) until the marrow inside is very soft, then scoop this out and use it on the vegetable like butter. A little pork dripping (make it by frying pieces of belly of pork) adds flavour. Mashed vegetables can look like hell. Make them more appetizing by fluffing the top and grilling it for a couple of minutes till the peaks brown (a few breadcrumbs scattered over it before grilling will help it go golden). A pinch of paprika or a spoonful of finely chopped hard-boiled egg yolk is also decorative.

Many vegetables benefit from a final few minutes in a pan with a little oil or butter. Drain fat off before serving.

Soup Making. Use a generous amount of the vegetable you choose – nothing can get over the lack of the basic flavour. For example, put half an onion finely chopped into a pan with some butter or oil. When the onion is golden, add two or three pounds of roughly chopped tomatoes, scattering salt, pepper, a little basil (*see* Herb section) and a small spoonful of sugar. Lid on – low heat, and you will find that the juice comes out of the tomatoes. When they are very soft (say half an hour), sieve. Now you can decide how much liquid to add. Use milk or stock or water. Add a knob of butter or cream. Adjust the seasoning. Serve.

Not all vegetables will make their own juice like tomatoes, so most will have to be started with water, but don't swamp your flavour with water – it tastes of nothing. Sieving helps to distribute the flavour through the liquid instead of providing a tasty mouthful of flavour, so only leave pieces in the soup if you have a generous amount of flavour already. The same basic system will give you thousands of soups. Try making soup from: cucumber, leeks, peas, white fish, asparagus, mushrooms, etc.

If you have no stock, remember that you can put some item in the soup that will add flavour (e.g. a ham bone). If you want your soup a little thicker, think before adding flour or even arrowroot. Grated potato (it will need a few minutes to cook) provides a thick creamy texture, but don't overdo it.

When buying remember that those large items that win prizes in displays are no friend to the cook. Better to choose the tiny, flavourful vegetables. Those enormous carrots, parsnips and beetroots may look gorgeous, but they have hearts of wood. Only enormous field mushrooms grow more flavourful with size. Tiny peas are no relation of the large ones, and the tiny flattened pods of peas (pois mange tout) that are eaten pods and all, are perhaps the finest vegetable there is.

Apples. A vast field of experiment and controversy. Learn a few types. There are apples from countries as near as France and as distant as New Zealand. They vary considerably in crispness. Three of the finest English apples (Cox's Orange Pippin, Ellison's Orange and Laxton's Superb) are fine eating apples of medium-crisp texture. Beauty of Bath and Jonathans are soft eating apples. Newtowns and Granny Smiths are quite hard quality eaters. Blenheim Orange is well worth searching for, it's a delicious English apple with a fine astringent flavour.

In England cooking apples are usually mushy – Victoria, Lord Derby or Bramley's Seedling; cooks who want apples that will retain their shapes should try using dessert apples, which are less acid, for their pies, etc., as they do in other countries.

Apricots. Too often regarded as a poor man's peach, they really have a life of their own. Available in winter from South Africa, but the Spanish ones on sale in the summer are great. Buy the biggest. Green ones will ripen in the sun. 'Peach apricots' from Murcia in Spain are superb dessert-quality ones.

Asparagus. Tips should be close and compact, stalks large and even in size. Cut away the tough white stalks. Dip the green tips into beaten egg, then fry gently. Or, after the beaten egg, dip into soft crumbs mixed with equal quantities of grated cheese before frying; or steam it and serve with butter.

Aubergines (Egg Plant or Brinjal). Look like black rubber truncheons. Go for a shiny, smooth, purple skin.

Fry or bake. These are generally sliced (thick or thin), then fried gently. Another way is to scoop out the interior, chop it small and fry it gently with some chopped onion. When it is quite soft, replace in the hollow aubergine. Bake at Regulo 5 (375° F.) for 30 minutes.

Avocadoes. Large, expensive, delicious cross between fruit and vegetable. Best eaten with simple vinaigrette sauce. Green ones may be a little under-ripe; test for softness around stalk or rely on your greengrocer. The biggest are not always the best, but those from Madeira or Israel are reliably excellent. They will ripen quickly in a warm place.

Banana. *See* pages 298–9.

Beans. This word is used to describe three different things in the kitchen. First there is the green vegetable eaten while the seeds inside are soft and only partly grown. These vary from the slim tiny ones to the gross coarse ones that are like boiled sandpaper to eat. Secondly there are the beans that are the seeds themselves. When young they are good to eat as they are, but old ones must have the outer layer of skin removed. Thirdly there are these same seeds dried to preserve them. I have listed these last beans as pulses.

Beetroot. Size doesn't matter. If you buy them ready-cooked make sure the skin is loose and flesh dark red. Cooked beetroots sometimes exude a mould; it is quite harmless – wash it off.

Blackberries. Cultivated ones are less flavourful than wild ones. Large bright ones are best.

Blackcurrants. Are mostly bought by the soft-drink industry, so price remains high. Large ones are easiest to trim. Be sure they are not leaking juice as it's a sign of bad condition.

Broccoli. A winter vegetable widely available frozen – try it fresh. Eat the stalks and flowers too, unless they are yellow, in which case don't buy any. Gardeners should plant 'Purple sprouting'.

Brussels Sprouts. Buy only the small, compact ones or, if possible, the very tiny ones. Mix sour cream with finely chopped onion, warm it, pour over cooked sprouts. Gardeners should try 'Aristocrat'.

Cabbage. Heaviness is good – it shows compactness. Gardeners might like 'Velocity'.
White is the crispest.

Red. Heavy, slightly tasteless – the correct thing for preparing with apple and sugar in the continental manner.
Savoy. Use this for eating raw (e.g. Coleslaw).
Drumhead. Good cooking cabbage.
Stuffed Cabbage. Remove large outer leaves of cabbage, give them a minute in boiling water. Drain and dry. Into each leaf wrap a heap of meat mixture, make it into a little parcel, fixing it with a toothpick. Bake in the oven at Regulo 2 (325° F.) for 40 minutes, either on a greased tin or in a sauce (a tin of soup: tomato, chicken or mushroom, etc.). The meat mixture can be ground beef, lamb, veal or pork (in which case make sure it is cooked right through – I cannot tell you the exact timing as it depends on the size of the 'parcels'). It should be well flavoured with spice, herbs, onion, salt and pepper.

Carrots. None in the shops equal fresh garden ones, and the jet-spray washed ones are awful. Gardeners should plant 'Early Nantes'. In the shops watch for the very first English ones for flavour, also the Dutch and French ones are very fine. Otherwise you can improve them by bringing out the flavour with a final sauté in butter to caramelize the sugar content.

Cauliflower. Buy them with plenty of leaf protecting the white part, and they will keep several days. The white must be hard and not discoloured. Cauliflower can be mashed and creamed, or puréed, with beaten egg, and steamed like a custard pudding. It can be fried or poached in stock. It can be served hot with a cheese sauce or fried almonds or chopped hard egg yolk as a garnish. It can be allowed to cool, and dressed with vinaigrette or deep-fried in batter. Or use it raw in salads.

Celeriac. Is a rough-looking root of a certain celery plant. Peel it, then treat the inside like a potato – cook it in salted water, drain, then roll it in butter.

Celery. Go for the large size with fresh-looking greenery still attached. If you can choose, buy the soil-encrusted ones. Wash well just before using it. Braise it in the oven with a little butter (well-fitting lid on casserole). The heart can be removed and gently fried. The extreme leaves are left in a warm place to dry, then used as a flavouring for soups and stews. Add pieces of celery to a stew five minutes before serving to get a crunchy fresh taste. Dip it into fondue or any cheese sauce, or spread cream cheese into hollow side for canapés.

Corn on the Cob. Choose large plump ears with even-sized kernels. Each kernel should be very juicy inside. Corn should be stripped of its outer leaf and put into fast-boiling, unsalted water for 10–20 minutes. Serve with plenty of melted butter, and a large napkin for wiping the mouth.

Cherries. Many varieties, when the season hits us. Napoleon is one fine example (piebald yellow and red), but unless you are sure of your knowledge, or your greengrocer, choose the darkest varieties for eating. Morello is a piquant cherry for cooking in pies or compotes.

Chicory (French: endive). Is like a small white artillery shell. It needs no washing and can be served raw, or braised (with stock or butter), but be sure that the tips of the leaf are yellow, not green. You will note that in England endive is a curly-leaved salad vegetable, which in U.S.A. is called escarole, and in France, chicorée. So sort that lot out.

Chillies. Are tiny red or green pods. They are very, very hot. Use them to flavour vinegar by leaving a couple in the bottle, or use them with discretion in a curry recipe. Note that long cooking lessens the strength somewhat. Unused chillies can be left to dry to a crisp, then stored in a jar. Warning: don't wipe your eyes after handling them.

Clementines. Are a type of tangerine without seeds. The Italian ones are the best. They are never very cheap.

Courgettes. Tiny marrows. Buy them only less than five inches long, cook gently without peeling until they are tender. Serve with butter.

Courgettes with Walnuts. Fry the tiny marrows in oil for five minutes (with a little onion if you wish). Add a little wine and water and a squeeze of lemon juice. Cook for ten minutes, then add walnuts.

Cranberries. In the late autumn they are widely available. Serve cooked unsweetened cranberries with game or poultry.

Cucumbers. Rough-skinned outdoor ones are richer in flavour, although sometimes a little bitter. Go for long slim ones. Colour doesn't matter except that yellowness is not good. Always cut them into chunks, and, unless you hate it, leave the skin on, for this makes them more digestible. Serve them lightly and very slowly cooked in butter, or raw; either way sour cream makes a great dressing.

Custard Apples. Large green fruit with creamy flesh. Eat it as it is. It is good with sugar and cream.

Endive (French: chicorée). It has a mild bitterness. In France it is often served cooked. Neither way is it very interesting to me, but use it as a salad vegetable, or braise it in stock or butter if you want to give it a whirl.

Fennel. Looks like pot-bellied celery, tastes like liquorice. Slice it or leave it whole, braise it or leave it raw.

Figs. Fresh figs make a pleasant end to a meal. Only the soft red inside is eaten. Sometimes cream is served with them, but a good one will stand alone.

Dried Figs. Ugh.

French Beans. Stringless, tender and flavourful. Cook them whole with butter. Gardeners should try 'The Prince'.

Globe Artichokes. Avoid ones with any trace of purple flower.

Gooseberries. Go for Sussex-grown ones. Some varieties are very sour, but are excellent for jams and jellies.

Grapes. Endless varieties from countless countries. Unless you are an expert, go for the dark ones (same for cherries). Colmar is a type of grape grown in many places. The English Colmar is a superb dessert grape. Belgian and South African Colmar are almost as good.

Small seedless grapes from various Mediterranean countries are a treat, unless you enjoy chewing the pips, and eating them, too, as they do in most grape-growing areas.

Grapefruit. Keep well. Buy heavy ones, they will be juiciest.

Green Beans. Must snap when broken and should be moist inside. Fry some chopped bacon and a diced red pepper (don't use the seeds). When cooked, add vinegar and sugar in about equal quantities. Some cooks add mustard or pepper sauce to this recipe. When sugar has dissolved, pour this over cooked beans. Mix well. Serve. (Wax beans are the yellow ones.)

Greengages. A member of the plum family. Unless you know someone who grows them you will be best advised to buy French ones. South African are quite good.

Green Peppers (Capsicums, Pimentoes or **Sweet Peppers).** Are a large firm vegetable, sometimes red, according to how long they are left to grow. Remove all the seeds, which are very peppery; the flesh can be eaten raw. In the Middle East they favour their green peppers scorched. In England they are generally stuffed with meat and rice, and cooked in a moderate oven. A simple way, however, is to quarter them, remove seeds, brush with oil and bake for 15 minutes at Regulo 4 (350° F.).

Japanese Artichokes are small twisted ones. Treat just like Jerusalem artichokes.

Jerusalem Artichokes are strange relatives of the sunflower, and have a delicate earthy taste. They are tricky to peel, so go for the smoothest ones. Boil or steam them until tender (30 minutes?), then peel them, roll in butter, serve. Another popular way is to sieve the skins away from purée after cooking, using the purée for soup, or adding cream and butter before serving as a vegetable. They can be eaten raw.

Kale. A rather tough cabbage-type vegetable with a taste resembling the spinach family. Gardeners should try 'Asparagus Kale'.

Leeks. Suspect any that are too carefully manicured. Small, even-sized ones are better in flavour than the very large ones. Leeks are superb braised in butter or stock. Serve them with a sauce (e.g. cheese), or make a leek-and-potato soup with a dash of cream. This latter is very good served chilled.

Lemons. Bad skins do not always indicate bad fruit, but the skin is a valuable item in kitchen and bar.

Lettuce. Buy fresh, sprightly ones that haven't been standing in water to revive them. Don't buy ones that already have the outer leaves removed, they are probably ancient. Ask for a 'Webbs Wonder', which is an especially crisp variety. Imported lettuces are just as good as home-grown, providing they are fresh. Gardeners might like 'Webbs Wonder', too.

Limes. These are less common than lemons. The juice is exquisite – iced lime juice (sweetened as you want) is a drink of the gods.

Loganberries are the big brothers of the raspberry. They are much more interesting for my money, especially to serve raw with cream and sugar. Nowadays you only see them in country towns.

Lychees are a soft juicy fruit with a flavour of roses. Discard the parchment-like outer skin, eat the soft flesh uncooked.

Mandarins. Just like tangerines. You either like them, or you don't. (*See* Oranges.)

Mangoes. Wildly expensive, but eaten fresh a sensation. Not to be confused with the tinned variety which is not sensational at all.

Marrow. A tough, tasteless vegetable that wins prizes at garden shows.

Medlars. Strange, stunted, apple-like fruit eaten when soft and seeming over-ripe. Worth trying, if only as a curiosity.

Melons

Cantaloupe. Go for those with thick, closely woven 'netting' with yellow or yellow/green between netting pattern. Tender orange inside. It should have a rich smell. Imported – expensive until summer. Don't cut more than a few minutes before serving, even to cool.
Tiger Melon. Is very similar, but with a smooth skin. A real Tiger Melon is even better than a Net Cantaloupe.
Honeydew. White rind is immature, it should be cream-colour. Flesh is more like that of a watermelon and so they are cheaper than the above varieties. Go for the ones from Spain, sometimes marked 'Elche'. On South African honeydews, 'Geest' is the label to search for. 'Prince of Wales' is another superb mark.
Charentais. Sent from France, are the kings of the melon world, although some gourmets go for Afghan ones. They are almost never cheap, but they are worth paying for – highly scented, sweet and pungent.
Watermelon. Very watery flesh. Beware of damaged ones as they rapidly deteriorate.

Mushrooms. Sensational whatever their size, shape or colour. The very light underside shows a very young mushroom, but gigantic plate-sized mushrooms have their place in cooking too. Try them all, and keep some in a dark place in the kitchen, but never in the refrigerator – they hate cold. Cultivated mushrooms do not need peeling. Sometimes wild mushrooms appear in the shops, but the real gourmet will stalk the choicest varieties with a good textbook in one hand.

Mustard and Cress is a mass of tiny green leaves on thin stalks, that looks like something out of a science-fiction film. It is really rape, and is useful for decorating hot or cold dishes, e.g. roast poultry, sliced galantine, or baked sole.

Nectarines. A superb type of plum. You must try one. South African ones in winter (*see* Food in Season section).

Onions. *See* pages 254–5.

Oranges. There are three different types of orange. There is the China or sweet orange – that's the ordinary orange as we know it. There is the Seville, which is a bitter orange for cooking with duck, pork, etc., and for making marmalade. Lastly, there is the mandarin, which is a small, flattened, loose-skinned type of orange that originated in China thousands of years ago. There are several varieties of mandarin – tangerine, satsuma and clementine – some of them have no pips. When buying ordinary oranges, choose the thin-skinned, smooth ones. Heaviest are best. Israel oranges are exceptionally good, particularly the real Jaffa. Outspan is a selection from the South African crop, and Navel is the choicest variety when the Spanish crop takes the stage. In January and February both Seville oranges and Aylesbury ducks are in the shops. Like all citrus fruits, oranges will give you more juice if heated before squeezing.

Parsnips. Should be white-fleshed, even if soil-encrusted. Don't buy them if they are very wrinkled.

Good parsnips are best braised or parboiled, drained, then fried in batter. Gardeners should try 'Student'.

Peaches. *Freestone* (English ones are all freestone) is perhaps the most delicious, but for cooking the *clingstone* holds its shape better. English peaches are perhaps the best, with Belgian and French running neck and neck. South African are less good, but reliable. Italian are inferior, but are good enough for compotes or bottling, etc. The best Italian peach is *Hales*, which sometimes is worth eating raw.

Pears. Can be bought a little under-ripe. They will ripen at room temperature in the fruit bowl.
William. A small, superb eating pear.
Conference. Slightly hard – good for eating or cooking.
Comice. Marvellous eater – late to ripen, tricky to grow. Home-grown Comice are best (e.g. Doyenne du Comice) but South African Comice are almost as good.

Peas. Well worth the trouble, in spite of the convenience of frozen peas. Ask greengrocer for Laxton or, if you are a gardener, grow Laxton Exquisite or Peter Pan. The flat type of pea which is cooked and eaten, pods and all, is perhaps the most delicious vegetable there is. English greengrocers call these *Sugar Peas.* Gardeners should plant 'Mange Tout'. Any sort of peas are best cooked very slowly in a covered pan containing lots of lettuce and butter. Add strips of thinly sliced ham and chopped onion. Serve.

Pineapple. Don't waste money on a dodgy one. If you can afford it, go for a St Michael's from the Azores. Note: an under-ripe fruit will ripen in a warm room, but watch it carefully. Refrigeration will ruin it.

Plums. For eating nothing can match a Victoria, although the people selling Laxtons sometimes say differently.

Pomegranate. A juicy dip into mythology, but take a big napkin.

Potatoes. Few shops – including Harrods – stock more than one sort of potato. This is usually the King Edward, which is a very dreary vegetable that dissolves into slush at the first sign of warm water. The waxy, yellow-fleshed ones (called in France 'Dutch potatoes') are much more interesting to the gourmet. They hold their shape and can be made into razor-thin fried potatoes, or puffy *pommes soufflées*. The potato-crisp companies are aware of this, and grow countless acres for their own use. Gardeners don't have to be a crisp-factory to plant *Record*.

Pulses

Beans. There are many of these; they are more or less interchangeable, except that traditional types are called for according to the region in which the recipe originated. Choose from: ***flageolet*** (small green), ***red kidney bean***, ***white haricot*** (butter beans). There are many more sub-varieties ranging in colour from white to purple.

Dried Peas. Various sizes from the large (marrowfat) to the small (petits pois). When soaked, cooked and tinned, these are called processed peas.

Lentils. Small split pulses of bright orange colour. If you can get ***brown lentils*** – get them. These are whole lentils with the skin still on; they are green/brown in colour.

Chick Peas. Used in *olla podrida* (Spain) and *couscous* (Algeria).

For all pulses:

Method. There is no need to soak them overnight. Give them two hours in cold water. (Note: Some cooks add one or two pinches of bicarbonate of soda to the soaking water.) Then put them in boiling water with:

1 A ham-bone.

2 Piece of bacon.

3 Piece of salt pork.

4 Piece of fresh pork skin.

5 Pork knuckle.

You can have any or all of them, but make sure that there is a piece of fat somewhere, as this has an important effect on the cooking of the beans.

The time of cooking depends upon the size of the pulses you are using and whether you wish them to go to a mash.

Use this method to prepare pulses as vegetable dishes. Cook them till tender. (Note: Pearl barley needs less cooking, but should be rinsed with warm water afterwards. Chick peas never go mashy.) Stir into the hot or cold pulses any of these: vinaigrette dressing, sour cream, crispy fried onion, toasted almonds, chopped herbs and butter, or very crisp streaky bacon broken up.

Cooked to a mash, dried peas become pease pudding, lentils become dhall. Pearl barley is a great switch as a breakfast cereal. Put sugar and cream on it.

Pumpkin. Leave it for Cinderella.

Radishes won't keep. Buy them crisp, use immediately. Gardeners should try 'Sparkler'.

Raspberries. Pick over, but don't wash.

Red Currants and Blackcurrants. Wash briefly.

Rhubarb is divided into outdoor and indoor varieties. The former is a more robust-looking plant that appears to bring prices very low. Cook without adding water, flavour it with lemon juice and sugar. Serve with cream. Gardeners might try 'Hawkes Champagne'.

Rice. *See* pages 156–7.

Runner Beans should be crisp. They need stringing.

Salsify (U.S.: Oyster Plant). Scrape the outside, cut into 2-in. lengths and drop into acidulated water (so it won't discolour). Then poach gently in flavoured water (here's where a tinned soup would do nicely) for about

two hours, and drain. Serve the final dish sautéed in butter or under a fine sauce – e.g. cheese sauce – or cover with thin cream.

Seakale. Steam it till tender – it may take almost an hour. Serve with butter for one of the taste-sensations of the year. Can be boiled or eaten raw.

Spinach can be anything from the tops of root crops to the real thing, imported from France at very high prices. Between these extremes are all manner of strange flora. You will probably get the value you pay for. Careful, diligent draining is the secret. A dish of spinach standing in a pool of water is most unpleasant. Mash it in a sieve until all the water is gone. Garnish with pieces of crisp grilled bacon and generous butter. Another way is to mix a cream sauce into the spinach; in this case it can be finished in the oven. Or yet another way: put well-drained spinach into a saucepan with plenty of butter, warm it. Add some beaten egg, stirring carefully over a tiny heat. You don't want flecks of scrambled egg in it. Add cream just before serving. (A blender makes this easy.)

Sprout Tops. Tender shoots – cook in butter.

Sorrel. Is not very popular in Britain because of its sour taste, but try it (as a vegetable soup or garnish) two or three times and you may well become an addict, or perhaps you are one already. (*See also* page 103.)

Strawberries. Judge them by the way the greengrocer treats them. They should be spread out thinly with no trace of leaking juice. The brightness of colour isn't a good guide, the tiny wood strawberries (if you are lucky enough to see them on sale) being dull brown, but they are without doubt the finest flavour.

Swedes. A great vegetable for mashing with fresh pepper and salt and butter.

Tomatoes. English ones are bred to look beautiful; generally speaking they are greatly inferior in flavour. French tomatoes are ugly brutes, but delicious for salads and cooking; we seldom see them here. Spanish are consistently excellent, if not the best we get. The Channel Islands also send excellent ones. Blues are the elongated ones like Siamese twins, wherever they originate. Gardeners should try 'Harbinger' and one of the yellow varieties never seen in the shops (not beautiful enough, I suppose) like 'Golden Sunrise'.

Turnips can be served raw in thin slices if you buy fine-quality ones. Otherwise boil and mash with lots of butter and plenty of freshly ground pepper, or use in a fatty pot-roast (e.g. duck or pork) where the turnip takes up the fattiness and is a perfect flavour-foil. Gardeners should try 'Golden Ball'.

Turnip Tops. A good variety of greens, but only if they are bright and fresh.

Watercress. Don't buy it if it's limp. Use immediately. Obviously useful for decoration but excellent inside sandwiches, soups and stews, or finely chopped and scattered. A sprig of watercress is almost always pushed to the side of the plate – try to make them eat it all up. It's delicious.

Ugli Fruit. Cross between orange and grapefruit. Try one.

THE SALAD COURSE. Ideally this is the course after the meat and before the cheese. It is the pause in the meal, and if you don't watch them, this is where the guests will whip out the fags and matches. A tempting salad may deter them. The greenery can be varied with spinach, watercress, raw cauliflower flowerets or white cabbage. Other ingredients: carrots, celery, cucumber (unpeeled chunks). Some cooks, influenced by America, will invent **fruit combinations.** For them I suggest: diced apples and raisins, orange pieces with celery, and their own permutations of cranberries, banana, pineapple, peach, sliced pear, watermelon pieces, grapefruit, etc.

VEGETABLE HORS D'ŒUVRES. Cold vegetables with oil and vinegar can be served as hors d'œuvres. Cold cooked beans with pieces of crisp fried bacon and green beans, tiny marrows, or aubergines are all good served in this way. Tomato, unlike the others, demands a place all alone – raw chopped onion being the only thing that will combine well with it.

Sour-cream dressing can replace vinaigrette. Mix sour cream with a little (very little) sugar, add salt and pepper. Some cooks add a squeeze of lemon. Serve this over the vegetables.

BACHELOR FOODS (THE QUICK COOK)

Everyone is in a hurry sometimes, but no one is ever in such a hurry that they should eat some of the pre-packaged foods I see on sale in my grocer's, let alone feed them to friends. The best course for people in a rush is to prepare the food well beforehand; e.g. cold roast chicken, baked lasagne or sherry trifle. But here are some ideas for when you are really pushed for time. The Blender chapter and the Delicatessen chapter will provide more suggestions.

THE SANDWICH

They say that the very first sandwich was two slices of bread with roast beef between. As a filling roast beef may never be beaten, but nowadays to serve a 'super sandwich' you would make a double-decker, using a thick slice of ham and a thick slice of chicken well seasoned. The whole thing would then be fastened with toothpicks, dipped into egg batter and fried in butter for a couple of minutes on each side. The outside should be golden brown and nicely crisp. The toothpicks are removed before serving.

Hero sandwiches are lengths of French bread split along their length. It is usual to have a profusion of content: cooked mushroom, hard-boiled eggs, ham, salami sausage, Gruyère cheese.

Lots of shapes and sizes is a good rule; have bridge rolls, brown rolls, home-made scones, sponge fingers with sweet fillings, French bread, pumpernickel. Use toast and various sorts of biscuit like Ryvita or MacVita, or discs of pastry and cheese fingers and vol-au-vents. Cream the butter with a fork to make it easy to use, and some portions of butter can be flavoured with spice, herbs, garlic, seasoning or mustard. Have at least one hot item – fried or toasted sandwiches or hot soup – at a sandwich party and bring it on halfway through the evening. Keep everything well tarted up with watercress and mustard and cress and coloured plates and paper d'oyleys, and I'm all in favour of those little paper flags that tell you what's in the heap. Have some pots of mustard, pickles and chutneys.

FILLING	DRESSING	BREAD
Smoked haddock warmed in butter. Remove skin and bone. Serve hot or cold.	Cheese sauce	PUMPERNICKEL
Steak Tartare (ground steak + chopped onion + capers + beaten egg)		FRESH WHITE
Liver sausage + tomato	Mayonnaise	FRENCH LOAF
Thick slice of ham fried in caramelized sugar	A thin smear of crushed pineapple	CURRANT BREAD
Veal escalope (cooked)	Toasted cheese	RYE BREAD
Liver sausage	Hot cheese sauce or a piquant tomato	WHITE BREAD
Cold scrambled egg	Anchovy fillets	WHITE
Crisp streaky bacon, underdone chicken liver		TOASTED CARAWAY
Cold chicken breast	Diced celery and diced black olive	FRENCH LOAF
Crisp streaky bacon	Peanut butter	WHOLEMEAL
Mashed crab + cream + whole shrimps	Good mayonnaise	BLACK BREAD
Creamed cold chicken	Chopped prunes	WHOLEMEAL

Here are some fish-based sandwiches:

1 Lobster creamed in cheese sauce
2 Shrimp chopped into scrambled egg
3 Sardine + butter and a dash of Worcestershire sauce
4 Fresh salmon + capers

Here are some things to mix into cream cheese (home-made tastes best):

1 Chopped dates or sultanas
2 Cucumber + chopped raw onion
3 Olives
4 Chinese ginger
5 Fried mushrooms + watercress

Here are some hot sandwiches:

1 Egg fried on both sides (not too much)
2 Frankfurters. Heat them in hot water, serve in a split soft bun
3 Roast beef + horseradish
4 Slice of pork + apple sauce

68

0 mins. to cook: APPETIZERS

1 Salami, garlic sausage, etc.
2 Tinned pâté.
3 Fresh chilled melon (don't cut it open till last moment).
4 Smoked back bacon sliced as thin as possible (eat it raw).
5 Caviare and its close and distant imitations (ask at your delicatessen).
6 Rollmops (bottled).
7 Sauerkraut.
8 All cheeses.

2 mins. to cook: SOUP

Tuna Fish Chowder. Heat a tin of tuna fish and a tin of sweet corn. Stir. Add a knob of butter and enough milk to make thick soup.

Lobster Bisque. Cream of chicken soup + tinned lobster. Mash lobster into soup, add butter, milk and sprinkle of paprika.

Chicken Celery. Can of each + milk and butter.

Mushroom Corn. Can of each + milk and butter. Garnish with crumpled streaky bacon grilled very crisp.

Green Pea Special. Blend, mash or beat a tin of peas, add Scotch broth, dilute with water.

Tomato Bean. Tin of tomato soup, add chopped pieces of sausage (cooked, any kind) and 2 dessertspoonfuls baked beans.

Consommé Special. A slug of sherry or Madeira and a squeeze of lemon juice will kill the oversweet flavour of tinned consommé.

Sherry can also spark up cans of luxury soups such as game soup, pheasant soup, etc., but you might have difficulty convincing your guests that you cooked it. Cream is another transformer of canned soup. Put it into any of the cream-style soups (e.g. chicken, lobster, tomato, Vichysoise, etc.).

4 mins. to cook: APPETIZERS AND SOUP

Vegetable hors d'œuvres. Drain the best-quality tinned vegetable you can get (for instance, French beans, mushrooms, white beans, artichoke hearts). Put a light vinaigrette dressing over them (*see* page 246 for recipe). If there is time, add capers or olives.

Cream can be used as a dressing over certain vegetables. For instance, stir it into a warmed can of sweet corn, or mushrooms, or artichoke hearts, or tiny green peas. The cream should be added at the last minute, of course, and never allowed to boil.

Clear soup, either canned or cubes, can be improved by having one beaten egg stirred into it a moment before serving. The heat of the soup will cook it into golden shreds. Another way of serving clear soup is with a whole raw egg yolk dropped into each serving.

Potage Saint Germain. Dilute a tin of pease pudding with milk and butter. Garnish with cubes of bread fried crisp in butter.

These tinned meals need more disguise than more complex efforts. Use cress, slices of lemon, warmed bread rolls to divert attention. Remember many soups can be served chilled.

5 mins. to cook: ICE CREAM DESSERT

Ice Cream can be given a lift by serving a warm sauce with it. There are many permutations, but try vanilla ice cream with these:

1 Melt a plain chocolate bar + one spoonful of water in a double boiler (or be extra careful over a low flame), add a big spoonful of rum, brandy or Tia Maria at the last moment. Serve.
2 Warm some very best-quality jam. Serve.

3 Heat honey, drop pieces of nut into it. Serve.

4 Warm some Chinese ginger in syrup. Serve.

5 A slug of crème de menthe + chocolate shavings as a garnish.

7 mins. to cook: VEGETABLE COURSE

Polish Beetroot. Fry a little chopped onion in plenty of butter. When it is golden, add a dessertspoonful of vinegar and a dessertspoonful of arrowroot which have been mixed together. When this has gone thick (3 minutes of constant stirring), add chopped cooked beetroot. Sprinkle with salt and pepper when it is quite hot, pour about 5 oz. of sour cream over it.

8 mins. to cook: DESSERT

Gâteau de Riz Sug Sug. Warm two tins of rice pudding into which you have put some chopped candied fruit and some sliced almonds. When the fruit has thoroughly warmed together, add two tablespoons brandy and a little thick cream. This dish is even better if allowed to get very cold before serving.

Any of this Gâteau that is left over can be used to make Rice Cakes. Mix cold cooked rice with egg yolk, raisins, grated lemon rind, chopped almonds (you may need to add a little flour if it seems too wet). Fry these little cakes, sprinkle with sugar, serve with coffee.

10 mins. to cook: VOL-AU-VENT

Ready-cooked vol-au-vent cases can be bought in many bakers' shops. Filled with a jar of chicken breasts mashed into a little cream of chicken soup, they will warm at Reg. 3 (330° F.), 7 mins.

12 mins. to cook: PHONEY CHINESE DISH

Phoney Chinese. Sauté (without browning) a little chopped onion in olive oil. Add a finely sliced green pepper (remove seeds). Some chunks of spring onion are also good. Before it has a chance to brown, pour this mixture into the pan: dessertspoonful of soy sauce + tablespoonful of arrowroot + ginger (any sort: amount depends on strength – its and yours) + 2 oz. sugar + 2 oz. vinegar (cider vinegar if possible). Stir this mix into the onion, etc., keep stirring for three minutes while it thickens. Now add a can of drained pineapple chunks, and plenty of shrimps (frozen, tinned, or fresh). Pieces of cooked chicken (e.g. tinned) can be added as well as, or instead of, the shrimps.

15 mins. to cook:
THE MEAT COURSE, OR A PASTA

Use ground beef to make **Hamburgers,** or use it to make **Chile con Carne.** Fry some onion in oil till it is brown. Add chilli powder, stir it into onion and oil, and cook it for three minutes. Add a tin of peeled tomatoes and some ground beef. Don't cook it – just let it get hot. Add a tin of baked beans. Stir, serve. A similar dish can be made by adding cooked rice instead of the beans, in which case omit the chilli. The tomato, meat and onion prepared this way is a **Bolognaise Sauce.** Pour it over any cooked pasta. In any case, it is most important not to cook the meat into small pellets. In no case should it have more than ten minutes over the flame.

The pasta will take about 13 mins. in boiling water. It can be drained and served with butter only; have grated cheese and fresh pepper (in a pepper mill) standing by.

Pasta Marinara is just a matter of chopping tinned anchovy fillets into the tomato sauce and using that over any cooked pasta. If you just gently warm a tin of tuna, and stir only that into cooked, buttered pasta, it is al tonno.

20 mins. to cook: SUKIYAKI (pretty phoney) and PÊCHES FLAMBÉES

Sukiyaki. The Japanese cook has always known a secret about cooking quickly – you *slice everything fine.* Have finely sliced ingredients standing by; to a little oil add onion and give it five minutes. Then turn the heat high and, stirring all the while, add: celery, mushrooms, spinach, spring onion, bean shoots (these can be tinned, but many shops sell them fresh). Stir it for five minutes, then add beef (the best you can afford). Give it three minutes, after which add two ounces soy sauce, one teaspoonful sugar and a mere trace of pepper. You can moisten it with a little stock (use tinned consommé or tomato juice if you like). Now serve it with rice.

The *sukiyaki* can be made in a chafing-dish (if you can get it hot enough). No bachelor should be without a chafing-dish. It gives a low romantic light. But space-age bachelors may prefer an electric frying pan, which is really a thermostat-controlled chafing-dish – scientific, but no glow! Here is another chafing-dish recipe:

Peach in Flames. If you use fresh peaches, blanch them to remove skins, otherwise use tinned ones. Sprinkle with sugar and some juice from the tin (or water on fresh ones) and a miniature bottle (or its equivalent) of brandy (peach brandy is even better). Light the fire underneath the chafing-dish. When it is all very hot, set fire to the juice. Don't singe your eyebrows.

You can do the same thing with skinned bananas (you won't need water or juice) using sherry instead of the brandy. A little butter goes well with bananas. At the end you can pour cream over it instead of setting it alight.

25 mins. to cook: A FISH MEAL

A Fish Meal. Put one plaice or sole per person on a buttered dish. Over the fish scatter peeled prawns (buy as such), or a little grated cheese (buy as such). Dot with butter. Protect with tinfoil. Bake for 20 minutes at Regulo 6 (400° F.). Serve with a chunk of lemon and brown bread and butter. Do the same thing with almost any white fish (a cod steak, rock salmon, etc.) with only a slight loss of elegance.

Another variation is to pour a tin of soup over the fish (e.g. tomato, obviously, but chicken is excellent, also asparagus, cream of lobster, etc.). Or cook the fish plain and drop a peeled, soft-boiled egg on it. The soft yolk makes a fine sauce. This is especially good with smoked haddock.

30 mins. to cook: GRILLS – meat and fish

You need at least half an hour to prepare any sort of grill. Firstly because the grill must be very hot indeed before popping the meat under it, and secondly because grilled food needs constant and careful attention, and you must be unflurried to do it. Switch the grill on first, then crush some garlic, salt, pepper and herbs (e.g. rosemary) into an eggcupful of olive oil. Brush the steak generously, pop it under the hot grill. From now on you are on your own. Make a note of the cooking time so that next time it will be perfect. Most steaks need 24 hours in a cool place (not a refrigerator) before cooking. If you are grilling fish it's quicker if you have the fishmonger split it open. Herrings are very flavourful if dipped into egg and rolled oats (a packet of porridge oats will do), then dotted with butter before being grilled.

35 mins. to cook: KEBAB

Buy tender lamb or beef (of frying quality), cut it into cubes one inch square. Spear meat, pieces of onion, pieces of pimento on to skewers (the butcher will give you some), dust with seasoning. Grill about 6 mins. per side until meat looks done.

Lamb kidneys with pieces of lambs' liver is perhaps the best of all. Put lots of lamb-kidney fat on the skewer; eat by pulling pieces off the skewer with wholemeal bread.

40 mins. to cook:
QUICHE and RICE PUDDING

Light the oven. Line a metal tin with a thin layer of ready-made short pastry. Prick pastry with a fork. Stir ½ pint cream into 3 beaten, seasoned eggs. Put chunks of ham into pastry, pour mixture over it. Give it 30 mins. at Regulo 3½ (350° F.).

Gâteau de Riz au Caramel. Coat a mould with caramel (scorched sugar – *see* Crème Caramel, page 276). Beat 2 egg yolks and add them to as much thick cream as you can spare. Mix this with two tins of rice pudding (sold ready-cooked). Stand it in the oven just like the Crème Caramel at Regulo 2 (325° F.) for 35 minutes. Let it cool or turn it out (this can be tricky, don't be too disappointed if it breaks up). Serve hot, or chill it and serve cold.

45 mins. to cook: sweet and savoury variations on the PANCAKE *see* page 158 for the recipe.

Pancakes will keep overnight (they must be thin). They can be drenched in brandy or orange curaçao, or have chopped ham put inside them and a cheese sauce over. Finish under grill.

Baked Pancakes. Buy some ready-made spaghetti

sauce; if you can't get it, use a tin of tomatoes (mash them and add to a roux, cook for three minutes till it is a creamy thickness). Pour half of this into a tin. Roll a mixture of cottage cheese and a little beaten egg into each pancake. Lay them in the baking tin. Pour rest of sauce over, scatter Parmesan cheese on top. Give it half an hour at Regulo 5 (375° F.)

50 mins. to cook: CHICKEN

Buy a good-quality frying chicken (e.g. a capon). If you must use a frozen one then be sure it is completely thawed. Have the shop cut it in half (or in portions, if you prefer it). Choose from any of the following flavour ideas. Rub chicken halves with: soy sauce, mustard oil, a cut lemon, a cut piece of fresh ginger, garlic, Worcestershire sauce, dusting of paprika. Smother the chicken with: peeled almonds, chopped nuts (egg + flour makes them stick), before putting strips of bacon fat over it, and giving it 45 mins. at Regulo 7 (430° F.). This is a particularly good way to cook chicken because the legs, which take longest to cook, are upward, while the breast, which cooks quickly, is protected. Test it with a needle; juice should run yellow, not pink, meat when cut should be moist.

The chicken can be covered in a can of soup (e.g. celery, green pea, tomato, asparagus, etc.) and cooked covered in a casserole for the same cooking time.

FOOD IN SEASON

The information in this section was supplied by Harrods and various information offices, to whom Len Deighton offers his sincere thanks. Like all seasonal events, the items mentioned (particularly home-grown produce) are dependent upon the vagaries of the climate. In some cases I have omitted items which, while in season, are not usually at their best.

Each onslaught of mechanized farming and agriculture brings us a step nearer to being battery hens ourselves. Where is the restaurant that serves a fine free-range chicken full of its own flavour, with just a background of freshly picked herbs? Where even is the restaurant that serves fresh unfrozen vegetables and fruit?

Restaurants cannot afford the labour cost of serving anything but deep-frozen, chemically fed, pre-packaged, forced food. Do not blame them – they have to compete in a highly competitive society. But your home is another thing again. If you buy frozen peas from your greengrocer and leave salsify on his hands, he will react accordingly.

No one can deny that frozen peas are convenient: the old-fashioned sort in pods take ages to prepare, have a high wastage, and deteriorate if unsold. Frozen peas are brightly coloured (altogether too brightly coloured to my suspicious mind), pre-cooked, sweetened and, if you are not careful, permeated with an overwhelming savour of chewing gum which the manufacturers think bears some sort of relationship to mint.

Every month the seasons disappear, for more and more foods are available permanently. I have therefore listed the seasons for the cook with a certain amount of trepidation. City-dwellers – never over-conscious of the natural cycle of the seasons – will soon lose their last point of reference: the food shop.

All the year round

Fish. Brill, cod, cockles, crabs, dogfish, eels, halibut, herrings, lobster, periwinkles, plaice, rainbow trout, saithe, shrimps, sole, turbot, whelks. (All fish are a bit out of condition during the spawning season.)
Home-grown fruit. Apples (Bramley's Seedlings).
Dried fruits. Prunes, apricots, figs and dates, also a variety of nuts.
Imported fruit. Avocado pears, bananas, grapes, grapefruit, lemons, melons, oranges, peaches, pears, pineapples.
Meat. All meat is good to eat all the year round: pork can be eaten in summer. Genuine Scotch beef is excellent all the year round and is more consistent in price, quality and supply than any other meat commodity.
Poultry and game. Capons, boiling and broiling chickens, ducks, ducklings, pigeons, rabbits, rooks, turkeys.
Home-grown vegetables. Artichokes, beetroot, cabbages, carrots, cauliflowers, cucumbers, leeks, lettuces, mushrooms, mustard and cress, parsley, potatoes, spinach, turnips, watercress.
Imported vegetables. Globe artichokes, asparagus, aubergines, chicory, courgettes, French beans and other dried pulses, haricot beans, Spanish onions, sweet peppers, tomatoes.

January

Fish. Carp, chub, coalfish, grayling, gurnard, haddock (fresh and smoked), hake, John Dory, lemon sole, ling, mackerel, megrim, mullet (grey), mussels, oysters, perch, pike, roker, scallops, skate, smelts, sprats, tench, whiting, witch.

Home-grown fruit. Apples (Cox's Orange Pippin, Newton Wonder, Worcester Pearmain, Laxton's Superb), pears (Conference, Comice), rhubarb (forced).

Imported fruit. Apricots, cranberries, granadillas, lychees, melons (honeydew), Seville oranges for making marmalade, nectarines and plums from South Africa.

Meat. All meat, but pork is especially good now. New Zealand lamb is at its wonderful best, but English lamb is out of season, though speciality shops stock housefed lamb.

Poultry and game. Aylesbury duck is excellent, also curlews, geese, goslings, hares, leverets, partridges, pheasants, plovers, quails, snipe, venison, widgeon, wild duck, wild geese, woodcock.

Home-grown vegetables. Jerusalem artichokes, broccoli (white and purple – Cornish), brussels sprouts, cabbages (January King and Savoy), celeriac, celery, kale and forced seakale if you look for it, mint, shallots, spring greens, swedes.

Imported vegetables. Endives, fennel, new potatoes, salsify.

February

Fish. Carp, catfish, chub, coalfish, cod's roe, grayling, gurnard, haddock (fresh and smoked), John Dory, lemon sole, ling, mackerel, megrim, mullet (grey), mussels, oysters, perch, pike, roker, salmon, scallops,

skate, smelts, sprats, tench, whitebait, whiting, witch.
Home-grown fruit. Apples (Cox's Orange Pippin),
pears (Conference, Comice), rhubarb (forced).
Imported fruit. Apricots, peaches and plums from
South Africa, granadillas, grapes (South African and
Californian), grapefruit (good now), lychees,
mangoes, nectarines, ortaniques, prunes, the last of
the Seville oranges (for marmalade), strawberries,
uglis.
Meat. All meat (especially pork), with New Zealand
lamb still superb. Scotch beef is also excellent now.
Poultry and game. Aylesbury duck is great, also
curlews, geese, goslings, hares, leverets, plovers,
quails, snipe, wild duck, wild geese, woodcock.
Home-grown vegetables. Jerusalem artichokes,
broccoli (Cornish), brussels sprouts, cabbages
(January King and Savoy), celeriac, celery, curly kale,
forced seakale, mint, parsnips, radishes, spring
greens, spring onions, swedes.
Imported vegetables. Endives, fennel, new potatoes,
salsify.

March

Fish. Carp (until the 14th), catfish, chub, cod's roe,
conger eels, gurnard, John Dory, lemon sole, ling,
mackerel, mussels, oysters, perch and pike (until the
14th), salmon, salmon-trout, scallops, smelts, tench
(until the 14th), whitebait, witch.
Home-grown fruit. Apples (Cox's Orange Pippin),
rhubarb (forced and outdoor), strawberries (hothouse).
Imported fruit. Apples, grapes and pears from South
Africa, granadillas, grapefruit (still very good),
mangoes, strawberries.
Meat. All meat; English lamb is sometimes available at
the end of this month.

Poultry and game. Guinea-fowl and very fine duckling.

Home-grown vegetables. Jerusalem artichokes, broccoli, brussels sprouts, cabbages (January King and Savoy), celeriac, kale and forced seakale, parsnips, potatoes (new), radishes, spring greens, spring onions, sprout tops, swedes, tomatoes.

Imported vegetables. Broad beans, endives, salsify, white cabbage.

April

Fish. Catfish, cod's roe, conger eels, crabs (abundant from now until June), gurnard, ling, mackerel, mussels, oysters, pollan, prawns, salmon, salmon-trout, whelks (at their best now), whitebait, witch.

Home-grown fruit. Apples (Cox's Orange Pippin), rhubarb (outdoor), strawberries (forced).

Imported fruit. Apples, granadillas, quinces.

Meat. All meats; English lamb appears – expensive, but at its very best.

Poultry and game. Excellent duckling and guinea-fowl.

Home-grown vegetables. Jerusalem artichokes, the first asparagus, beans (hothouse), broccoli, brussels sprouts, cabbages (Savoy), horseradish, marrows, mint, parsnips (good now), potatoes (new), radishes, real seakale (brief season begins), spring onion, swedes, tomatoes.

May

Fish. Bass, bloaters, catfish, conger eels, crabs, crayfish, haddock, ling, mackerel's roe, prawns, salmon, salmon-trout (now in its prime), whitebait.

Home-grown fruit. The first of the cooking

gooseberries, early raspberries and strawberries, rhubarb (outdoor).

Imported fruit. Granadillas, quinces.

Meat. All meat. With the approach of summer beef and mutton become less fine and will remain so until the autumn. During these summer months veal is the most reliable choice of meat. With modern refrigeration, however, even pork can be bought at any time of the year.

Poultry and game. Duckling is still fine, also guinea-fowl.

Home-grown vegetables. Jerusalem artichokes, asparagus, beans (hothouse), broccoli, courgettes, endives, the first green peas, horseradish, parsnips, potatoes (new), radishes, seakale, spring greens, spring onions, swedes, tomatoes.

June

Fish. Bass, bloaters, bream, catfish, chub, cockles (at their best from now until November), conger eels, crabs, crayfish, grilse, haddock, hake, mackerel's roe, mullet (red), prawns, perch, salmon, salmon-trout, whitebait. Carp, perch, pike and tench after the 16th.

Home-grown fruit. Blackberries, cherries, gooseberries, loganberries, melons, peaches, raspberries, rhubarb, strawberries; blackcurrants and red currants begin at the end of this month.

Imported fruit. Apples, cherries, granadillas, grapes (hothouse), grapefruit (South African), naartjes, nectarines.

Buy **Herbs** now: mint, tarragon, lemon thyme and rosemary, for drying or making flavoured vinegars.

Meat. All meat; lamb is still good and is lower in cost.

Poultry and game. Guinea-fowl. Excellent duckling.
Home-grown vegetables. Jerusalem artichokes, asparagus in full growth, beans (broad beans begin, also dwarf, French, kidney, and hothouse runner beans), cabbage (Primo), courgettes, endives, green peas, horseradish, marrow, potatoes (new), radishes, seakale (after this no more), possibly the first sweet corn, spring onions, tomatoes.

July

Fish. Bass, bloaters, bream, carp, catfish, chub, conger eels, crayfish, grilse, gurnard, haddock, hake, mullet (red and grey), mussels (at the end of this month), perch, pike, prawns, salmon, salmon-trout, tench, whitebait, whiting.
Home-grown fruit. Apples (Beauty of Bath, Early Victoria, Grenadier, Lord Derby), cherries, blackberries, blackcurrants (at their best now), large dessert gooseberries begin, loganberries, nectarines, peaches, plums, red currants, raspberries and strawberries (at their best), rhubarb (outdoor).
Imported fruit. Apples, apricots, cherries, fresh figs, naartjes, nectarines, plums.
Herbs to buy and dry now: marjoram, nasturtium seed for making capers (*see* Flavourings section).
Meat. All meat.
Poultry and game. Guinea-fowl, excellent gosling and duckling.
Home-grown vegetables. Artichokes (Jerusalem and globe), the last asparagus, beans (broad, dwarf, French, kidney, and the first tender scarlet-runner beans), cabbages (Primo), courgettes, endives, green peas, marrow, mint, potatoes (new), radishes, sweet corn, spring onions, tomatoes.

August

Fish. Bass, bloaters, bream, carp, chub, conger eels, crayfish, gurnard, haddock, hake, ling, mullet (red and grey), perch, pike, prawns, salmon, salmon-trout, tench, whiting, witch.

Home-grown fruit. Apples (Worcester Pearmain, Beauty of Bath, Early Victoria, Grenadier, Lord Derby, Warner, Miller's Seedling), blackberries, blackcurrants (they are ending – make the most of them), cherries, damsons, gooseberries, loganberries, melons, nectarines, plums, pears (Laxton, Dr Jules, Clapps, Williams), red currants, raspberries and strawberries, white currants.

Imported fruit. Apricots, figs, greengages, naartjes, pears (watch out for Italian Williams).

Herbs. Buy and dry sage and thyme (*see* Flavourings section).

Meat. All meat; lamb is still a good buy.

Poultry and game. Capercaillie and blackcock (from the 20th), grouse (from the 12th), guinea-fowl, hares, leverets. Also excellent gosling and duckling.

Home-grown vegetables. Globe artichokes, beans (the last of the broad beans, also dwarf, French runner and white haricot beans), brussels sprouts, cabbages (drumhead and Primo), celery, courgettes, endives, green peas, marrow, mint, parsnips, potatoes (new), radishes, spring onions, sweet corn, tomatoes.

September

Fish. Bass, bloaters, bream, carp, chub, coalfish, conger eels, crayfish, gurnard, haddock, hake, ling, megrim, mullet (red and grey), mussels, oysters (back again), perch, pike, pollan, prawns, roker, skate, smelts, tench, whiting, witch.

Home-grown fruit. Apples (Cox's Orange Pippin, Newton Wonder, Worcester Pearmain, Lord Derby, Warner, James Grieve), blackberries, bullaces, damsons, fresh figs, gooseberries, greengages, melons, nectarines, peaches, pears (Laxton, Dr Jules, Clapps, Williams), plums, quinces.

Imported fruit. Cherries, hothouse grapes, naartjes.

Meat. All meat; pork is getting very good again.

Poultry and game. Blackcock, capercaillie, curlews, geese, goslings, green geese, grouse, hares, leverets, partridges, plovers, quails, snipe, widgeon, wild duck, wild geese, woodcock.

Home-grown vegetables. Globe artichokes, beans (French and runner), brussels sprouts, cabbages (drumhead and Savoy), celeriac, celery, courgettes, cucumbers (ridge), endives, marrows, mint, parsnips, peas, pumpkins, radishes, spring onions, swedes, sweet corn, tomatoes.

October

Fish. Barbel, bass, bloaters, bream, carp, chub, coalfish, conger eels, crayfish, grayling, gurnard, haddock, hake, ling, megrim, mullet (grey), mussels, oysters, perch, pike, pollan, prawns, roker, scallops, skate, smelts, sprats, tench, whiting, witch.

Home-grown fruit. Apples (Cox's Orange Pippin, Newton Wonder, Worcester Pearmain, Laxton's Superb, Lord Derby, James Grieve, Charles Ross, Lord Lambourne), blackberries, bullaces, damsons, filberts, nectarines, peaches, pears (Conference, Comice), end of the English plums, quinces.

Imported fruit. Figs, naartjes.

Meat. All meat; pork is good now.

Poultry and game. Blackcock, capercaillie, curlews, geese, goslings, green geese, grouse, hares, leverets, partridges, pheasants, plovers, quails, snipe, venison, widgeon, wild duck, wild geese, woodcock (excellent now).

Home-grown vegetables. Globe artichokes, beans (hothouse – French and white haricot beans are nearly over), broccoli, brussels sprouts, cabbages (drumhead, January King), celeriac, celery, endives, horseradish, kale, marrows, mint, onions, parsnips, peas, pumpkins, radishes, swedes, sweet corn, tomatoes.

November

Fish. Bream, carp, chub, coalfish, grayling, gurnard, haddock, hake, ling, mackerel, megrim, mullet (grey), mussels, oysters, perch, pike, roker, scallops, skate, smelts, sprats, tench, whiting, witch.

Home-grown fruit. Apples (Cox's Orange Pippin, Newton Wonder, Worcester Pearmain, Laxton's Superb, Lord Derby, Lord Lambourne), colmar, filberts, grapes (muscat), medlars, peaches, pears (Conference, Comice).

Imported fruit. Cranberries, filberts, pomegranates.

Meat. All meats. Australian lamb appears; it is cheaper than New Zealand, but not as good.

Poultry and game. Blackcock, capercaillie, curlews, geese, goslings, green geese, grouse, hares, leverets, partridges. Pheasants are at their best. There are still plovers, quails, snipe, venison, widgeon, wild duck, wild geese. Woodcock are excellent.

Home-grown vegetables. Jerusalem artichokes, beans (hothouse), broccoli, brussels sprouts, cabbages (January King, drumhead and Savoy), celeriac, celery, endives, horseradish, kale, mint, onions, parsnips, shallots, swedes, tomatoes.

December

Fish. Barbel, bream, carp, chub, coalfish, grayling, gurnard, haddock, hake, lemon sole, ling, mackerel, megrim, mullet (grey), mussels, oysters, perch, pike, roker, scallops, skate, smelts, sprats, tench, whiting, witch.

Home-grown fruit. Apples (Cox's Orange Pippin, Newton Wonder, Worcester Pearmain, Laxton's Superb, Blenheim Orange), colmar, grapes (muscat), pears (Conference, Comice), rhubarb (forced).

Imported fruit. Cranberries, filberts, peaches (the first South African ones), and round about Christmas mandarin oranges (large tangerines), clementines and satsumas.

Meat. All meat; pork is very good.

Poultry and game. Blackcock (until the 20th), capercaillie are fading a bit now, but Aylesbury duck are super. Still some curlews, geese, goslings, green geese, grouse (until the 20th), hares, leverets, partridges, pheasants, plovers, quails, snipe, venison, widgeon, wild duck, wild geese, woodcock.

Home-grown vegetables. Jerusalem artichokes, beans (hothouse), brussels sprouts, cabbages (January King, drumhead, Savoy and red), celeriac, celery, horseradish, kale (Scotch), mint, onions, parsnips, shallots, swedes.

Imported vegetables. Endives, salsify.

WHAT'S WHAT IN THE DELICATESSEN

The delicatessen shop has brought a new range of foods to every part of Britain (there are over 10,000 shops). Health-food shops are also helping discriminating shoppers get what they want. Chemists, too, sell bay leaf, saffron, sea salt and certain oils. A first-class wine merchant stocks the most superb-quality olive oils. If you are not within easy reach of the food you want you can arrange to have it sent by post.

Vinegar. Many foodstuffs in delicatessens are pickled. Buy your vinegar here. Vinegar can be made from any liquid from beer to milk. Watch for cider vinegar, milder than average; wine vinegar (all German vinegars are wine vinegars), best for salads and cooking; malt vinegar, cheaper than wine vinegar, is made from barley. It is amber in colour; use it for pickling. Distilled vinegar is clear, therefore it should be used when you wish to avoid darkening (e.g. in mayonnaise). There are vinegars flavoured with garlic, onion, shallot, mint, chillies, and all kinds of herbs, which are sometimes displayed decoratively inside the bottle. These flavourings can easily be added to your own vinegar.

Sauerkraut (French: choucroute) is a German speciality. Around Stuttgart there is a region which specializes not only in the production of the special cabbage from which sauerkraut is made, but also in wine-vinegar production. Great sauerkraut comes from this region. It is in tins.

Mustards are ranged around delicatessen shops in all manner of fancy packs and pots. English mustard (the very best is marked 'G.D.S.F.') is the fiercest, German (often marked 'Düsseldorfer Senf') is milder, and French (often marked 'Dijon') milder still. The lighter the appearance, the hotter it is likely to be.

Sausages. Liver sausage is Leberwurst. Watch for Landeleberwurst (pork liver + fat) and Kalbsleberwurst (calf liver). Blutwurst is black pudding, and if it is coarse in texture it will be called Blutschwartenmagen. Gänseleberwurst is goose-liver sausage. Zungenwurst is a sausage made from tongue. As you see, there is a whole lifetime of eating at the sausage counter; as this is a German contribution to world eating, learn a few more German names. Jagdwurst is a coarse ham sausage, and Lachsschinken is ready-cooked smoked pork loin; Probakalbsleberwurst is smoked liver sausage.

The best-known sausages are probably Frankfurters; these need warming in boiling water for four minutes. Sausages which need cooking are marked 'zum Kochen', and a type of salami which needs cooking is marked 'Kochsalami', but most salami is ready to eat cold. Large horseshoe-shaped sausages are called 'boiling rings' or Krakauer rings or Polish rings (pölnische Ringe) – they need four minutes in boiling water too. 'm. Knoblauch' means 'with garlic'.

Some sausages are intended for spreading, like pâté: kugenwalder Turist is one of these; ask for others. Chorizos are a special sort of Spanish sausages. They are made from beef, pork and paprika. They are very hot. Essential in Paella, they are wonderful in any food which needs sparking up. Slice fine and use sparingly until you gauge how hot they are.

Fish. Smoked cod's roe is sold in jars, or by weight. Use it (sparsely) as a spread or snack. Smoked trout, sprats, buckling, smoked salmon, smoked saithe (much cheaper) and smoked mackerel are served with a slice of lemon and brown bread and butter. No preparation is needed. They are all delicious and make the easiest possible fish course. The trout, mackerel and buckling are served whole (one per person). Herring can be bought in aspic, and herring fillets appear in the most amazing dressings, from fruit sauce (Lukullustunke) to red wine and madeira sauce (Rotwein- and Madeira-tunke), but my favourite is marked 'geräuchert im eigenen Saft' (smoked in its own juice). Eel can be bought smoked (very expensive), or prepared in oil or dill, etc. Anchovy fillets are a useful item, sometimes available loose. There are also the Rollmops and Bismarck herring which you already know.

Cheeses are equally various, from the soft, blue-veined Bresse bleu to the nasty processed varieties. Here are some others: Demi-sel is a whole-cream cheese from Normandy; Fromage de Monsieur is a soft creamy cheese of the Camembert family; Roquefort is a fierce blue cheese made from ewe's milk; Räucherkäse mit Salami is a smoked cheese with salami pieces; Schinkenkäse is ham cheese which may also be smoked. Buy grated Parmesan in the delicatessen. It is cheaper bought by weight than in fancy little tins.

Breads and biscuits are here in profusion. Buy the small packets of ready-sliced, foil-wrapped black bread (pumpernickel types); use it for open sandwiches or serve it with a heavy peasant (one-course-meal type) soup, or with the cheese as a second type of bread. It may be too sweet for some tastes.

There are lots of strange items in tins and jars, and this is a good way of acquainting yourself with the wilder growths from afar, e.g. buy prepared pigs' feet and you may like them enough to prepare some yourself.

Coffee. Delicatessen shops are often well stocked with coffee. Nothing can compare with freshly roasted coffee that is ground in the kitchen one minute before the kettle boils, but vacuum-packed is the next-best thing. Coffee marked 'French' generally has chicory in it. Austrian coffee means that it has fig essence added (it's not as bad as it sounds).

Pasta and egg noodles (Eiernudeln) should be carefully examined. British-made ones are not nearly as good as continental ones, in my experience.

Odds and Ends. Chillies may be dried or tinned or bottled. The small ones are very hot. Peppers (green or red) are available in tins. Add them to casseroles, etc. – they are quite mild in flavour.

Large blocks of unsweetened chocolate are now seldom seen in any sort of shop, but a helpful grocer will get some for you. Order a reasonable amount to make it worth while – it will keep.

Flour. Wholemeal is the only flour that has none of the germ removed (the germ is sold under various brand names and is very expensive). Some experts feel that *stoneground wholemeal* is even better. *Wheatmeal* means that they have replaced certain parts of the germ by means of chemicals. *White flour* has had the germ extracted, after which it has been bleached by chemicals.

Self-raising flour is plain flour that has a raising agent added. You should have both kinds. Plain is best for bread, pastry and batter mix and quite a few other things. Unless otherwise directed (by a recipe), use plain. Cornflour is a maize flour for thickening sauces, etc.

Buckwheat Flour is strong-flavoured (so often mixed with ordinary flour).

Potato Flour: great for thickening, leaves no raw taste. Use one-third normal amount.

Rye Flour: this is what makes pumpernickel as heavy as lead.

Soy Flour: high protein. Use to enrich as directed.

Arrowroot: clear thickening agent. Tasteless, therefore perhaps the best one.

Cornstarch/Cornflour: a refined thickening flour.

Corn Meal: high nutrition value, found throughout world. Worth experimenting with, e.g. for pancakes, cornbread.

Oatmeal. The packet variety is not as flavourful as the real thing. See if you can get oatmeal loose; ask for 'pin-head cut' for the greatest dish of porridge you ever tasted. A health-food shop is your best bet for this.

Salt. *Sea salt* is something you must try. *Maldon salt* is one very excellent variety.

Tea, like coffee, is mostly sold blended. If you wish to taste unblended tea, many tea and coffee merchants will be only too happy to send even small amounts (½ lb.) through the post. Ask for Darjeeling, Assam and Dooars; these are three contrasting types of Indian tea. The merchant will probably send you his list; it might

also mention Lapsang Souchong, which is a heavy, smoky tea; Keemun and Chingwos, lighter teas (these are all China); Earl Grey, generally a China tea (but it is a generic name unless it comes from Jackson's, the most important supplier).

Tea as we normally buy it is called 'black tea'. 'Green tea' is an unfermented tea and the only one you are likely to see is Gunpowder. Oolong is halfway between black and green (it has a faint fruity scent).

Olives can be bought loose or in bottles. In each case they come black, green, or green and stuffed with a chunk of red pepper. The black ones are 'ripe' olives; they can be rolled in a little garlicky olive oil. (If you wish the oil can be heated and the olives served hot on sticks – but warn your guests or they may think they are going crazy when they get a hot olive in the kisser.) Green olives are equally good – serve them as they are.

Olive Oil. The king of all cooking oil is the 'virgin' first-pressed oil from choicest olives. It is expensive and not so easy to find (ask the best wine merchant you know for details). Other pressings are variously priced, as also are the many other oils: cotton-seed, peanut, sunflower, etc., which are all quite excellent in their way.

Sour cream is used in savoury dishes (e.g. Chicken Paprika) and also on fruit, pies, etc. Not good in cakes or for making ice cream. Sometimes marked 'cultured cream'.

Soy (sauce). A thin, dark-brown, very salty liquid made from soya beans. There are several different qualities. This is useful in the kitchen, for it will give a rich brown colour and a piquant saltiness, plus a slight flavour that is all its own. It should be put on the table as a condiment when Chinese food is served. A splash of soy into a thin chicken broth (or similar) is more interesting than salt, but put it on the table and let your guests help themselves. Similarly, in Chinese cooking, it is best to give each guest a tiny saucer (e.g. a demi-tasse saucer) into which he can pour soy and after that dip pieces of food into it before eating them. Soy sauce is never normally poured over rice.

Anchovy. A dark, small, very salty fish. Available in brine, salt or oil. Those in tins are filleted; usually therefore much more expensive. Wonderful in pizza with tomato, mushroom and meat. It is a strange fish, for it will mix with all sort of unlikely items, so experiment – but with great care.

Delicatessens also sell cooked items – pâté, terrine, chicken in aspic, pizza, Quiche Lorraine, vol-au-vents, meat pies. Although these tend to be more carbohydrate than protein, they can sometimes be good.

Take a good look at items that attract you – it is a good way to learn professional garnishings and presentation.

Some delicatessens have speciality items available only one day per week – many of them made on the premises. Freshly made pasta and pastry are not uncommon.

HERBS, SPICES, SEEDS AND OTHER FLAVOURINGS

As a rough definition, spices are stamens, shells, bark, etc., from tropical zones, and herbs are the leaves of plants grown in temperate climates. The former are used more sparingly in most dishes. Whole spices and seeds are either crushed before use or are used in long, simmering types of cooking. Crushed spices are best added only a quarter of an hour before serving, and there is no need to retrieve them from the cooking pot before serving. Store all flavourings in airtight containers (chemical jars are excellent) in a cool dark place. Buy in small amounts, store in small containers. I have designed a small herb rack (the Len Deighton Herb Rack, manufactured by Marler and Haley Ltd) which has instructions for use actually baked on to the glass jar, so I may as well give it a plug here.

HERBS

Basil. There are people who won't touch a tomato without it. Tomato soup, tomato sauce, grilled tomatoes and tomato omelette are all perfected with a trace of basil. Lamb chops can be sprinkled with a little just before they finish cooking.

Supper dishes that are mainly egg or cheese will respond well, as will plain vegetables like peas or creamed potatoes.

It is a very widely distributed herb, and features in Italian and Spanish cooking. Put it in home-made sausages or meat balls.

Capers. These are buds of a plant that grows around the Mediterranean, and are sold bottled. Add them to mayonnaise when making Sauce Tartare. They give piquancy to cold meat or poultry. People who like them very much will eat them with almost anything. Particularly good as an appetizer.

Caraway. There are three usable parts: the root, seeds and leaf. The roots can be eaten (cooked) as a vegetable, the leaves can be used chopped and sprinkled into salads. It is mostly used in conjunction with vegetables, but also goes well with pork.

Celery. This is a great flavouring which can be used in such a variety of foods that it is very difficult to go wrong with it. Fish, eggs, any stews, salads and stuffings – all these are suitable. When you are using fresh celery, cut off the green leaves and hang them in the kitchen to dry. When they are dry, they can be put into a jar. These dry crisp leaves are a wonderful flavouring ingredient. Celery seed should always be on the herb shelf. Celery salt is also useful.

Chervil. Well known in French cooking, it is strangely neglected in English and American cooking. There are quite a lot of recipes that call for a combination of green herbs, and this is the one that is all too often left out. Use it in Sauce Béarnaise and in Omelettes Fines Herbes. This is a herb that blends well with others. Use it with delicately flavoured foods, e.g. eggs, white fish and mild vegetables.

Chives. This is a sort of milder-than-mild version of the spring onion, and looks like a blade of grass. Of all the herbs this is the one to use fresh if you possibly can, otherwise it is possible to buy it as chive salt. Chives will fit anywhere where a touch of onion flavour will be welcome. Some cooks insist that the finest omelette is a chopped-chive omelette. Some types of cottage cheese are sold with the chives already in it. Wonderful with tomato.

Dill. This is as common in North America as it is rare in Europe, being used only as a flavour for pickling. Chop the tips of the stems and use them in a poultry stuffing, or scatter them over halibut, salmon or the oily fish like mackerel, before putting under the grill. It will make a fresh, uncooked garnish for salad vegetables like cucumber and avocado pears. The pulse-type vegetables also go well with it – pea soup, for instance.

Fennel. This has a wonderful flavour. The stems and root are eaten like celery, and it has as wide an application as celery has, but this is not a meat flavouring. Use it with fish (this is good with oily fish such as mackerel – eels too). Experiment with vegetables (especially parsnips).

It can be added to the water before poaching fish (e.g. salmon, cod, halibut), globe artichokes or eggs.

Fish soups (e.g. bouillabaisse), sauerkraut, potato salad and pickled beetroot call for it, and some apple-pie experts regard it as an essential ingredient.

Garlic. Controversial as a flavouring element, although I can hardly imagine life without it. Fanatics like me will add it to almost everything, but everyone should try it with steak, any beef stew, and green salads; it will even spark up the flavourless battery hen. A clove or two can be put into a bottle of vinegar or oil to make a flavoured dressing – the bottle should stand a couple of weeks to take on the flavour. Don't put pieces of garlic into a dish unless you either crush them thoroughly or fry the garlic in oil and then remove it.

People who don't like garlic will go out of their minds if they get pieces in their mouths.

Horseradish. It amazes me how much bottled horseradish sauce is sold, even when the fresh vegetable is available in the shops. Everyone has his own way of preparing it. In any case grate it very finely, adding a good, light, wine vinegar, cream, a touch of mustard and sugar, etc. Or just serve the plain grated stuff with nothing added.

It is wonderful with boiled beef, trout, steak, etc., etc. There is a recipe for horseradish sauce (*see* page 232).

Marjoram. A relation of mint and such a close relation of oregano (which is a wild variety) that it can be used as a substitute. It is a fragrant and versatile flavouring, but should be used with care. Good in minced beef (hamburgers, meat loaf, etc.) or with baked sole; it has a wide variety of uses in soups and stews. Baked-cheese recipes react well, and it is sometimes used with roast pork as a change from sage.

Mint. Mostly associated with roast lamb – if you use mint sauce, then make your own rather than buy it in bottles, and you won't have to have the flavour of mint and lamb both swamped by the taste of sugar. It is great chopped into fresh fruit – try it in fresh fruit salad or scattered on grapefruit. Make tea Arab-style, using a big sprig of mint instead of milk. Use a little on fish. With savoury things use it sparingly, but with jams and jellies you can go to town.

Nasturtium. For a really wild idea, try using petals and even small leaves in a salad (go and visit a friend's garden). The seeds can be pickled in vinegar and after eight weeks can be used just like capers.

Oregano. This is a wild marjoram. Use it as marjoram. It is especially good if you make pork sausages at home, and is good inside a roast chicken or pheasant. Mostly called for in Italian recipes – try it in tomato, beans or onions.

Parsley. Perhaps the most widely used single herb. What a pity it is mostly relegated to the position of garnish. Try it in recipes that will extract the flavour – fish stock is better for it, and there is no meat or fish that you can't use it with. Add it early during the cooking process, even if this means replacing it with some more before it goes to the table – after all, how much is a piece of parsley?

Rosemary. Roast mutton or lamb is never the same without it. Combined with garlic, it goes well with roast beef or sprinkled on a steak. Brown stews (beef or rabbit), vegetable or meat soups benefit, as do pickles, jams and jellies. Some cooks like it with white sauces, white fish, poultry and cakes, but it should be used with discretion in the case of the last four.

Sage. Best known in the stuffing for roast pork, duck or goose, it is sometimes used to flavour cheeses. If added to liquid, it is apt to taste bitter unless used towards the end of the cooking. An essential ingredient for pork pies, it also goes well with various dried beans (lentil-soup recipes generally call for it) and green beans. Experiment with it on baked fish and in green salads.

Savory. Another Mediterranean plant, it is especially good with green vegetables. It is one of those herbs which is especially good fresh – grow a little if you can. It has a very wide variety of uses: stuffings for lamb, beef or any poultry. It is used in certain parts of Germany – sauerkraut is given that authentic flavour with a little savory.

Sorrel. This is a less common herb, due no doubt to the sour bitter flavour. That makes it sound terrible, but it hasn't been going since 3000 B.C. for nothing. Cook the under leaves like spinach – sometimes its flavour is modified by using it mixed with other green leaf-vegetables. The real enthusiast, however, will take it straight. On French menus it is called Oseille – try some.

Tarragon. We find this in the luxury dishes of France – in the shellfish, scattered over the finest steaks, flavouring the asparagus, in the chicken soups, the roasted duck and in the Béarnaise sauce. Also good with game – hare and rabbit especially. Failing all

that, have it mixed into your scrambled egg.

Thyme. Many varieties exist of this sweet aromatic herb. It adds interest to food that would otherwise taste too bland. It is wonderful on fresh poached salmon, in an oyster stew or with most shellfish recipes. For more everyday uses try it with beef or with braised beef liver. Grilled tomatoes can be sprinkled with thyme before cooking. It is a good herb to experiment with; try using it in stuffings or clear soups.

Watercress. Generally stuffed under the steak and left uneaten, watercress is a highly nutritious food and flavouring. If you leave it whole, it is more awkward to use, so chop the leaves finely and sprinkle it into vegetables like beans, carrots and potatoes, and into any sort of vegetable or fish soup (it makes a fine splash of colour for the white cream soups). Scatter it over cooked steaks and poultry. As a salad ingredient, it is better to chop the leaves from the stalks.

SPICES

Allspice. This is not the same as mixed spice. It got its name because people couldn't decide which spice it resembled. It comes in berries, or ground as a powder. It is good with ground meats (especially beef) and sausages. Apple pie gains a lift from it, so do most cooked-fruit recipes. You would be equally correct to use it in a court-bouillon and with vegetables (especially tomato), but I warn you, a little goes a long way in these latter cases.

Cayenne. This bottle should be marked with a skull and crossbones – this is dynamite. Use it with great caution. It is made by grinding up tiny dried chillies. I make my own form of cayenne by buying more chillies than I need (who needs many chillies?) when cooking with them. I let the surplus ones dry out and then give them a few minutes in my blender – voilà cayenne! If you don't have a blender you will find it easy to crush the brittle pods in your hand – but don't wipe your eyes afterwards. Another advantage of rolling your own cayenne is that you remember that it is powerful stuff.

Chilli Powder. It is virtually the same as cayenne, but varies in strength. It can be used when making a Chile con Carne; a typical flavour combination for Chile con Carne is:

    2 cloves garlic (crushed)
    ½ teaspoon cumin
    1 teaspoon oregano
    1½ teaspoons chilli powder

pinch of cinnamon

½ teaspoon sugar

Of course the other ingredients are tomato, soaked red kidney beans, some lightly fried onion, a sprinkle of salt and, five minutes before serving, ground beef (about a pound will go with this amount of flavouring).

Cinnamon. When you use cloves with meat (e.g. ham, smoked pork, etc.), then cinnamon will go well too. Pork of all kinds goes well with it, as it cuts down the richness rather as apple sauce does. I don't have to tell you that it is terrific with apple pie and in hot wine punch, but what about sprinkling it on rice pudding or custard tarts, or popping a small piece into the coffee pot once in a while?

Cloves. Most prejudice against cloves comes from finding one in your mouth when you are eating a piece of apple pie. For this reason many cooks use ground cloves. Better to crush the head of the clove between thumb and forefinger before adding it, throwing the stalk away. Clove is obviously great in apple pie, ground meat, in terrines and in any of those rich, piquant tomato sauces. Use it in hot wine punches, pork and boiled vegetables.

Ginger. It is imported in many different forms – do not mix them. There is the candied ginger which is good to eat as it is, or can be chopped as a garnish on fruit or ice cream. There is ginger in sugar syrup – great as a sauce over vanilla ice cream, bananas, and many other desserts. The root itself is used to make ginger beer and ginger wine, and to flavour alcoholic drinks and fruit punch. The fresh soft ginger in tins (not sweetened) is something to be kept in the store cupboard. Buy the smallest tin there is, for it must be finely sliced, therefore it goes a long way and is not easy to keep once the tin is open. Ginger Beef is a favourite recipe in South America, and this flavouring can be introduced discreetly into any beef dish. Use it chopped in a casserole, or rub it on steak before grilling it. Use it even more discreetly with chicken – rub it over a bird before roasting, or add it to a piquant sauce which can be served with it. Casseroled chicken can also be cooked in ginger sauce.

Mace. Part of the nutmeg fruit, but rather more powerful; some say it tastes a little like cinnamon. Use it with cooked cheese, ground meats (including sausages) and, of course, sweet fruit or egg or milk dishes. Creamy savoury things also react well, like rich soups and stews (e.g. oyster stew, bisque, cream of mushroom soup, etc.).

Mustard. The crushed mustard seed is mentioned in the Seeds section. It is sometimes adulterated – turmeric is added to make it more yellow. The best mustard is marked G.D.S.F. (Genuine Double Super Fine). While you may prefer mustards in tubes, always keep a tin of good powdered mustard for use in cooking, for the ready-made variety can produce some nasty flavours if mixed with other things.

Mustard Oil is a useful addition to the flavourings. Use sparingly. For other sorts of mustard *see* the Delicatessen section.

Nutmeg. An important ingredient in French cooking. It is worth the trouble of grating it yourself, as it is more flavourful then. Any ground meat reacts well: sausages, meat balls, hamburgers, terrines, pâtés, etc. Use it also with any milk pudding. Put it on to cream soups, chicken soups and Scotch broths.

Paprika. A sweet pepper made from dried capsicum pods, it is native to Central America. Too often confused with the more fiery cayenne. Paprika can be used fairly generously in pâtés, stuffings and any meat dishes. It is essential in goulash and, of course, Chicken Paprika. It contains vitamins A and C and aids digestion. Its value as a colouring and a garnish (on sour cream, cottage cheese) should not blind the cook to its importance as a flavouring. Buy only the very best-quality Hungarian paprika, and you will use no other.

Pepper. This is a small, wrinkled, black berry – there is no other true kind. White pepper is merely the same berry with its outer skin missing. Red pepper is not pepper at all – it is finely ground-up capsicums. As for that stuff marked pepper that looks like grey flour – that is quite possibly grey flour.

You must have a pepper mill so that the pepper is used one moment after it has been ground, thus retaining the aromatic oils. There are an enormous variety of types: 'Singapore' is perhaps the finest.

Saffron. There are five thousand buds in every ounce of saffron – no wonder it is so very expensive. Best known as an ingredient in bouillabaisse and as a colouring for rice in both Italian and Indian cooking. I personally think it is enormously overrated.

Turmeric. This is the ingredient that makes curry yellow. It is called 'haldi' in Indian cookery. It is used to colour many packaged foods from mustard to custard, through pancake mixes. It has quite a rich flavour and a little bit added to a real batter mixture gives it new taste. Good with any cake mixtures, and in pickle-making and relishes. Beware of adding too much, for although the flavour is mild, the colour goes much more violent when heat is applied.

SEEDS

Anise Seed. This can be very widely used if you keep the flavour-level low. It is usually found scattered over breads and pastries. Use it when poaching shellfish and in making home-made sausages. Superb in fruit salads and any kind of fruit compote. Use it very carefully and you can bring a sweet interest to veal or pork, braised or stewed.

Caraway Seed. Like anise seed, this is best known as the flavour of a drink, but in Central European cooking it holds an important place. Great in baked apple or apple pie, also in potato soup or sauerkraut. Like aniseed, it can go into veal or pork whether it is braised or stewed. Beware – some people hate it.

Cardamon Seed. This is of Indian origin and I only use it when cooking boiled rice. However, in Northern Europe it is found in all manner of things from hot wine punch to fruit salad. If you want to experiment, use it in fruity things – it will transfer its flavour very readily.

Celery Seed. *See* Herbs section.

Coriander Seed. For my money just about the greatest flavouring matter there is. Crush some in a warm hand and inhale it – if you don't agree that it is the greatest thing you ever inhaled, don't write and tell me. Hurl crushed coriander seed into any open pot you see. It's marvellous for stuffings, soups, stews and sausages. It can be put into the pepper mill along with peppercorns and everyone will ask where you bought the pepper. One crushed seed can be dropped into a cup of coffee. Use it in stewed fruit (great for baked apple). Use it with pork, braised or roasted; milk puddings and vegetable soups. Just one thing: the crushed seeds will not dissolve, so grind them fine (e.g. in a pepper mill) or use ground coriander. The latter is not so aromatic in my opinion. Caution – you may not share my enthusiasm.

Cumin Seed. Strongly associated with hot dishes and dishes from the East. In Indian cookery it is called 'zeera' and is found in most curry mixtures. In Mexican cooking it is called 'comino'. In the Middle East, the kebab is almost invariably sprinkled with lots of it. It has a powdery, musty flavour that can be discreetly added to meat stew and poultry stew. I have heard that fruit that already has cloves or spices added to it benefits from a touch of cumin seed. I don't think so, but go ahead and try it for yourself.

Dill Seed. *See* Herbs section.

Fennel Seed. *See* Herbs section.

Juniper. Best known as an ingredient of gin, it is connected with the cooking of game and poultry. Use it also in strong-flavoured wine sauces. It has a strong, almost bitter taste, and should be used where the recipe includes other strong flavours. Popular as a marinade ingredient, it therefore is a natural if you marinade venison. Use it also in stews which have been flavoured with wine.

Mustard Seed. Remarkably tiny seeds that can be used wherever the flavour of mustard would not be out of place. It has the advantage that it can be scattered over foods, e.g. hot vegetables or salads, providing a flavourful garnish. I need hardly say that it must be used with care.

Nasturtium Seeds. *See* Herbs section.

Poppy Seed. Usually found on tops of loaves, it is wonderful in breads and cakes. Use it also in hot vegetables like carrots, potatoes, and those frozen peas that are dying for want of flavour. Goes well with cheese – cream cheese can be decorated with it – and when you have a taste for it, put it on fruit compotes.

Sesame Seed. Known in Indian cookery as 'til', it is also widely used in China. Best known here as an ingredient of Halva. Use it as a garnish for the blander types of food, e.g. potatoes, scones, toast, rice, noodles, cheese and white fish. It can be sprinkled over the food just before taking it to the table, but adding it before the cooking process will not harm it or detract from its flavouring qualities.

OTHER FLAVOURINGS

Chilli Sauce. *See* Cayenne and Chilli Powder in Spices section.

Monosodium Glutamate (M.S.G.). This is a glutamic acid produced from soya beans. It has little or no flavour of its own, but 'brings up' the flavour of other ingredients. Don't use it with milk, fruit or cereals.

Vanilla Pod. This is the seed-pod of a Mexican orchid. It is about the size and shape of a half-used pencil. It is dropped into hot milk, custard, sauce, etc., and imparts a wonderful flavour. After use it should be washed in warm water, dried, and used again. It will gradually lose its flavour, but don't be mean – buy a new one now and again. Keep a jar of castor sugar with a vanilla pod in it.

Peel (orange or lemon). Wonderful as a flavouring element. Take it from fresh fruit with a potato peeler. Avoid white pith.

BASIC STORE CUPBOARD

A well-stocked larder needs all these items. Check with these three lists before you go shopping. Replace as used to keep items circulating.

Most flavourings: *see* Flavourings section, page 97.

Flour: plain and self-raising.

Cornflour or arrowroot.

Baking powder.

Cooking chocolate.

Gelatine.

Dried yeast.

Oatmeal, packaged or loose.

Tinned coffee.

Tinned milk. Get evaporated and condensed.

Tinned fish (tuna, sardine, pilchard, anchovy). Tuna + tinned corn makes a soup.

Fish in jars (Rollmops, etc.).

Tinned soups (*all kinds*). Choose some for suitability as sauces. The condensed ones are best for this. Consommé can be used as stock; cream of chicken as a chicken sauce.

Tinned meat: corned beef, beef casserole, Danish pork, Frankfurters.

Tinned vegetables: corn, mushrooms, tomatoes, sauerkraut, pimentoes, artichoke hearts, asparagus, beans, carrots, processed peas (soaked dried peas) and garden peas, etc.

Tinned prepared meals: cassoulet, whole chicken, whole ham (latter can be wrapped in pastry, cooked in oven – impressive).

Dried fruit (large): figs, dates, prunes, apricots, apple rings, peaches, plums (these are great – ask for them), pears and mixed fruit.

Dried fruit (small): currants, raisins and sultanas. If you scatter them over your cornflakes you will soon get through them.

Nuts (canned or loose): almonds (ask for soft-shelled ones), hazels, brazils, pecans and walnuts. Walnuts don't keep so well.

Tinned pulses: tinned baked beans can be used in an emergency to put a sort of Chile con Carne together. Tins of butter beans, tins of peas (processed or garden) can be sieved to make thick purées or soups.

Alcohol: red wine, a dry white wine, a sweet white wine (can hide a multitude of tins). These are best bought in half-bottles. Brandy (for cooking it can be

less than perfect but it shouldn't be too beastly).
Madeira.

Tinned cream. Has a distinctive taste – a little vanilla helps to disguise it.

Tinfoil and greaseproof paper: also rolls of absorbent paper for cleaning omelette pans, etc.

Cake decor: angelica, silver balls, chocolate decoration.

Milk drinks: unsweetened chocolate for flavourings or making cocoa; drinking chocolate, Horlicks, Bournvita, etc., to personal taste.

Sugar: castor for creaming or for dusting pies, etc.; granulated (there are various qualities). Barbados – the most flavourful sugar. Decorative coffee sugar. Golden syrup, icing and preserving sugars if you use them.

Dried vegetables (for quick purées you can grind these items in a blender before cooking – which is then very quick).

Rice (long and short grain – buy best of each).

Semolina (doesn't keep all that well).

Tapioca (buy the smallest sort, unless you like those big chunks of 'goo').

Split peas and dried peas.

Lentils: the green continental ones are better than the bright orange English ones. Chick peas, haricot beans, red kidney beans.

Jams and marmalade: useful as pancake fillings, flavourings; and diluted slightly will make a sauce. If you can't afford the best, make them yourself – it's not difficult.

Honey: great variety available. Can be used in luxury cooking.

Pickles and chutneys. Shops selling curry constituents have wonderful ones, but most shops have a couple.

Vinegar: *see* Delicatessen section (page 90) for varieties.

Tea: *see* Delicatessen section for varieties.

Tomato in tins or tomato purée: both useful in a hundred ways. Buy lots of small tins rather than one huge one that will go bad. Purée is best in tubes.

Meat extracts and bouillon cubes. Best to make your own (*see* Rich Stock grid), but Marmite is the one I use otherwise.

Salami. Buy a whole (small) sausage. It does not have to be salami – choose one you like.

A piece of streaky bacon: will keep well if wrapped and stored in the cool.

Pasta: take your choice of shapes and sizes.

Oil: olive or nut oil.

BUY THESE ITEMS EACH WEEK

Coffee beans. There is a vast range of coffees blended and unblended and a choice of light or dark roasts. If you are not happy with your local supplier, have coffee mailed to you at prearranged intervals.

Bacon, smoked or unsmoked. Have it sliced to the thickness you want, for whatever you want. Try it very very thin for a change. Smoked back sliced as fine as possible can be served raw. O.K. – don't believe me – try it.

Butter. I always buy unsalted even though it does not keep as well as salted. It is a good rule to buy your salted butter of a brand that does an unsalted one too. Danish Lurpak is one of the world's great (mass-production) butters.

Cheese (cream-types). It is worth finding out which day the fresh cheese comes to your local shop. Buy accordingly; buy a fresh cream-type cheese if it will be served within a couple of days of arriving at the shop, otherwise choose one that will ripen or remain unchanged.

Cooking fat. There is nothing to beat fine pork fat for many things. Ask your butcher for a chunk of pig fat, slice it finely and fry very gently; when just 'crackling' remains, pour off the dripping for use. Branded fats you see in ads on TV are good for flavourless cookery.

Suet. If you want to make dumplings or suet pudding, ask your butcher for a piece of **suet** and grate it yourself (*see* Steak and Kidney Pudding grid).

Packet suet: pieces of beef fat rolled in flour. It keeps very well and is good to use when you have no alternative.

Mutton, beef (including items to make stock once a week), or **game.** This is often too fresh. Hang in a cool airy place. It costs money for the food industry to use storage space – it costs you nothing. You will be amazed at the difference in tenderness and flavour. If in doubt ask advice from a shop in which you have confidence.

Soft drinks: orange juice (it's better to make your own), blackcurrant juice, soda water, tonic water, lemon juice (all these are best bought in large bottles for use in the kitchen), tomato juice and cider (come in very large tins), beer and lager.

Sterilized milk: usually the bottle with the crown cap. Keeps very well, useful as an extra.

Garlic.

BUY AND EAT AS SOON AS POSSIBLE

Eggs.

Green vegetables. The 'greens' and also the extra items like tomatoes, mushrooms, avocado pears, lettuces, etc.

Root vegetables: potatoes, swedes, turnips, carrots, parsnips. Can be kept for a few days.

Fruit. Certain items (melons, pears, etc.) can be bought a little under-ripe if you want to buy in advance.

Frozen food. If you can get it back to your freezer before the temperature rises above 0° F. and if your freezer can keep it at zero, then you can buy frozen food months in advance. Otherwise buy it and use immediately.

Milk, yoghourt and cream. Most households have these delivered. In many areas it is possible to obtain 'farm-bottled' tuberculin-tested milk. This is pure raw milk and tastes different from the bulk of milk delivered to the towns (ask your dairy). Homogenized means that the cream and milk are mixed together. Pasteurized means rendered free from any possible infection by heat; this also means it will keep better, but some flavour is lost. (Most milk is pasteurized.) Yoghourt is undoubtedly beneficial to digestion and well-being. Can be eaten or used in cooking.

Cream (comes single or double – the latter for whipping thick). It is mostly pasteurized or sterilized, and some have preservative added so that it can grow dusty on the grocer's shelf without concern to him. Unless it goes bad quickly, it is not fresh cream.

Clotted cream can be bought by post; this is highly recommended unless you can find fresh untreated cream (I can't).

Bread. Try some unusual ones now and again.

Fish. *Note:* kippers do not keep well. Eat fresh.

Chicken. Pork. Veal. Lamb.

Ice. Can be ordered in cubes or blocks from the local ice company. Having lots and lots of ice is essential for even a small party.

DRINKING

Drink experts should skip this chapter. They might get annoyed at the generalizations I have made.

The Restaurant Wine List. (*see* table on page 121.) Chat up the wine waiter, call him 'sommelier' for a good start. Ask his advice if in doubt; if you are going to try to bluff your friends, let the wine waiter get out of earshot first.

In the list I have mixed Châteaux, communes and districts: e.g. Margaux is a commune in the district of Médoc.

With this oversimplified framework committed to memory, remember these wines too:

Hock (Rhine) and Moselle. Nearly all exported ones are white. Experts choose them by reading the name of the grape-type (Riesling, Sylvaner, etc.) and the selection (Auslese, Spätlese, etc.) from the label, as well as the vintage. All are fragrant, some are fruity.

Alsace. Dry white table wine, taking its name from the grape (Riesling, Traminer, Sylvaner) and tending to be more fragrant than the German counterpart.

Rhône. The Châteauneuf du Pape is the best-known one. It is a fine strong red. Hermitage is a good buy nowadays, since it is out of fashion. Tavel is perhaps the finest rosé in the world.

continued page 124

If you are eating:	Turn wine list page to:	Look down the page for this:	Say this to your guests:	It will taste:
FISH, SHELLFISH	White Burgundy	Chablis Pouilly-Fuissé Meursault Montrachet	Scarce Very fine Variable Great	Very dry
LIGHT MEATS, e.g. PORK, VEAL or CHICKEN	Red Bordeaux (it might say Claret)	Médoc St Émilion St Julien Margaux	Pot luck Big claret Haut Médoc Commune	Light dry
RICH FOOD, e.g. STEWS, STEAK, etc. CHEESE too	Red Burgundy	Vosne-Romanée Beaune Nuits-St-Georges Chambertin	Luxury Ordinary Average Possibly superb	Heavy dry
DESSERT	White Bordeaux	Graves Entre Deux Mers Sauternes Château Yquem	Might be dry Average Aromatic Aristocrat	Fruity, sweet

In order both to illustrate and augment the simple notes on the previous page, here is a list of ideal partners that Cyril Ray, the wine expert, and I worked out one frivolous, post-prandial work-session.

Food	Drink
Oysters/shellfish	A very dry light white wine. Any white Burgundy or a dry Moselle. Stout and oysters are superb. Champagne will do.
Fish plainly served	Dry Graves, dry Moselle or hock.
Fish more elaborate	Fuller-flavoured white, e.g. a 'big' hock or a full-flavoured Alsatian such as Gewürztraminer.
Pasta with just butter	A dry white Italian – Soave or a dry white Orvieto.
Pasta in rich sauce	Red Chianti or cold beer.
Lamb or duck	A light red such as Claret or Beaujolais.
Veal, pork or goose	A not too heavy red (e.g. a Beaujolais, or a Valpolicella or a Bardolino from Italy). An even lighter wine, e.g. a Tavel rosé, may be better. Be guided by the richness of sauce, if any. N.B. Any of these can be served cool.

Food	Drink
Beef, grilled or roast	Cyril Ray preferred a claret, Len Deighton a red Burgundy.
Rich stew, game or cheese	A full-bodied red: a fine Burgundy, a Châteauneuf du Pape, Rioja (Spain), a red Chianti or a 'big' claret, i.e. a St Émilion or Pomerol.
Chicken roasted, fried or in a dark sauce	A light red, i.e. any claret.
Chicken in white sauce or with rice	A dry but fragrant white (hock, Moselle or an Alsatian Riesling or Sylvaner). A fine white Burgundy would do well if you can afford it.
Curry, or goulash with dumplings	Ice-cold lager, or ice-cold light beer. Hungarians drink white wine diluted with equal part soda.
Dessert	The sweet wines – white Bordeaux (Sauternes), sweet champagne, or similar sparkler. Sweet Lacrimae Christi, or pink bubbling Portuguese Mateus rosé.
For vegetarians and T.T.-ers serve	Soda water, Ribena, lime juice or Shloer apple juice. With a hot curry or other piquant food you may care to try yoghourt + ice water mixed in equal quantities.

Chianti. One of the most unreliable guides to wine, since even the district is not clearly defined, although it should be Tuscany between Florence and Siena. You are best advised to ask for something more specific, like a Valpolicella (a little like a red Bordeaux), or a Barolo (like a red Burgundy).

Loire. These white wines range from Muscadet – white, dry, fresh wine, not unlike Chablis, with which it used to be blended – to the light fruity Vouvray and the fine Pouilly Blanc Fumé, which is a little like the Pouilly-Fuissé (White Burgundy) with which its name is frequently confused. Anjou is another Loire wine. It is usually a rosé but not always.

Having worked your frontal lobes like an IBM machine, you are suddenly faced with the problem that everyone has ordered something different to eat.

When this happens:
1 Order in half-bottles. Most restaurants stock plenty of half-bottles because of this very fact (they are only slightly dearer).
2 Watch the future course. You can hit the second half of a bottle of red Burgundy with the cheese course if you intend having one.
3 Move *up* the above list when you have to compromise, i.e. you can drink white Burgundy with anything; or: cheese, steak and stew are good with red Bordeaux if someone else is having chicken.

A BASIC WINE CELLAR

No. of bottles	On the label	Type	Bring it out
3	Meursault	White Burgundy	Fine dry whites for luxury
3	Pouilly	White Burgundy	Fine dry whites for luxury
6	Dry Graves	White Bordeaux	Dry enough to serve with oysters or anything
4	Château Margaux	A really fine red Bordeaux	With steak and chicken
12	Pomerol	A heavier red Bordeaux	Suitable for steak, cheese, etc. (like a red Burgundy)
4	Beaujolais	A lighter red Burgundy	As Château Margaux (*above*)
3	Sparkling Vouvray	A sweet, champagne-like drink	On not-quite-champagne occasions
3	Gewürztraminer	A fruity Alsace	Serve this with dessert

DRINKING AT HOME

1. Your cellar

If you are planning drink to accompany food at home you have more time to dwell upon the problem, and maybe to experiment. Rather than run down to the off-licence as the first guests are arriving, why not plan well ahead – plan a cellar?

If you don't have a cellar, find a quiet cupboard, bearing in mind that it should be cool (55° F. if possible, but certainly not above 65° F.). This means it must not be draughty either. Light will affect wine (yes, even artificial light), so keep it dim; and lastly, no vibration – and that means not letting your visitors heave all the bottles out to see what you have in stock. See table on page 125 for the most tentative of suggestions for a beginning for a wine cellar. I have chosen for variety, value and versatility.

DRINKING AT HOME

2. Throwing a party

A bottle holds 25·6 oz. and in the U.S.A. is often called 'a fifth' because that is a fifth of a gallon. A bartender pours you a drink using a small measure called 'a six out' in the trade, because it gives six drinks out of a gill of hard stuff. Perhaps you belong to some generous ritzy club where they use a 'five out', and even a 'four out' is not beyond the realms of possibility. However, you will not be wanting to give your guests these tiny commercial measures of drink. I would suggest that you calculate for doubles, i.e. a 1½-oz. tot – roughly 17 drinks per bottle. For larger calculations reckon that three bottles will give you 50 drinks and a case (12 bottles) will supply 200 drinks.

A rougher way to calculate is half a bottle per head each two hours. Oddly enough, for each subsequent two hours you must allow three-quarters of a bottle per head, since drinking will increase if they haven't gone home by then. Here's a rough guide:

No. of guests	2-HOUR PARTY		4-HOUR PARTY	
	hard drink (bottles)	mixes (baby size)	hard drink (bottles)	mixes (baby size)
10	5	60	12	144
20	10	120	24	288
40	20	240	48	576

Of course, this is only a rough calculation. How can I know whether your friends are boozers? In practice you probably wouldn't want 576 baby mixes – you would buy the mixes in large-size bottles. You may wish to include some fancy soft drinks like Shloer apple juice and blackcurrant juice. Friends on the wagon appreciate having something worth drinking. Whatever you are ordering, your supplier will probably agree to take back the unopened ones, so to overstock will be in the interests of your guests and your supplier.

You can throw an excellent party without using spirits at all. A wine bottle also holds 26 oz., but wine glasses can hold anything from 4 oz. to 9 oz. without being very different in appearance. A choice of small cheap glasses means that you are not distressed when one is broken, and the small size gives your guests a chance to keep a score on their drinking. I would allow about three-quarters of a wine bottle per head. You may wish to have several wines, or only one. If you choose a white wine (very good with hot snacks – stuffed crêpes, for example), give it enough time to get cold. A bathful of ice cubes from the ice company is best. Bury the wine in it.

You may like to serve only beer at your party. It is

very good with hot cheese savouries, or with hot dogs. Choose your beer carefully if you have only one sort. Some of the light ales chill excellently and have better flavour than many lagers. Ladies seldom like the dark varieties, so have an alternative drink for them. You may like to buy a cask of beer, in which case ask for a Pin which holds 4½ gallons. Beer consumption is the most difficult to calculate, but 1¾ pints per head would be an average to base your guess upon. You know your friends best.

Champagne is often a sole performer at a party. Allow half a bottle per guest. There are five main types, from brut, the driest, through the extra sec, sec and demi-sec, to the sweet doux. It comes in all sizes, from quarter bottles, magnums (2 quarts), Jeroboams (4 quarts), Methuselahs (8 quarts), Balthazars (16 quarts), to the Nebuchadnezzar (20 quarts). Vintage champagne is a blend of one particular year, and non-vintage is a blend from several different years – it is not necessarily inferior. If served with dinner in Britain or U.S.A. it will probably be a dry one served all through the meal, but in France it is more likely to be a sweeter one served with the dessert. There are many other sparkling wines less expensive than champagne, and I strongly recommend that you try some of them. Burgundies come as sparkling reds, sparkling whites and even sparkling pinks. Also from France there are sparkling versions of Muscatel and Vouvray. From Germany there are sparkling hocks (especially fine), Moselles and Liebfraumilch. From Italy there is a sparkling version of red Valpolicella and, perhaps best known of all, the sweet Asti Spumante.

For regular entertaining you may prefer to stock a bar. This may be anything from a card-table and cupboard to a full-scale carpentry job with footrail and back-lit aperitif bottles.

A BASIS FOR YOUR BAR

Gadgets

Ice bucket (lined with cork or similar to stay cold)

Lemon squeezer (any kind)

Can opener and/or beer-can opener

Good sharp knife and cutting board

Glass jug for your use

Spoon or stick or muddler

Paper towels

Cocktail sticks

Cloths

Cork screw

Peeler

Jug of iced water

Bottle opener

Extras

Lots of ice cubes (order from the local ice company. The fish shop buys ice – ask them)

Oranges and lemons

Angostura bitters

Castor sugar

Stuffed green olives

Tomato juice (a big tin is better than tiny expensive bottles)

Worcestershire sauce

Bottle of cherries

Soda water

Tonic water (big bottles are cheaper)

Ginger ale

Coca-cola

The Hard Stuff

Bottle of gin (e.g. London Dry) or vodka

Noilly Prat (or some other dry vermouth)

Scotch whisky (e.g. Long John)

Pale sherry (e.g. Tio Pepe or San Patricio)

Lager (or pale ale) on ice

1 liqueur (e.g. Benedictine)

Brandy (one of medium quality for mixes – Hennessy*** – and one for drinking – Otard or Rémy Martin)

Red and white wine for 'spritzers'

Champagne (e.g. Pol Roger). There are 8 glasses in a bottle, 34 in a Jeroboam. What about 2 of each size?

FOR A MORE COMPLEX BAR ADD THESE THINGS

Gadgets	Extras	The Hard Stuff
Ice-crushing tongs	Bottled pearl onions	Vodka (e.g. Samovar Stolichnaya)
Beer mats	Lime juice	Vermouth bianco (sweet) (Martini or Cinzano)
Shaker	Fresh mint	Medium sherry (Dry Sack or Bristol Milk)
Egg yolk separator	Nutmeg, cloves, cinnamon, etc.	Rum (e.g. Ron Bacardi)
Strainer	Canapés	The strong beers
Big bath of crushed ice to put wine, lager and champagne into	Nuts (cashews, brazils)	Rye or bourbon (e.g. I. W. Harper bourbon)
	Orange juice	Madeira or port (e.g. Harvey's Directors' Bin)
	Blackcurrant juice	More liqueurs: Drambuie, Irish Mist, Crème de menthe, Green Chartreuse, etc.
		Campari, Dubonnet (and other aperitifs)

PRE-DINNER DRINKS

Offer a dry sherry (e.g. Tio Pepe) or dry vermouth served with ice and a piece of lemon, or with one-third gin or vodka. Ladies might prefer vermouth bianco (sweet), in which case add ice and lemon, and let them add soda if they wish. Campari is a type of bitters (herb-flavoured spirits) which are all expensive.

Campari-soda is merely that mixed to a rose colour, but unless the soda is ice-cold you'll need ice. Equal parts of Campari, gin and vermouth go well together, and any of the three go well with each other. An *Americano* is equal parts Campari and sweet vermouth, with a slice of lemon. Soda water is optional.

Wine aperitifs (e.g. Byrrh, Lillet, Dubonnet) all need ice and lemon. Experiment with gin if you want to live dangerously. Two aperitifs that deserve to be tasted alone are Punt e Mes from Italy, and Chambéry from France.

Although I don't think whisky of any sort is a good pre-dinner drink, it is very popular in all its many varieties.

Since 1909 Scotch whisky is defined as three-year-old whisky from Scotland, even if it's a blend of grain- and malt-spirit. These blends are lighter than pure malt whisky and the brands sold in the U.S.A. are lighter still (e.g. Cutty Sark and J & B Rare). Liqueur whisky is a slightly better, older version of a blended whisky. Pure malt whiskies are usually eight to twelve years old, and are different from blended whisky and different from each other too, although they are all soft and heavy, with a smoky, almost medicinal flavour. The modern trend in world whisky drinking is away from the heaviness of pure malts to the blends which are light in both colour and texture as already mentioned. Such blends use the pure malt as an ingredient, adding it to grain spirit in unrevealed proportions. The actual blending is very skilful and secrets are jealously guarded. Irish whiskey is made in a slightly different way whereby the malt does not take on the flavour of peat.

Bourbon is made from at least (by law) 51 per cent corn, with some rye and barley malt around in the blend. It is something of an acquired taste and a Scotch-whisky drinker is usually appalled by it. The bourbon drinker, however, goes for a 'sour-mash' type bourbon (not a sweet-mash type), which has given a distinctive flavour to the better brands.

Rye is like bourbon except that it's the rye that is at least 51 per cent. It is usually pretty brutal stuff drunk by heavies in Hollywood B pictures. It is a rarity in England, although there is some Canadian rye around. This Canadian stuff is lighter than its U.S. version.

Rum is made from sugar or molasses. The expert will prefer an unblended rum; preferably from one chosen, named estate. So far these are not available in the U.K. but probably someone will begin to import them soon. A good unblended Barbados rum – best of the B.W.I. rums – is light and dry with a very delicate bouquet. An unblended Martinique is very similar. In France this is sold as 'St James Rhum'. Trinidad rum is a little heavier, darker and sweeter. The best of the Jamaica rums are fresh-tasting, golden yellow, just a little heavier than the South Caribbean rums. However, there are quantities of Jamaican white rum around in the U.K. (much of it illegally imported). It is a rather toxic, semi-fermented drink, often loaded with impurities. Not recommended. On the other hand 'Exel' is a superb British Guiana rum, perhaps the greatest rum of all.

The rums on sale in U.K. at present are heavy

cloying blends which I don't find very interesting, but they are fine for a Rum Punch. Make it like this:

1 part sour (e.g. lime juice)

2 parts sweet (syrup or honey)

3 parts strong (rum)

4 parts weak (water)

Strong drink can be made from almost anything, including your front door. Potatoes, for instance, not only make the notorious Irish poteen, but the respectable aquavit. Slivovitz is made from plums, Kümmel from caraway, and kirsch from the glut of the cherry crop. Drink usually originates from a superabundance of its basis, and so vodka is made from wheat, rum from sugar, saké from rice, etc.

Dutch gin is a special sort of clear drink made in Holland from grain alcohol. It has a slight taste of raisins and, once you get over the original shock, is drunk in tiny glasses thrown into the back of your throat with mad abandon, often as an aperitif. This is the only way to handle it and it should not be used in mixed drinks, unless you want to experiment.

Gin is the stuff that naval officers throw a globule of bitters into and drink neat. It is usually clear, but some manufacturers produce aged ones which are very slightly yellowish. Arguments abound as to whether it improves with age. Gin is the basis of most cocktails, and the different brands are substantially different in flavour. For instance, Plymouth (which the Navy buy) is very different from Old Tom, which is a sweet gin, and different again from London Dry, which is unsweetened, and therefore the favourite cocktail gin.

Vodka is the nearest thing to a flavourless alcohol yet produced. It is sold in many strengths, from a British label at 65° to a Polish label that boasts 140°, at about double the price.

It may be that you are a cocktail fanatic and enjoy

making 200 varieties of gin sling – if so, you will already have a book containing a thousand cross-indexed permutations and will need no help from me. For the sake of the others, here are a few simple drinks to offer your guests. Note: you may wish to put a guest in charge of the bar – it is a good way to get everyone talking (or perhaps even fighting).

Spritzer. Pour 3 oz. of white (dryish) wine. Add ice. Fill up with plenty of soda.

Cooler. As Spritzer, but using red wine.

Whisky Sour (can be gin or rum). 2 oz. whisky + juice of half a lemon + teaspoon sugar + ice. Shake. Strain. Garnish with cherry and lemon slice.

Bloody Mary. 3 oz. vodka + 4 oz. tomato juice + just a squeeze of lemon + dash of Worcester sauce + ice. Shake. Strain. Offer salt and pepper.

A Screwdriver is vodka + as much orange juice as you like.

A Gimlet is 2 oz. vodka + 4 oz. lime juice.

Brandy Cocktail. 1½ oz. brandy + 1½ oz. French (dry) vermouth + dash bitters.

Dry Martini. 2 oz. gin + 1 oz. French (dry) vermouth + ice. Stir. Strain. Add lemon twist and a green olive or cocktail onion.

Vodka Martini. Use vodka for gin.

Sweet Martini. 2 oz. gin + 2 oz. Italian (sweet)

vermouth + ice. Strain, add lemon twist and a green olive or a cherry. N.B. Americans make Martinis with 99.9 per cent gin or vodka.

Tom Collins. Juice of a lemon + teaspoon sugar + 1½ oz. gin + plenty of ice (crushed if possible), all in a tall glass. Fill it with soda water (ice-cold). Serve with a swizzle-stick to stir sugar.

Champagne Cocktail. (Use another dry, sparkling white wine if you like.) Dash a lump of sugar with bitters and put it into a champagne glass with a piece of ice and a teaspoon of brandy. Twist a piece of lemon peel and fill the glass with cold champagne. Serve with a stick to prod at the sugar.

Gin and tonic is just gin with tonic added no matter what rituals may be demonstrated under its name.

Pink Gin is gin + a dash of bitters.

FOR COLD NIGHTS

Simple Hot Punch. Put 2 bottles of red wine into a saucepan and pour ½ lb. of sugar into it + 6 cloves + a piece of cinnamon + the outer peel of a lemon and its juice. Heat it almost to boiling point and serve it. There are many variations on this recipe. These hot wines are often called Glühwein – it is a great greeting on a freezing night, or as one for the road, but don't give it to drivers as hot wine is deceptive stuff.

Mulled wine is similar, sometimes having brandy – into which the yolks of 4 eggs have been thoroughly beaten – mixed into the hot wine. This must not boil. Put a pinch of grated nutmeg on each serving.

Rum Punch has equal parts of rum and cider warmed with cloves, cinnamon, nutmeg and a slice of orange for each serving floating in it.

These have all been hot drinks, but there are cold ones too. If you order a large block of ice for your party, a hot saucepan stood on it will sink in as it melts the ice. Remove the saucepan and you will have an ice block with a cavity in which the cold punch can be served, or a **Frozen Eggnog** like this:

Beat 6 egg yolks and add ½ lb. of sugar to them when it is nicely gooey. Mix in 2 pints of cream (it is cheaper than whisky, isn't it?) and chill it overnight. Before serving, pour half a bottle of rum and half a bottle of brandy on to it and churn it into something that doesn't need a spoon – in a word, a drink.

COOKING TERMS

AB

Acidulate. Add vinegar or lemon juice.

Ail. Garlic (aioli – a powerful garlic mayonnaise).

A la meunière. Dipped in flour, cooked in butter, usually fish.

Al burro. (Pasta) in butter.

All-purpose flour (U.S.). Plain flour.

Al sugo. (Pasta) in sauce.

Aloyau. Sirloin.

Antipasto. Hors d'œuvre.

Aspic. A cold jelly (generally savoury).

Au gratin. Breadcrumb-topped and browned.

Bain-marie. A tray of water in which basins or pots stand to keep warm.

Baking powder, double acting (U.S.). Use 25 per cent more.

Bard. To protect with thin slices of pork fat (often placed over poultry while it's roasting).

Baste. To moisten with spoonfuls of gravy or fat during cooking.

Béchamel. A white sauce.

Beurre noir. Black butter – used on fish, brains or similar.

Biftek. 'Beefsteak'; it can be a slice of fillet or ground beef.

Bigarade. Made with peel and juice of bitter oranges.

Bind. To make something glue together or become thicker in texture.

Blanch (Fr. **blanchir**). Cook in boiling water, often for a very short time (e.g. when skinning almonds or tomatoes).

Blend. Mix very well.

Blind. Empty pie-crust.

Blini. Tiny Russian pancakes.

Bonne femme. Simply cooked (housewife-style) – often includes potato.

Boudin. Black-pudding sausage made from pigs' blood (called in U.S.A. 'blood pudding').

Bouillabaisse. Fish and fish stock cooked as a stew, but often served separately (as a Pot-au-feu).

Bouilli. Boiled meat from a Pot-au-feu (Bœuf bouilli).

Bouillon. Clear meat stock.

Bouquet garni. A bunch of herbs, parsley, thyme, etc.

Braise. To cook gently in a covered pot with a minimum amount of liquid, basting or moistening frequently. If meat is braised it is usually seared first. (*See also* **Daube**.)

Broil. American word for grill.

C

Calamari. Squid.

Cervelas. A large, garlic-flavoured pork sausage.

Chafing-dish. Used on dining-table to keep food hot or even cook it. There is a flame under it.

Chair à saucisses. Sausage meat.

Chantilly. Whipped cream to which sugar and vanilla have been added.

Char (Fr. **Omble chevalier**). Something like trout from the Savoy region – highly esteemed.

Chateaubriand. A thick slice of meat through the

sirloin and fillet (rather like a Porterhouse steak, but with the bone removed). The Chateaubriand can weigh up to 1¾ lb. It should be cooked more slowly than the smaller steaks, because of its thickness. Very often a double-thick slice of fillet steak is called a Chateaubriand.

Clam (U.S.). A not-well-defined type of edible bivalve mollusc. Oyster or mussel can substitute.

Cocotte. Casserole.

Compote. Fruit (fresh or dried) cooked in syrup.

Contre-filet. *See* **Faux-filet.**

Couenne (Fr.). Thick pork skin, a highly regarded flavouring ingredient for stews, etc. Ask your butcher for some.

Coulibiac. A Russian hot fish-pie.

Cream 18 per cent (U.S.). Single cream.

Crêpe (Fr.). A pancake.

Crépinettes (Fr.). Little flat sausages wrapped in caul (crépine), which is the membrane enclosing paunch.

Croquettes (Fr.). Cakes of meat or fish.

Croûtons. Small shapes of bread fried crisp. Used as a garnish (especially for soup).

Cure. To preserve by hanging in smoke or by salting or drying.

D

Daube. Originally meat cooked in a daubière and then served cold. Now it means meat cooked in a covered pot. Usually the meat is larded and marinaded. Unlike a braise it is never seared before cooking. A sealed casserole in a low oven (often means beef in wine).

Decant. To pour out, letting sediment remain.

Déglacer. To rinse out, e.g. meat juices from a pan with brandy.

Dice. To cube or cut small.

Duxelles. A mushroom paste.

E

Entrecôte. Sirloin steak.

Épigramme. A slice of breast of lamb and a lamb chop dipped in egg and breadcrumbs and fried.

Escalope (or Collop). Thin slice of meat (sometimes pounded flat), very often veal.

Escargots. Snails (the vineyard snail is the best). Generally cooked with garlic and butter.

Estouffade. Strictly speaking a stew (sometimes like a cassoulet) cooked à l'étuvée (*see* **étuver**), but it is generally used exactly as daube.

Étuver. To cook in a covered pot, using no liquid but plenty of fat – usually butter – at a temperature lower than the boiling point of water. Put the pot in the lowest oven you can get for 4 to 7 hours. Meat or poultry cooked this way is usually cut into pieces first. Vegetables are sometimes cooked like this too.

FG

Faux-filet or Contre-filet. Part of sirloin other than the fillet.

Fifth. A fifth of a gallon. An American description of the standard-size bottle.

Filet. 'Le filet' is the undercut or fillet of steak; 'un filet' is a flat piece of meat or fish without bone.

Fines herbes. Selected mixture of herbs. In France, however, it often only means parsley.

Flambé. In flames; it is alcohol burning.

Fricassée. Poultry (sometimes vegetables, too) in a cream-and-egg sauce.

Fritto-misto. Mixed items fried (Italian cooking).

Fry. To cook in fat. It is important that the heat be regulated to remain below the burning point of the sort of fat you are using (*see* Measuring section, page 32). There are two basic methods: total immersion known as deep frying, and shallow frying or sautéing. In both cases the outside of the food must be very dry. Flour it if in doubt. *See also* Meat, page 147.

Gratin. To brown under the grill, or a dish so treated.
Grill. To cook by radiant heat near to heat source and not in an enclosed box. *See* Meat, page 151.
Gulyas. Hungarian stew.

HJ

Hacher. Chop or grind.
Hachis. Chopped or ground.
Haricot. Beans (white, brown or green). *See* Pulses in Vegetables section.

Jarret. Knuckle.
Jigger. A one-and-a-half-ounce measure.

Julienne. Shredded foodstuffs (usually means vegetable cut in strips).
Jus. Gravy.

LM

Lard. A piece of pork fat used for larding meat, or dripping made by slowly cooking chopped pork fat (used in south-west France). This is easy to do and well worth while.
Longè. The top end of loin.

Mariné. Pickled.
Marinade. Oil, wine, herbs, spices, onions, vinegar, etc., in which meat (or fish) is soaked to soften the fibres.
Marmite. Tall narrow-topped vessel with minimum evaporation area, for lengthy cooking of stocks.
Marmite (Petite). A superb clear broth.

Matelote. Fish stew.

Médaillons. *See* **Tournedos**.

Meunière. *See* **A la meunière**.

Mignon (Filet). *See* **Tournedos**.

Mignonnettes. *See* **Tournedos**. Also name for coarsely ground pepper.

Mimosa. Garnished with chopped hard-boiled egg yolk.

Minestrone. A thick Italian soup.

Mode (A la). In the fashion. This is usually followed by the name of place where the fashion prevails. In the case of Bœuf à la mode Française, which is a large piece of braised beef, the final word is omitted. In U.S.A. à la mode means with a serving of ice cream.

Molasses (U.S.). Black treacle.

Mornay. With a cheese sauce.

Moussaka. Balkan dish made with ground meat, onions and either potatoes or aubergines.

NO

Navarin. A mutton stew containing onions and potatoes.

Navy bean (U.S.). Haricot beans.

Niçoise (A la). A dish containing tomatoes and garlic.

Noisettes. *See* **Tournedos**.

Noodles. Flat strips of pasta.

Oiseaux sans tête. A thin, flattened slice of steak rolled around a savoury stuffing and cooked in a closed pot.

Olla podrida. A Spanish stew of ham and chick peas.

Oyster plant. Salsify. *See* Vegetables section.

P

Pané (Fr.). Coated with breadcrumbs.

Papillote. An oiled paper case or envelope in which

fish or meat is cooked in the oven. (Metal foil will substitute.) The juices and aroma are captured inside it. Can also be a paper decoration.

Parboil. Pre-cook.

Parmentier. A Frenchman responsible for the popularity of the potato. His name is often attached to potato dishes.

Pâte. Pastry.

Pâté. Meat or fish enclosed in pastry on all sides (*see also* **Terrine**).

Paupiette. A thin slice of meat used for wrapping round various stuffings, or minced meat.

Pistou (Pesta or **Pesto).** This is a sauce put on pasta or stirred into minestrone or soupe au pistou. Make it by dripping olive oil on to crushed garlic, basil, tomato purée and Parmesan cheese while stirring frantically.

Poach. *See* Simmer.

Poêle (A la). Literally to cook in a shallow pan, but when it appears on menus it means étuver (*see above, and also* page 195).

Pot-au-feu. Meat, vegetables and broth cooked together but sometimes served separately.

Purée. Thick sieved pulp.

Q

Quenelles. Lightweight dumplings of meat or fish, used as a garnish for meat, fish or soup.

Quiche. Various savoury tarts from Lorraine and Alsace. Quiche Lorraine is an egg, cream, and ham tart.

R

Ravigote. A piquant white sauce.

Reduce. To evaporate by rapid boiling.

Remoulade. A mayonnaise with capers, onion, chervil, tarragon, anchovy, etc., added.

Render. Remove fat by heating gently.

Roast. Meat exposed to heat so that, as the bulk shrinks and the juices come to the surface, they dry and form a dark flavourful crust. Pot-roasting is done in a covered pot rather like braising, and in this case there is no luscious outer crust.

Roux. Flour and fat mixed over heat until the flour is cooked.

S

Salmi. Game or meat cooked almost through, then given final cooking at the dinner table.

Salpicon. Meat, fish or vegetable pieces held in a good sauce, used to make croquettes, etc., or fill vol-au-vents or canapés.

Sauté. Cooked in fat over a moderate heat.

Scald. To bring almost to boiling point. Sometimes it is to pour boiling water on to things.

Scallion. Spring onion.

Sear. To fry the outside, e.g. of a piece of meat before braising it.

Shortening (U.S.). Best-quality cooking fat.

Simmer (or **poach).** To cook in liquid below the boil. The surface of the water vibrates slightly.

Sommelier. Man in charge of the cellar (wine waiter).

Soubise. Purée of onion and rice.

Soupe (Fr.). A peasant soup laden with vegetables and usually bread.

Soups (Fr. **Potages**).

Thick: *Velouté* is a very thick creamy soup with added egg yolk. *Purée* has starchy vegetables as a base. *Crème* is a creamy (shellfish) type (based upon Béchamel sauce).

Clear: Potage is unthickened soup containing meat, vegetables, etc. *Consommé* is clear broth.

Steam. To cook in steam without the food touching the water. A pressure cooker is a special type of steamer.

Stew. Cook in liquid kept below boiling point, i.e. to simmer.

T

Tartare. Mayonnaise made by dripping oil on to hard-boiled egg yolks while stirring. Other flavourings exactly as **Remoulade**.

Tartare (A la). Ground beef with capers, chopped onions, parsley and egg yolk.

Terrine. Fish or meat (generally chopped or ground) baked in the oven. If surrounded with pastry this is a pâté. The pâté can be served hot or cold, but terrine is always served cold. The pot in which a terrine is cooked is also called a terrine.

Timbales. Any preparation served in a pie-crust.

Tournedos. Slices of fillet of beef weighing about 100 grammes (3½ oz.). 'Médaillons', 'Noisettes' and 'Mignonnettes' are exactly the same.

Z

Zabaglione (Fr. **Sabayon**). A hot dessert made from sugar, beaten egg and alcohol.

Zest. Oily, thin, flavourful outer skin of oranges, lemons, etc. 'A twist of lemon' is a squeeze to get a drip of oil from the zest.

Ziste. The bitter white pith under the zest. It is a confusing world, isn't it?

ACTION COOK STRIPS

All meat contains moisture, and the retention of this moisture means the retention of flavour. When meat is heated it shrinks in bulk. This means that it can no longer hold the same moisture-content and the moisture escapes. The object of a cook must be to minimize this escape. The simplest way of cooking meat is to put it in the oven, where radiant heat dries the moisture as it comes to the surface of the meat. Everyone appreciates and prefers the outside juice-encrusted slices. Similarly, grilling will bring moisture to the surface. Many cooks prefer to sprinkle the outside of meat with flour in order that these juices should dry rather than drip to the bottom of the pan. In shallow frying, too, the cooking will result in a loss of this moisture-content, therefore the gravy remaining in a frying-pan should never be wasted. In deep frying the meat (ground or not) should be dipped into a heavy batter to prevent the escape of the juices. In Chinese cookery the meat is sometimes wrapped in thin pastry and then steamed, or poached. Either way you get small, juicy meat dumplings.

When making a stew the loss of juices into the liquid surround is nothing to be deplored. However, a new danger shows itself. When it is boiling (with bubbles coming through it), the meat is getting harder. Therefore the stew should do what the professional cook calls 'smile'. This is especially true of boiling beef, mutton or pork. In these cases the loss of flavour into the liquid is not good because the liquid will be thrown away.

While the cooking period for pot-roasting or boiling is essentially calculated by the weight of the piece of meat, a stew consisting of similarly-sized cubes will take the same amount of time whether there is one pound of meat or four pounds of meat involved in the cooking.

COOKING BEEF (Part 1) cooking means making its centre **hot!**

1. ROAST

All around heat

HEAT OVEN FIRST. THEN COOK FOR 15 m. per lb. + 15 m. at Reg 7.

to stand the joint in a tray of fat is to half fry it!

A thin Joint needs less cooking than a thick one of the same weight

A meat thermometer will give perfect results every time

DON'T PROD MEAT

2. GRILL (FILLET RUMP ETC.)

Get grill **very** hot before starting

Brush ↓↓↓↓↓↓↓↓↓ with oil

Rough Guide 4 min. per side

3. SHALLOW FRY (FILLET RUMP ETC.)

Make gravy with juices that remain in the pan (Add the last of the '04 Claret) For **Steak au Poivre** add lots of Freshly Ground Pepper

Oil (or oil & Butter) pan just enough to prevent sticking

Sprinkle meat with Salt and Pepper

Rub with garlic

Many Indian recipes use a low oven and a carefully fitting lid to the casserole. It is surprising how seldom one needs to add any liquid at all, especially if tomatoes and onions are among the ingredients. Needless to say, you will have to check with the casserole frequently.

Although most civilized people agree that beef is best eaten rare, arguments abound as to the desirability of eating undercooked chicken and lamb. Whatever your feelings about this, neither lamb, nor chicken, nor any other meat benefits from overcooking; for this same moisture-content that we were talking about vanishes and leaves us with a powdery texture that can be 'eaten with a spoon' – very nasty.

It is not possible to give exact cooking times, since ovens vary, and therefore you should write in the margin of this book the cooking times which suit your tastes and your kitchen best. Here are the comparative times for veal, pork, beef, lamb and poultry:

Beef and Mutton:	thick cut: 20 mins. per lb. + 20 mins. thin cut: 15 mins. per lb. + 15 mins.
Lamb and Venison:	20 mins. per lb. + 20 mins.
Pork:	thick cut: 30 mins. per lb. + 30 mins. thin cut: 25 mins. per lb. + 25 mins.
Veal:	25 mins. per lb. + 25 mins.
Chicken or Duck:	20 mins. per lb. *See* pages 188–9
Goose:	Medium size: 1½ hours, large: 2 hours
Turkey:	*See* pages 188–9

149

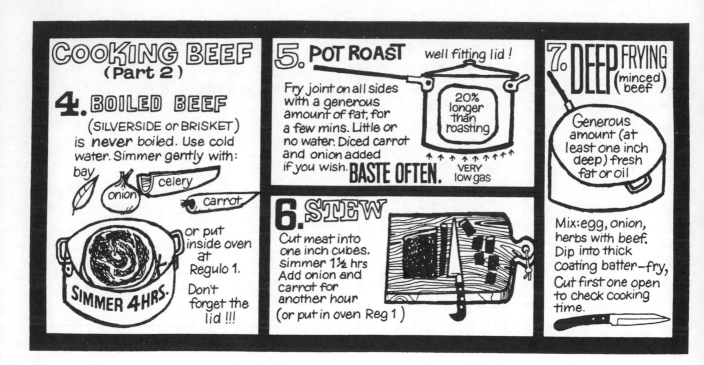

COOKING BEEF
(Part 2)

4. BOILED BEEF

(SILVERSIDE or BRISKET) is **never** boiled. Use cold water. Simmer gently with:

bay
onion
celery
carrot

or put inside oven at Regulo 1.

Don't forget the lid !!!

SIMMER 4 HRS.

5. POT ROAST

Fry joint on all sides with a generous amount of fat, for a few mins. Little or no water. Diced carrot and onion added if you wish. **BASTE OFTEN.**

well fitting lid !

20% longer than roasting

VERY low gas

6. STEW

Cut meat into one inch cubes. Simmer 1½ hrs Add onion and carrot for another hour (or put in oven Reg 1)

7. DEEP FRYING (minced) beef

Generous amount (at least one inch deep) fresh fat or oil

Mix: egg, onion, herbs with beef. Dip into thick coating batter–fry, Cut first one open to check cooking time.

Grilling. The more contrast you want between the well-done outer crust and the underdone centre, the nearer the meat must be to the heat source. (It obeys the inverse square law.)

A meat thermometer is stuck into the meat to take a reading from the very centre of the joint. The thermometer is marked with temperatures for different types of meat. Put it deep into the joint, but don't let it touch the bone. The thermometer stays in the joint while it's in the oven. Some oven manufacturers (e.g. Moffat) have a built-in thermometer which rings a buzzer when the meat is cooked (*see* Utensils section, page 37).

Rich Stock

1. BUY 2 or 3 lb. of leg of beef. Ask for marrow-bones chopped into SHORT LENGTHS!

cover with **COLD** water

CUT MEAT INTO CHUNKS

Add ½ teaspoon SALT per pint of water

DON'T BOIL simmer (covered) for 3 hrs. BETTER <u>UNDER</u> BOILING POINT THAN OVER IT!

SKIM top as often as you can.

2. AFTER 3 hrs. Add:

turnip

bay

peppers

carrot

leek

celery seed

(or as many of them as you have). Also add a large onion, **RAW** for light stock. e.g. chicken or veal, or **FRIED** dark brown in butter if you prefer dark stock. **COOK FOR ANOTHER 1½ hrs.**

3. STRAIN into BOWL or JUG. Leave over-night. Remove **FAT.**

4. IF YOU NOW HAVE TOO MUCH STOCK, OR IF FLAVOUR IS NOT STRONG ENOUGH, **REDUCE** over fierce flame – CAREFUL NOW!

5. OTHER FLAVOURS. INSTEAD OF THE BEEF USE EITHER:

CHICKEN + giblets if available. Cut cooking time by half.

or **VEAL** A knuckle is best + some ham if you have it.

or FISH Court Bouillon use about 2 lb. (heads are fine!) Add a glass of Rhine Wine, lemon peel and thyme. Cook 1 hr. strain. When boiling: lower (freshwater) fish into this stock. Poach gently. Remove carefully. – SERVE.

152

Since the finished product cannot be served to the table as it is, this isn't so much a recipe, a method or a list of ingredients: it is a way of life, for if there is fresh stock made every week, a reputation as a good cook will almost inevitably follow. Cooking times don't indicate the amount of *bother* a recipe will require; stock will happily work at preparing itself hour after hour in repayment for an occasional peep and stir.

Le Jus Brun. The instructions in the grid should be followed closely. For example, if you add hot water instead of cold, the resulting stock will be considerably less flavourful. Bacon, bacon rinds, chicken carcass, calf's foot, chicken feet, or a piece of ham are useful additions. Remove the scum, especially if you are aiming for a clear soup eventually. In this case don't disturb the bones and meat while they are simmering, and remove them at the end of the cooking rather than tip the saucepan to pour the contents through a strainer, for this will raise sediment. Finally, a cup of cold water will help to clear. When the stock has been strained, the result will be what the French cook calls le jus brun; from this he makes sauce demi-glacé, which I will describe in a moment. Meanwhile, the same lot of meat and bones can be used to make another wonderful ingredient for soups, stews and gravies – your own meat extract, which in French is called la glace de viande.

Glace de Viande. Cover the same bones and meat with cold water and simmer for a long time, anything from 2 to 8 hours. Strain, and this time throw away the meat and bones. Turn up the gas and boil this second lot of stock furiously, reducing it until you have something like a cupful of thick, dark-brown syrup. Pour this into a pot. When it is cool you will have a substance that is better than any meat-extract you ever bought over a counter. It is slightly harder than commercial brands. It will last a long time if only you can restrain yourself from using it up like mad.

Demi-Glacé. With the first lot of stock (le jus brun) you can make the half-glaze sauce. This should be done by cooking fat (not butter, because it burns) and flour in equal quantities together over heat, letting them cook together (this is a roux). The stock should be added to form a thin brown sauce. A little tomato purée should be beaten into the sauce; let it come to the boil, then put it over a tiny flame unstirred for 2 hours. Skim occasionally. This will keep for several days and is the basis of many sauces; it will be referred to in later recipes.

Pot-au-feu. The process of making a jus brun is so like that of making the classic Pot-au-feu that this seems a good place to mention it. Use a nicer piece of meat (e.g. shoulder or brisket), and when you add the vegetables, add perhaps 2 parsnips, some parsley, thyme and bay leaf. Remove fat with a ladle while it is still hot. Serve the bouillon first, then follow with the meat (sliced) served with the vegetables. Many people favour mustard or horseradish sauce served with the meat. In some parts of France, poultry shares the pot-au-feu with the beef.

Petite Marmite Henri IV. If you have bouillon from the pot-au-feu left over, then the next day will provide you with a chance to make the mighty Petite Marmite Henri IV, considered by many to be the ultimate soup of French cuisine.

La Petite Marmite is merely a pot-au-feu + chicken pieces or giblets. If the chicken is a tender fleshy one, this dish can be called Poule-au-pot, and since Henri IV thought every Frenchman deserved one, it is sometimes called **Poule-au-pot Henri IV.** It is served with toast and grated cheese. There are a few embroideries you can add:

1 The words *Henri IV* to the name of the dish.
2 An oxtail.
3 Chicken feet – they make it more glutinous.
4 Slices of marrow bone half an inch thick (the butcher will cut them) poached gently for a minute or so, and served in or with the soup. (Careful not to lose the jelly-like marrow when dishing them up.)

All non-edibles, chicken feet, etc., are discarded, and edibles (vegetables, meat, chicken) are cut into small slices before serving.

OTHER TYPES OF STOCK

The standard beef stock is the most common one and probably the most useful, but if a recipe calls for a chicken to be poached in stock, or you need to make a jelly for a chicken aspic, then the beef stock will be too strong.

A white stock is made from veal. Use neck, knuckle or trimmings, which are often sold in Britain as 'pie veal'. If possible add a chicken carcass, chicken giblets and a little ham to strengthen the flavour. Proceed as in Rich Stock grid, but use no beef or beef bones.

To make a chicken stock the procedure is exactly the same as for white stock, but instead of the chicken carcass use a whole chicken. The chicken must of course be cleaned, but the feet (cleaned) are included, and many cooks would also include the head.

Another, lesser known, is a vegetable stock. Although mostly used for people on diets it can be useful when you have no meat. Brown the chopped vegetables in butter; use onions, celery, leeks, parsnips, mushrooms or as many of them as you have. This is one of the few items that is boiled furiously. After an hour's boiling add some herbs and strain, pressing the vegetables to extract all the water.

RICE (MY WAY)

1.
WASH LIKE MAD FOR FEW MIN. (to remove mill flour).

SOME RICE IS PRE-COOKED; IF YOU USE IT FOLLOW THE INSTRUCTIONS ON THE PACKET.

2.
COVER WITH COLD WATER TO ¼" ABOVE LEVEL OF RICE.

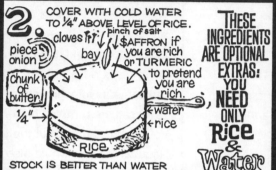

piece onion, chunk of butter, cloves, pinch of salt, bay, SAFFRON if you are rich, or TURMERIC to pretend you are rich.

¼"

←water
←rice

RICE

STOCK IS BETTER THAN WATER

THESE INGREDIENTS ARE OPTIONAL EXTRAS: YOU NEED ONLY Rice & Water

3.
BRING WATER TO BOIL. STIR.

Cover with a well-fitting lid. TURN GAS AS LOW AS IT WILL GO. Cook 20 min. — NO PEEPING! Turn out gas. Leave 5-10 min. — SERVE

4.

SERVE IN WARM BUTTERED DISH.

BUY GOOD-QUALITY RICE (If you have cheap broken rice — throw it at a bride). 1. LONG GRAIN patna style rice (PILAU) is best for curries. 2. SHORT GRAIN for RISOTTO. 3. VERY SMALL long grain requires extra cooking
1. 2. 3.

Added to meat or fish rice becomes:

RISI-PISI : AUSTRIA, HUNGARY
PAELLA : SPAIN, S. AMERICA
HAR CHOW FAN : CHINA
PILAU : IRAN, CAROLINA
RIJSTAFEL : INDONESIA
RISOTTO : ITALY
PULAO : INDIA
PILAF : EGYPT

in JAPAN rice is served as a **sticky** mass rather than as separate grains. In CHINA cold rice is fried with lightly beaten eggs; other uses — rice pudding.

The long-grain variety is most often referred to as *Patna*, the finest sub-division of this type is called *Pilau*, which has introduced the words Pilaw and Pilaf into French menus. The word Risotto on a French menu refers to the plump short-grain variety generally called short or Italian rice (although the trade often calls it Japan).

Use the long grain for curries and recipes calling for the rice grains to be separate, and the short for soft, absorbent-type cooking like risotto or rice pudding. A third type called Bismati is a small, dark, long grain. It is highly regarded by Indian cooks, but will require longer cooking time.

Vary my cooking times if you find the result not to your taste, and after that *stick to the same timing and buy your rice from the same shop always.*

Cooked Rice: Use it as stuffing (+ flavourings) in tomatoes, peppers, vine leaves, poultry or pancakes. It's a fine garnish for soups or can be served cold, with an oil-and-vinegar dressing, with vegetables, shrimps, etc.

The Japanese cook it into a glutinous mass (omit washing), one product being a type of canapé (*sushi*). The still-warm rice is pushed into a mould or cut into small slabs, then decorated with fish, shellfish, anchovy, etc.

Treat cooked rice with care, for it is easily crushed and damaged.

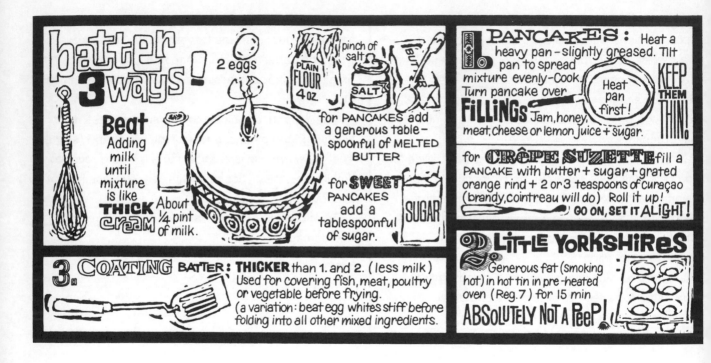

batter 3 ways!

2 eggs

PLAIN FLOUR 4 oz

pinch of salt

SALT

BUTTER

Beat Adding milk until mixture is like **THICK cream**

About 1/4 pint of milk.

for PANCAKES add a generous table-spoonful of MELTED BUTTER

for **SWEET** PANCAKES add a tablespoonful of sugar.

SUGAR

3. COATING BATTER: **THICKER** than 1. and 2. (less milk)
Used for covering fish, meat, poultry or vegetable before frying.
(a variation: beat egg whites stiff before folding into all other mixed ingredients.

1. PANCAKES: Heat a heavy pan – slightly greased. Tilt pan to spread mixture evenly–Cook. Turn pancake over

Heat pan first!

KEEP THEM THIN!

FILLINGS Jam, honey, meat, cheese or lemon juice + sugar.

for **CRÊPE SUZETTE** fill a PANCAKE with butter + sugar + grated orange rind + 2 or 3 teaspoons of curaçao (brandy, cointreau will do) Roll it up! GO ON, SET IT ALIGHT!

2 LITTLE YORKSHIRES:
Generous fat (smoking hot) in hot tin in pre-heated oven (Reg. 7) for 15 min
ABSOLUTELY NOT A PEEP!

Shallow frying calls for the simplest possible coating mixtures, the normal ones being flour, egg and breadcrumb applications. Fresh breadcrumbs which absorb the egg mixture are considerably better than the packaged dry variety. (A blender makes the production of fresh breadcrumbs a very simple matter. *See* page 23.)

The *deep frying* of vegetables and meat presents very different problems due to the rapid shrinkage of the materials. Here the purpose of the batter coating is something more than a garnish: it is designed to hold the meat juices inside. The batter texture can be considerably heavier than that for making Yorkshire puddings, as it does not have to rise and it must cling to the meat or vegetable in order to provide an adequate layer. Each item dropped into deep fat will naturally lower the temperature and therefore small quantities should be cooked at a time. Cold vegetables are made especially attractive by deep frying.

In England the pancake is too often eaten only on Shrove Tuesday, with sugar and lemon. Hashed chicken, corned beef, etc., can be rolled into pancakes and covered in a cheese sauce and quickly grilled to brown the top; or the pancake contents can be of a more luxurious nature, as the Crêpe Suzette demonstrates. N.B. Only warm alcohol ignites. For dinner parties the pancake is that useful item that can be prepared well in advance.

In China the long flat noodle is the symbol of longevity. It is found in the cuisine of the world.

When cooking the noodles in fast-boiling water, remember that fresh home-made noodles will cook more quickly than hard shop-bought ones. Have a big bowl warmed with a little hot oil or butter in it. Drain the cooked noodles carefully (in a large sieve), then put them into the warm bowl, stirring well to cover the pasta with the oil or butter. It can be eaten in its simplest possible form, and in fact, grated Parmesan cheese, butter and freshly ground black pepper is probably as fine a dressing as can be thought of.

Pastry: Coolness is the secret of pastry making, and this is why the use of finger-tips is so essential. Anything that can be done to keep the temperature low will improve the pastry. When heat is applied to the pastry the small particles of fat melt and the adjacent particles of air expand. This is the principle involved in any similar cooking process. Recipes specify sieved flour in order that the greatest possible amount of air shall be trapped in the mixture. (Flour can be given two or three minutes in the blender which will have exactly the same result.) Many cooks prefer to bring the fat down to a very low temperature in a refrigerator and grate it into the mixture, but even so, unless the grated pieces are very small, it will need further rubbing.

LONG NOODLES

1. 1lb. flour, pinch of salt, mix to a stiff elastic dough. a LITTLE water. 5 beaten eggs

2. Roll out as THIN and EVEN as you can — REST 1 HR.

VIVE LA DIFFERENCE: Purists use (per 1lb. of flour) 4 yolks + 6 whites for TAGLIATELLE (Italy) 8 yolks + 3 whites for NOUILLES (France).

3. Sprinkle with flour. Roll up loosely. Cut into noodles.

Widths:
1½" LASAGNE
¼" TAGLIATELLE
⅛" FETTUCCINE
All equally PAPER-THIN!

4. HANG THEM UP IN A WARM PLACE TO DRY FOR AN HOUR OR SO

Cook in lots of BOILING WATER (about 5 mins.) serve with melted butter for NOUILLES AU BEURRE. Add grated Parmesan + fresh pepper for TAGLIATELLE AL BURRO.

SHORT PASTRY

1. (Utensils and ingredients should be cold)

COMBINE: 1lb. flour
¼lb. butter for flavour
¼lb. lard for texture
pinch of salt
Drip of Rum or Lemon?

Egg, optional but cook at Reg.5 (380°) if you use it.

Castor sugar?

FOR PASTRY CASES (Pâte à Foncer) USE 2 EGGS — OMIT LARD.

2.

Handle lightly — use finger **TIPS.** Gently rub fat SMALLER, SMALLER, AND SMALLER until it is like breadcrumbs. ANOTHER METHOD. use 2 knives to slice the mixture into 'breadcrumbs' KEEP IT COOL BE THOROUGH Don't Rush it! Take about 5 min.

3. Sprinkle water (iced if possible) into mixture a LITTLE at a time. **Too Wet is FATAL!** End with it too dry to pick up the tiniest pieces. Roll out gently. Bake at Reg.6 (400°F).

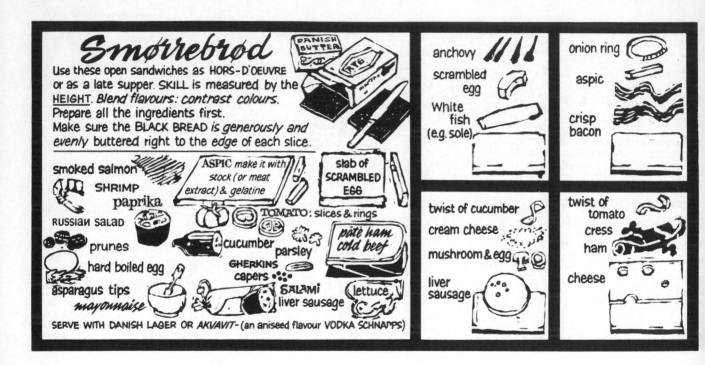

Smørrebrød

Use these open sandwiches as HORS-D'OEUVRE or as a late supper. SKILL is measured by the HEIGHT. *Blend flavours: contrast colours.* Prepare all the ingredients first. Make sure the BLACK BREAD *is generously and evenly buttered* right to the *edge* of each slice.

DANISH BUTTER

smoked salmon
SHRIMP
paprika
RUSSIAN SALAD
prunes
hard boiled egg
asparagus tips
mayonnaise

ASPIC make it with stock (or meat extract) & gelatine

slab of SCRAMBLED EGG

TOMATO: slices & rings
cucumber
parsley
GHERKINS
capers
SALAMI
liver sausage

pâté ham cold beef

lettuce

SERVE WITH DANISH LAGER OR *AKVAVIT* - (an aniseed flavour VODKA SCHNAPPS)

anchovy
scrambled egg
White fish (e.g. sole)

onion ring
aspic
crisp bacon

twist of cucumber
cream cheese
mushroom & egg
liver sausage

twist of tomato
cress
ham
cheese

In Denmark it is said that, unless the butter is spread thick enough to leave tooth-marks after biting it, it is not a real **smørrebrød.** The butter must be spread thickly and to the extreme edge, since this anchors the filling and prevents moisture saturating the bread. The ingredients are all made ready before you begin, and height is the criterion of skill. The ingredients should be meaty and tempting: Danish smoked pork loin; Danish blue cheese with cocktail cherries; cold sliced beef with horseradish cream and beetroot; pickled herring with onion and tomato.

For a flat base, the meat or cheese slices should be carefully trimmed to the exact dimension of the bread. Garnishings of onion rings, radishes, lemon, cucumber, tomato, etc., should be carefully done, as this is very much an appearance dish. Should you wish to serve them without knives and forks the slices of bread should be cut in half, in which case they are called *snitter.* Don't prepare them more than two hours in advance, unless you have carefully chosen ingredients that will not deteriorate. For an hors d'œuvre or an entrée at a dinner party, the cook should limit the ingredients; for instance, rich meat smørrebrød would be ill suited to precede a fish course.

Chicken Soup

THIS IS **GILDERNE**... A CLEAR SOUP EATEN ON JEWISH SABBATH AND HOLIDAYS. | The amounts will give 8 portions. OR USE as a very fine white stock.

I **CUT UP A CHICKEN** (include gizzard, heart, neck and feet – but remove excess fat.)

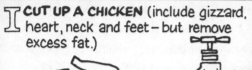

A 4-5 lb. boiling fowl will be just right.

COVER with cold water

BRING TO BOIL – SKIM.

II **SIMMER**

cover

anything from 45 mins. to 2½ hours.

Then TEST for flavour: if too weak, reduce over a high flame.

III **ADD** – A bay leaf
–2 peppercorns –1 carrot ⎫
1 onion ⎬ chopped

– celery leaves (or celery seed)

SIMMER another ½ hour
STRAIN – SERVE.

Variations... FOR SERVING

1. Drop one raw egg yolk into each bowl.
2. Scatter finely-chopped parsley.
3. Add noodles (or any pasta) a few mins. before serving.
4. Leave some pieces of lean chicken in soup when serving.

This is a gourmet dish. Don't give it to anyone who is likely to think that you have made it from a cube. It's simple to make this soup into a thick creamy one by adding flour and cream, but a fine, clear soup is unbeatable as it is.

This recipe will give you a good chicken stock which can become a basis for many other dishes. For instance, the minestrone recipe (*see* pages 170–1) will be superlative if based upon chicken stock, and so will any other recipe where a white stock is called for.

After you have made this soup the remaining pieces of chicken and vegetable can be used again with fresh water to make a second lot of stock. This will not be good enough to serve as soup, but will be better than bouillon cubes for cooking purposes.

бσрщ BORSCHT

A soup made with meat, vegetable stock and beets, sometimes garnished with dumplings, sausage & meat.

THE SIMPLEST VERSION:

2 medium-sized chopped, cooked beetroots.

1 teaspoon (or more) sugar.

Juice of ½ lemon

½ pint white stock

Season. Cook 10 min.

THEN

sieve. Chill at least 3 hours.

1 onion

Sauté onion in SCANT butter.

SLIGHTLY HEAVIER... *Barszcz* (A Polish variation)

Soak some lima beans overnight; cook them in the soup until tender (*which may be a long time*). Add: shredded cabbage,

HARICOT BEANS will do!

chopped apple and tomato. **Serve hot** before these last 3 are fully cooked.

A MAIN DISH

Replace the ½ pint white stock with up to a pint of beef stew. Add cabbage, apple and tomato, but beans are optional.

Serve hot.

ALL 3 should be served with a generous ladle of sour cream.

Or mix cream with yoghurt.

Served in iced soup plates with a generous spoonful of sour cream dropped into each at the last moment. If you want to be authentic, shredded crabmeat, chopped hard-boiled egg, chopped cucumber and caviare are passed around among the guests. They put a little of what they fancy into the cold borscht before stirring the cream in.

Borscht has as many variations as minestrone: one of them, less well known in the West, is **Shchi.** To make it, use the first recipe, but use either sauerkraut (pickled cabbage) or fresh cabbage in place of the beetroot. Shchi is served hot and the stock must be light in colour (be sure not to brown the onion for any of these recipes). If you use fresh cabbage, serve the shchi with a ladleful of sour cream, but if you use sauerkraut it is traditional to serve fresh cream with it.

Another way of making borscht is to grate raw beef into the stock, which means it will need longer cooking: proceed as in the first recipe.

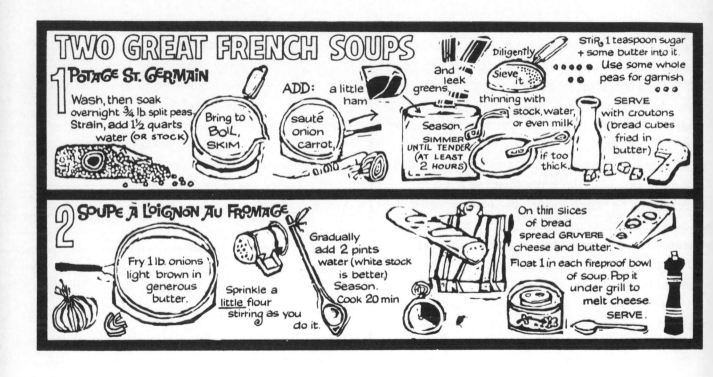

TWO GREAT FRENCH SOUPS

1 POTAGE ST. GERMAIN

Wash, then soak overnight ¾ lb. split peas. Strain, add 1½ quarts water (OR STOCK)

Bring to BOIL, SKIM

ADD: sauté onion carrot, a little ham and leek greens, Diligently Sieve it thinning with stock, water, or even milk, if too thick.

Season. SIMMER UNTIL TENDER (AT LEAST 2 HOURS)

STIR, 1 teaspoon sugar + some butter into it. Use some whole peas for garnish

SERVE with croutons (bread cubes fried in butter)

2 SOUPE À L'OIGNON AU FROMAGE

Fry 1 lb. onions light brown in generous butter.

Sprinkle a little flour stirring as you do it.

Gradually add 2 pints water (white stock is better.) Season. Cook 20 min

On thin slices of bread spread GRUYERE cheese and butter.

Float 1 in each fireproof bowl of soup. Pop it under grill to melt cheese. SERVE.

The quality of **French Onion Soup** will stand or fall upon the quality of the stock on which it is based. The hearty peasant-soup recipe pours the onion soup on to large chunks of bread and a quarter-of-an-inch layer of grated cheese is added. The individual bowls should then be grilled until the cheese bubbles. A complex dinner party, however, calls for a much thinner variation and the onion should be quite finely chopped. In this case it is more usual to pass a bowl of grated cheese among the diners. **Garlic bread** (a French loaf sliced lengthwise and copiously spread with butter to which crushed garlic has been added) is served hot from the oven.

There are probably more variations on **Potage St Germain** than on any other soup. **Fontanges** uses two egg yolks to thicken it and garnishes with lightly fried shredded lettuce and a sprinkling of chervil. If in addition to that you add a little cooked rice before serving, you will have **Ambassador** soup. Add sliced cooked string beans and lettuce to make **Marigny** soup.

Lamballe soup reduces the amount of dried peas by a third and uses three spoonfuls of tapioca to increase the thickness. (Buy the smallest variety of tapioca. Use it to thicken other recipes; it is very useful.) A **Longchamp** is St Germain with vermicelli and sorrel. **Mimi** soup has pearl barley with a garnish of cooked carrots added last.

MINESTRONE

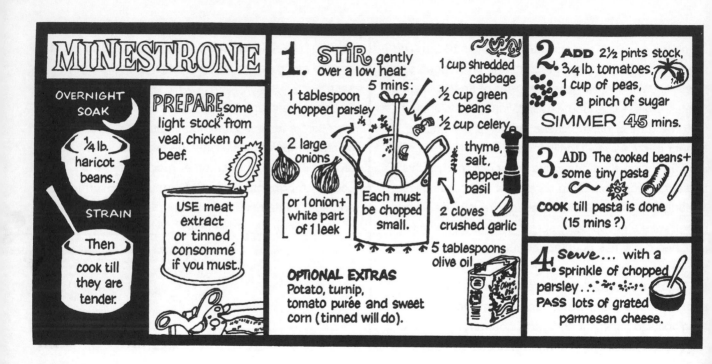

OVERNIGHT SOAK

¼ lb. haricot beans.

STRAIN

Then cook till they are tender.

PREPARE some light stock* from veal, chicken or beef.

USE meat extract or tinned consommé if you must.

1. STIR gently over a low heat 5 mins:

1 tablespoon chopped parsley

2 large onions

[or 1 onion + white part of 1 leek]

Each must be chopped small.

1 cup shredded cabbage
½ cup green beans
½ cup celery

thyme, salt, pepper, basil

2 cloves crushed garlic

5 tablespoons olive oil

OPTIONAL EXTRAS
Potato, turnip, tomato purée and sweet corn (tinned will do).

2. ADD 2½ pints stock, ¾ lb. tomatoes, 1 cup of peas, a pinch of sugar
SIMMER 45 mins.

3. ADD The cooked beans + some tiny pasta
COOK till pasta is done (15 mins?)

4. Serve... with a sprinkle of chopped parsley...
PASS lots of grated parmesan cheese.

Naturally enough the ingredients will be those in plentiful supply. It won't be ruined by leaving one or two things out. Fresh basil would be considered very important by an Italian cook, and he might very well add small pieces of salt pork. The pork can be fried first, or not, as you prefer.

Another authentic ingredient that an Italian might add is 'pesto'. This is made by carefully pounding two tablespoonfuls of Parmesan cheese (grated) and the same amount of basil. Add a spoonful of olive oil and a clove of garlic and mash it up diligently. A pestle and mortar is useful here, but a wooden spoon and a small bowl will do. This pesto is dropped into the hot soup as it goes to the table. Stir it well in before ladling the soup. In Italy minestrone is served as a first course in the evening meal. Follow it with a light meaty course.

An acceptable quick version of this can be made by using canned bouillon and small cans of beans, tomatoes, sweet corn, green beans, peas. You merely fry some onion and chopped cabbage, adding the canned vegetables. Open a can of grated Parmesan – everyone sit down!

BŒUF BOURGUIGNON
THE FATHER-FIGURE OF THE BEEF STEW

* parsley
* thyme
bay

1. SEAR cubes of 2 lb. leg of Beef in pork dripping.

↕ 1½"

1 carrot.

6 shallots – small onions will do.

Make pork dripping by frying chopped pieces of belly of pork.

A veal knuckle optional but wonderful (have it chopped)

3. PUT INTO PAN WITH **WELL-FITTING LID**

½ bot. BURGUNDY

2. BROWN ½ lb. chopped onion + a clove of garlic (finely chopped) in the same dripping.

4. COVER.
SIMMER for 3½ hours. IT MUST NOT BUBBLE. If it begins to get dry add water as needed.
↑ ↑ ↑ ↑ ↑

5. ADD 3 tablespoons of BRANDY and/or a wineglass of MADEIRA 30 mins before serving. Remove vegetable pieces — bay leaf, knuckle, etc. — then SERVE

OPTIONAL ¼ lb. mushrooms fried in butter added 15 mins before serving

* NOTE ABOUT MEAT: LEG OF BEEF will give the best flavour for this dish. **CHUCK BEEF** will need about 1 hour less cooking. **ROUND** needs somewhere in between. In any case test for tenderness, SERVE when meat is TENDER — but not soft or flaking — **UGH H !!!**

In this classic dish of French provincial cooking wine is used both to tenderize and provide flavour. With any kind of stew it is as bad to overcook as it is to undercook. It is better, by far, to stop the cooking process by turning the gas out and warming it later, than to serve a mashy stew.

Whenever alcohol is heated during a cooking process it is essential that it should be cooked. Most recipes will tell you to reduce by half, and sometimes to add water after to increase bulk, which sounds the sheerest nonsense; but this is merely to make sure that the alcohol is well cooked. Similarly when a frying pan is swilled out (déglacé) with wine or brandy to make the juices there into a small amount of fine gravy, the alcohol must be subjected to a high blast of heat.

Some cooks roll the meat cubes in flour before frying them – this makes the gravy slightly thicker in texture – but this is not really necessary, and quite superfluous if you include the veal knuckle. Another technique is to seal the lid on with a thick paste made from flour and water, but if you have a heavy well-fitting lid on the casserole this will not be needed. Incidentally, if you have an iron pot this is the dish for it.

There are certainly plenty of shapes and sizes to choose from, and if you want to be correct in serving them, you should check with the man behind the counter.

In soup one finds the tiny stars, angels' hair, snail shells, or the pasta called melon seeds. For past'asciutta (dry pasta) there is an even greater range of shapes and sizes; all sizes of wheels, conch shells, butterflies, and the huge tubes which are stuffed with meat (cool them under the tap or you'll burn your fingers) then covered with a creamy cheese sauce before being finished in a hot oven or grill.

For the evening meal, the pasta course in Italy will probably be pasta in soup. For midday it will be past'asciutta. Normally the pasta course precedes the main dish.

Ravioli are the most difficult to make. When they float to the top of the water they are cooked. Drain them well. If they burst open you probably have the water boiling too fiercely.

Italians have very uncomplimentary names for the way the British cook pasta. The Italian prefers his pasta 'al dente', that is, needing to be bitten (undercooked by our standards). A carefully cooked pasta can be served 'al burro'; take it to the table in a warmed pot. Hand large amounts of butter (warmed if you wish), grated cheese (Parmesan if possible) and a pepper mill.

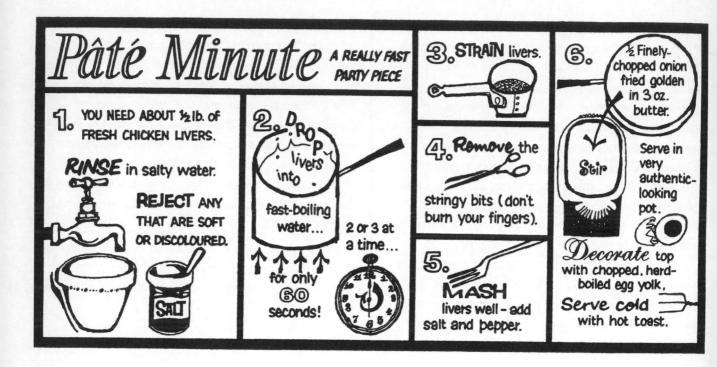

Pâté Minute

A REALLY FAST PARTY PIECE

1. YOU NEED ABOUT ½ lb. of FRESH CHICKEN LIVERS.

RINSE in salty water.

REJECT ANY THAT ARE SOFT OR DISCOLOURED.

SALT

2. DROP livers into fast-boiling water... 2 or 3 at a time... for only **60** seconds!

3. STRAIN livers.

4. Remove the stringy bits (don't burn your fingers).

5. MASH livers well - add salt and pepper.

6. ½ Finely-chopped onion fried golden in 3 oz. butter.

Stir

Serve in very authentic-looking pot.

Decorate top with chopped, hard-boiled egg yolk.

Serve cold with hot toast.

Now that it's possible to buy chicken livers by the pound in Britain there are all manner of uses for them. Perhaps soon poulterers will sell legs, wings and breasts of chicken by the pound, too, so that we need not buy four chickens in order to serve eight guests with Chicken Kiev.

This purée of chicken livers occurs in Belgian, Jewish and American cooking. In America it is generally used as a sandwich filling, garnished with crispy pieces of bacon. In Jewish cooking the unmoulded liver will be garnished with bright yellow 'schmalz' or chicken fat, and decorated with chopped hard-boiled egg.

Brochettes de Foies de volailles are chicken livers impaled on a metal skewer, dipped into warm butter and grilled.

When you make the Pâté Minute shown here, don't overcook the livers. The mashed livers should be soft and pink. Don't attempt to cut the mould into slices, it should be served with a spoon in dollops. This pâté, unlike almost any other, is normally served very cold, and for this reason serve hot, dry toast with it.

A TERRINE

CAN BE MADE FROM RAW FILLETED...... { CHICKEN
RABBIT
HARE
PIGEON —

OR FROM: PORK, PORK-LIVER, VEAL, ETC.

1. I suggest you ask your butcher to grind 2 lb Pig Liver + ½ lb. Belly of Pork. [He will hate to dirty his machine — but insist or change your butcher.]

MARINADE the meat overnight; **in**

½ bot. DRY WHITE WINE

A spoonful of brandy will make it even better.

2. ADD:
1 teaspoon salt
2 beaten eggs
and any of the following that you can find:
2 minced cloves of garlic
2 heads of cloves (crush them)
minced bacon
teaspoon basil
½ finely-chopped onion
chopped parsley
8 oz. breadcrumbs (soaked in milk, then squeezed)

STIR IT ALL!

3. DUMP this into a terrine (or similar pot) lined with streaky bacon sliced as fine

as your grocer can

slice it. Remove rind and pieces of bone. **WHEN FULL** close bacon ends over top..

4. You can arrange other items to make pretty patterns — very impressive!

PISTACHIO NUTS
HAM SLICE
TRUFFLES
STRIPS HAM FAT
HAM SLICES ROLLED

5. COVER DISH with metal foil or put a split calf's foot on top. **COOK** in a ← water jacket — Reg 4 (360°F) 2 hours.

6. 2 lb. Leave to get cold. **A FINAL TOUCH.** Add a cup of warm clear aspic. (If it comes from a tin don't admit it)

7. SERVE in thin slices; they should be at room temperature.

A PÂTÉ is a terrine cooked in pastry.

If it says 'pâté maison' on a menu it is most probably made from veal, pork belly and pork liver. If there is any game, etc., in it, it takes its name from that item. A game terrine is not made from one hundred per cent game, but from the chosen item added to veal and pork. The proportions are up to you.

If there is reason to believe that the game might be tough, extend the marinade period.

If you can get crépine – pig caul – from your butcher, use this as a surround to the filling instead of the thin slices of bacon. Or another alternative is to use thin slices of pork fat. Those from the outer fat of the loin are best.

If you pour clear-jellied stock into the terrine (as section 6), then the terrine should be used within four or five days. To keep it longer than this take the cooked filling out of the dish and wipe away all traces of moisture with a cloth. Replace it and pour fat over it to seal. Refrigerated, it will keep for several months.

Although it looks good on a table the best way to serve terrine is to remove only as much as is to be eaten, slice it, and leave for an hour at room temperature.

CASSOULET

A French peasant dish from the LANGUEDOC Region

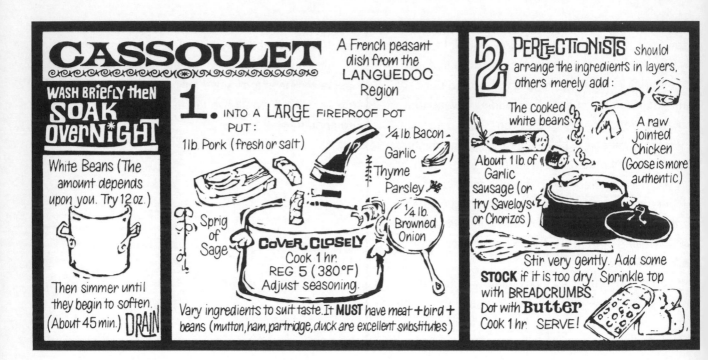

WASH BRIEFLY then SOAK OVERNIGHT

White Beans (The amount depends upon you. Try 12 oz.)

Then simmer until they begin to soften. (About 45 min.) DRAIN

1. INTO A LARGE FIREPROOF POT PUT:

1 lb. Pork (fresh or salt)

¼ lb. Bacon

Garlic

Thyme

Parsley

Sprig of Sage

¼ lb. Browned Onion

COVER CLOSELY
Cook 1 hr.
REG 5 (380°F)
Adjust seasoning.

Vary ingredients to suit taste. It MUST have meat + bird + beans (mutton, ham, partridge, duck are excellent substitutes)

2. PERFECTIONISTS should arrange the ingredients in layers, others merely add:

The cooked white beans

A raw jointed Chicken (Goose is more authentic.)

About 1 lb. of Garlic sausage (or try Saveloys or Chorizos)

Stir very gently. Add some STOCK if it is too dry. Sprinkle top with BREADCRUMBS. Dot with Butter Cook 1 hr. SERVE!

It is no longer possible to say what is the right way of preparing a cassoulet, nor even exactly how it originated. Most of these recipes involved the use of the local baker's oven which gave a lengthy gentle cooking. Similarly today, if time permits, a long period at a lower temperature will give its reward in flavour and tenderness. The beans should be medium-sized white haricot beans. The sausage should ideally be Toulouse sausage, but failing this, it must be one with a high meat-content. Should you use Chorizos, they should be only a small proportion of the total since they are exceedingly hot in character. Few French cooks would fail to add a generous amount of pork rind (couenne) which most butchers will give you upon request. Don't remove the fat from the pork, since the cassoulet is essentially fatty in character; this is countered by the absorbency of the beans. Green vegetables of any kind would be an embarrassment with this dish, which should be served in bowls accompanied only by a not-too-rough claret and argumentative conversation.

Choice of a cut of pork is not critical, but a combination of knuckle (for body) and breast (for fat) will be found very satisfactory. Do not add too much sage – it is very pungent. Pieces of rind, herbs, etc., which you wish to retrieve before serving should be tied in a bundle.

CHILE CON CARNE
(PEPPERS + MEAT)

THIS IS A DISH OF THE AMERICAN SOUTH-WEST [ESPECIALLY TEXAS], IT IS UNKNOWN IN MEXICO. THIS RECIPE FEEDS 4 – 6

There is no classic way of making this dish nor even a standard hot ingredient. This is the way I do it, but some cooks omit tomatoes, and in the U.S. sometimes the beans (frijoles) too.

SOAK OVERNIGHT

RED KIDNEY BEANS

½ lb.

1. COOK BEANS
IN SAME WATER **UNTIL ALMOST** *TENDER.*

SIMMER GENTLY

Some unscrupulous cooks even use a can of cooked beans. (e.g. BUTTER BEANS). Disgusting, isn't it?

2. FRY 1 onion (chopped) in beef dripping.

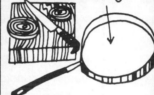

WHEN BROWN ADD:
- the **HOT** bit – (see grid)
1 teaspoon cumin
½ teaspoon oregano
STIR, –then add 1 lb. chopped skinned TOMATOES

THE HOT BIT: use any of following

(A) 1 green or red

small hot-type pepper chopped small.

(B) A pea-sized shot of hot pepper sauce e.g. TABASCO.

(C) 2 teaspoons

CHILLI POWDER

(D) 1 teaspoonful of PAPRIKA + a trace of CAYENNE.

3. ADD BEANS and 1½ lb. of ground beef.
Cook over medium heat 4 minutes.
SERVE: This is all the cooking the minced-up pieces of meat need. Longer will make them shrivel into hard pellets. If the meat is *finely* chopped by hand, flavour will be better.

This is not a Mexican dish, though nowadays there are plenty of Mexican roads littered with Chile signs. That's to attract American tourists, for Chile con Carne is an American dish – specifically a dish from the U.S. south-west. Like chop suey, spaghetti and pizza, it has become a part of the American diet, and a housewife who would balk at steak and kidney pudding will take these dishes in her stride.

There is certainly an enormous selection of beans available: all kinds of yellow, red, brown spotted ones, and black-eyed ones too. (Information about pulses is given in the Vegetables section, pages 59–60.) Everyone has his own method for dried beans (fresh beans make it even better, if you get some). Don't cook the beans to a mush. If you use any sort of powder for the hot bit, cook it gently for at least three minutes. Tiny hot peppers are the best, but chop them very

small, and don't wipe your eyes with the hand that's touched them – it will hurt. Lastly, don't overcook the meat. The moisture should still be in it when it's served. Exactly the same advice goes for the meat in a spaghetti sauce. Such tiny pieces of meat cook almost immediately upon entering the saucepan.

Bachelor cooks should use tabasco sauce (needs no cooking or chopping), canned beans (baked beans will do at a pinch) and tinned tomatoes; proceed as number three. A five-minute meal.

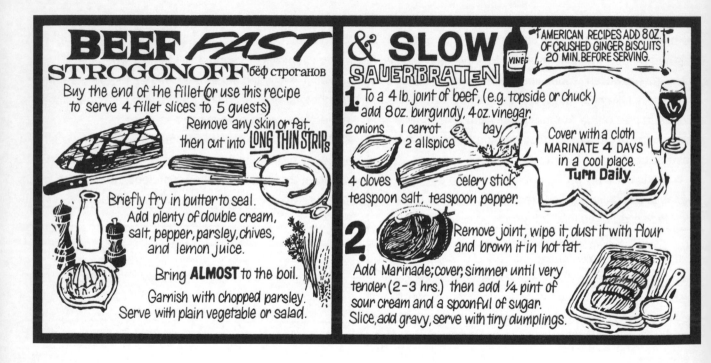

BEEF *FAST*
STROGONOFF бёф строганов

Buy the end of the fillet (or use this recipe to serve 4 fillet slices to 5 guests)

Remove any skin or fat, then cut into LONG THIN STRIPs

Briefly fry in butter to seal.
Add plenty of double cream, salt, pepper, parsley, chives, and lemon juice.

Bring **ALMOST** to the boil.

Garnish with chopped parsley.
Serve with plain vegetable or salad.

& SLOW
SAUERBRATEN

AMERICAN RECIPES ADD 8 OZ. OF CRUSHED GINGER BISCUITS 20 MIN. BEFORE SERVING.

1. To a 4 lb. joint of beef, (e.g. topside or chuck) add 8 oz. burgundy, 4 oz. vinegar.

2 onions   1 carrot   bay
           2 allspice

4 cloves   celery stick
teaspoon salt, teaspoon pepper.

Cover with a cloth MARINATE 4 DAYS in a cool place. **Turn Daily**.

2. Remove joint, wipe it, dust it with flour and brown it in hot fat.

Add Marinade; cover, simmer until very tender (2-3 hrs.) then add ¼ pint of sour cream and a spoonful of sugar.
Slice, add gravy, serve with tiny dumplings.

A marinade is any solution which will break down the fibres of a piece of meat. Generally their strong flavour prohibits their use on plainly prepared dishes. Yoghourt and tomato are two tenderizing materials that leave only a very slight flavour. The marinade is sometimes discarded after use, but sometimes provides the liquid in which the finished dish is served. Most marinades contain vinegar, onion and herbs.

When preparing a Strogonoff, a very great saving of money can be effected by buying skirt steak instead of the usual fillet steak. Remove the fibrous layers before slicing it, and it must be sliced across the grain. A piece of meat is like a bundle of string. If you cut across the bundle, you will have dozens of tiny pieces of string; cut it longways and you will get a few long fibres.

In cooking Strogonoff I have found it best to remove the meat from the pan while it is still slightly underdone, and then reduce the remaining sauce furiously until it is thick. So far I have never found the sauce disintegrates, but if you have trouble in this way, you should reduce the speed of the final boiling up. In French cooking the cream is always fresh, but in authentic Russian versions it is soured cream and in this case is more likely to curdle – so beware.

Cervelle de veau au beurre noir

1. Get yourself a decent set of BRAINS (and one set for each guest)

CAlves Brains are best, but **lamb**, **PORK** or **OX** are O.K.

Immediately after purchase soak in salt water for an hour or so.

Remove skin and blood **DON'T** buy sets that are broken or covered in bone chips

2. Cover with fresh water

Add : 2 tablespoons vinegar

salt onion

BAY THYME WILL ADD flavour

SIMMER 30 min.

Then leave in this liquid until ready to continue

3. Dry on a cloth, dust with flour. Sauté gently in plenty of butter. Remove brains. Cook butter dark brown (not too noir) Pour over brains. Add a thread of vinegar (and some capers if possible)

Au Beurre Noisette Cook the butter light brown — no capers.

À LA ROBERT Serve cold with dressing of cream mixed with mustard. Add a little shredded celery.

VINAIGRETTE Brains hot or cold + vinaigrette dressing

SLICED, BREADCRUMBED and fried in oil + butter. GARNISH with lemon

It has been said that brains are the only foodstuff that cannot be overcooked. Escoffier said that even two hours' cooking will only make them firmer. Brains are a very fine nutritive food. They are simple to prepare and, once blanched, can be used a day later, having been stored in the refrigerator overnight. The final preparation can be as simple or as complex as the cook wishes. Even should the finished article break into a scrambled-egg-like mixture, the final dish will taste just as delicious. Brains are a very good constituent for a soufflé. They are delicious fried, or in any of the piquant wine sauces.

Some General Rules about Offal

Sweetbreads, like brains, should be blanched soon after purchase. They can then be refrigerated. Many cooks are also in favour of a few minutes' parboiling for veal and beef kidneys, although lamb kidneys are never treated in this way. Liver and kidneys are best sliced very thinly and cooked over a high heat. Sheep's kidney is a particularly good ingredient for kebab. In kebab made in this way you should leave generous pieces of lamb kidney fat on the slices, or put pieces of fat between the pieces of kidney.

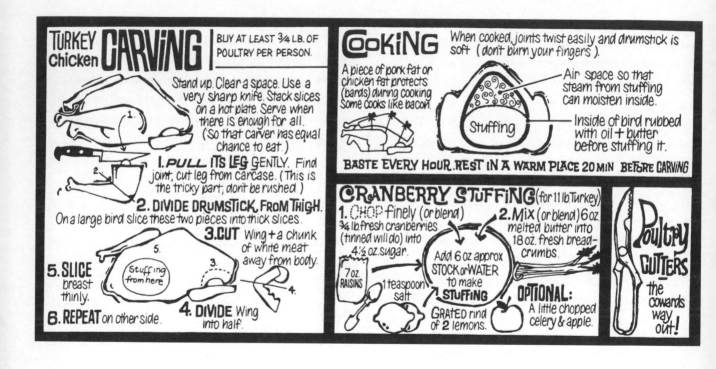

TURKEY Chicken CARViNG

BUY AT LEAST ¾ LB. OF POULTRY PER PERSON.

Stand up. Clear a space. Use a very sharp knife. Stack slices on a hot plate. Serve when there is enough for all. (So that carver has equal chance to eat.)

1. *PULL* ITS LEG GENTLY. Find joint, cut leg from carcase. (This is the tricky part; don't be rushed.)

2. DIVIDE DRUMSTICK FROM THIGH. On a large bird slice these two pieces into thick slices.

3. CUT Wing + a chunk of white meat away from body.

5. SLICE breast thinly.

Stuffing from here

4. DIVIDE Wing into half.

6. REPEAT on other side.

COOKiNG

When cooked, joints twist easily and drumstick is soft (don't burn your fingers).

A piece of pork fat or chicken fat protects (bards) during cooking. Some cooks like bacon.

Air space so that steam from stuffing can moisten inside.

Stuffing

Inside of bird rubbed with oil + butter before stuffing it.

BASTE EVERY HOUR. REST IN A WARM PLACE 20 MIN BEFORE CARViNG

CRANBERRY STUFFiNG (for 11 lb Turkey)

1. CHOP finely (or blend) ¾ lb. fresh cranberries (tinned will do) into 4½ oz. sugar.

2. MIX (or blend) 6 oz. melted butter into 18 oz. fresh bread-crumbs.

7 oz. RAISINS

Add 6 oz approx STOCK or WATER to make **STUFFING**

1 teaspoon salt

GRATED rind of 2 lemons.

OPTIONAL: A little chopped celery & apple.

Poultry CUTTERS

the cowards way out!

Most poultry prepared outside France is overcooked. Under no circumstances should a roast bird be white and so dry as to be almost dusty. Serve your poultry moist and flavourful. Remember that the breast needs less cooking than other parts. If the chicken is sectioned, it is best to add the breast only at a late stage of the cooking. When roasting, protect it with a piece of pork fat secured firmly over the bird.

A chicken without stuffing is like a hollow tube and consequently will cook quickly like a thin lamb chop. If you fill it with stuffing, it will need a great deal longer, unless the stuffing is cooked before being added.

Here is a good general rule: Switch oven to Regulo 7 (420° F.) and give it 15 minutes to get warm before starting to cook. Put half a lemon inside the chicken and paint outside with a mixture of olive oil and soy sauce. Place the chicken upside down on the tray for 15 minutes. Then tip it so that it rests on the other side (but still bottom up) for another 15 minutes. Finally, put it the right way up for 15 minutes. Test for doneness (prick deep – it should run yellow juice, not red). Serve it.

A sprig of fresh tarragon or thyme inside a roasted chicken gives a fabulous flavour. One last word; avoid deep-frozen poultry unless you intend to add plenty of flavour by means of the cooking process, or give it 24 hours' hanging.

The Chicken Paprika can be made into *Porkolt* merely by substituting pork for the chicken, or *Veal Porkolt* by using veal.

A Chicken Paprika deserves a fairly good-quality chicken, but there are many chicken recipes of the casserole type which can be left in the oven until the damn bird does get tender. Here are two classics.

The story goes that on June 14th, 1800, after the battle of Marengo, Dunand, the chef of Napoleon, produced this invention for his master from the only ingredients available.

Chicken Sauté à la Marengo: Brown a jointed chicken in oil. Fry three eggs in the same oil, add a clove of crushed garlic, and four chopped tomatoes. Splash some brandy over it (the story says that this came from Napoleon's hip-flask), putting six crayfish on top to cook in the steam. Serve when all is tender.

That is the original recipe as near as I can discover. Most cooks nowadays would prepare the eggs separately as a final garnish, in which case this could be casseroled to the point of succulent tenderness.

Pollo alla Cacciatora (Hunter's Chicken) is a very similar recipe. Brown the chicken and add tomatoes and garlic, but also add two small green peppers (but not the tiny fiery kind) from which the seeds have been removed. When it is nearly done, add plenty of mushrooms.

Both these recipes should be cooked in a casserole with a well-fitting lid, either over a very low flame or in a low oven.

Both the recipes would work O.K. with veal, but you'll have to name them yourself.

CHICKEN PAPRIKA

1 SIMMER
½ lb. chopped onion

in lots of butter

till it's golden.

2 ADD
a boiling-fowl cut into bits

SPRINKLE
1½ tablespoons of very good-quality paprika pepper over it.

3 COVER
with a well-fitting lid.

Simmer
for 1–1½ hours (less if you use a frying chicken)

Add water if it goes dry.

4 MIX
1 tablespoon of flour into half pint sour cream.

NO LUMPS!...

SPOON that into the gravy of the chicken

Keep stirring

5 Keep
on stirring it

over a tiny flame for about 10 mins.

DON'T boil it or it will CURDLE!

6 SERVE
it, and to make it pretty add a spoonful of

sour cream to each portion — and dust with a pinch of paprika.
Accompany with rice, noodles or tiny dumplings.

CHICKEN À LA KIEV

1. BUY 1 chicken for every two diners.

CAREFULLY PARE WHOLE BREASTS AWAY FROM BONE — REMOVE SKIN.

French cooks leave this first wing-bone attached to the breast meat so that it looks like a leg when it's served. CRAZY, eh?

SOME COOKS HAVE SECRET ADDITIONS like grated parmesan cheese or fried mushroom tucked inside.

2. Roll the meat out flat on a piece of wax paper — put another piece on top of it, then...

But it must not break or tear!

THUMP it with the side of a cleaver or a rolling-pin.

3. This is cold butter. Sprinkle it with parsley, salt and pepper.

Fold it up like a little parcel. It sticks to itself.

If you left a piece of main wing-bone on, it looks like this.

4. Roll in egg and breadcrumbs. Put it in the cold for at least 2 hours.

5 mins. should do.

DROP into deep fat. DRAIN—SERVE.

Chicken à la Kiev is a really impressive dinner-party feat. You cut carefully into each one when serving because your guests might stab them hastily and get an eyeful of hot butter.

There is nothing at all difficult about the preparation. Don't be in too much of a hurry. Have a very sharp knife when you cut the breasts away from the bone. If you break the meat even slightly at stage 2 then don't try to continue with that one, because it will leak and mess up your cooking fat when frying. When I do it I hold the chicken, still in the wax paper, up against the light. This way you can see where the flesh is thin and where it is still thick and needs more thumping.

Another time that this trick is useful is in the preparation of steak and kidney pudding. If you line a transparent heat-proof basin with the dough you can hold that against the light to help you press it to an even thickness.

The Parmesan-cheese stuffing is a secret from the Trattoria Terrazza restaurant, where one new chef was so shocked by the idea that he could not bring himself to do it.

CANETON à l'orange

THIS RECIPE FOR DUCKLING WITH ORANGE IS THAT OF M. FAUVEL *OF* RENAISSANCE RESTAURANT, FOSSEBOUDOT, *NEAR* BLAYE, GIRONDE.

Everything depends on the quality of the duckling and <u>NOT</u> having very sweet oranges.....

1. ROAST
a duckling

For a 2-3lb. duckling about 1 hour at Reg.6 (400°F) should have it about right, –but watch it!

Ladle fat away from gravy.

2. Make a ROUX, i.e.
cook a tablespoon butter and tablespoon flour over a low flame 3 mins.

3. Into ROUX put:

giblets   1 carrot

big wine-glass dry white wine

COVER-COOK GENTLY 1 HOUR

bouquet garni (parsley, thyme, bay leaf etc.) if you have it. STRAIN.

4. Into the giblet gravy put:
gravy from duckling [Remove fat first–see 1. Keep duckling warm]

<u>juice</u> of 3 oranges (Ask your greengrocer for oranges that are NOT sweet).

5. Make the gravy the texture of thick cream by adding cooked potato and beating it in. (Tiny bits of potato cook in no time).

6. PUT  8 to 12
quarters of peeled, seeded orange into the gravy.

Cook for 5 mins. to soften.

7. POUR sauce over duckling to glaze it; arrange orange pieces.

CARVE AT TABLE.

194

I like chicken, but better still I like duck or goose. There is much prejudice against these fatty poultry, but with careful cooking the fat comes away, and it's wonderful to have it in the kitchen or, better still, to eat it spread on hot toast.

If you are lucky enough to get a very young duckling – say under 5 months – it should be prepared in the simplest possible way, for a strong flavour of orange or sage will swamp the flavour of the duckling.

When buying a duck be sure the feet are soft and pliable. Dark-red feet and bill are a sign of age.

Duck *à l'anglaise* means roasted with a sage and onion stuffing, apple sauce, and thin gravy. The French, who loathe sage and onion stuffing, are more likely to cook the duck *poêle aux navets,* which means in a covered casserole at a very low temperature, adding sliced parboiled turnips towards the end of the cooking. The turnips take up the heavy fat and make the final dish less rich, although some cooks would ladle some of the fat away before adding them.

a Persian meal
CHELO KEBAB

1 2 cartons yoghourt

salt
pepper
fine-chopped onion

1½ lb. cubes of lamb (loin or leg)

MARINADE OVERNIGHT

2 Put cubes on skewer.

OPTIONAL: *3 MIN. BEFORE COOKING IS FINISHED ADD ONE WHOLE TOMATO.*

GRILL it 5 min. Turn it over for another 5 min.
Meat should be *slightly* pink. **SERVE** or...

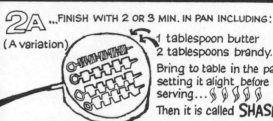

2A ...FINISH WITH 2 OR 3 MIN. IN PAN INCLUDING:

(A variation)

1 tablespoon butter
2 tablespoons brandy.

Bring to table in the pan, setting it alight before serving...

Then it is called **SHASHLIK**

ACCOMPANY with RICE
You can blanch some almonds, peel them, fry them for half a minute in butter, then add to rice..... but it is not strictly Persian any more.

WITH THE MEAL: Drink **YOGHOURT** beaten into an equal quantity of iced water

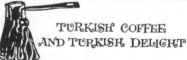

AFTER:

TURKISH COFFEE
AND TURKISH DELIGHT

When this strip appeared, a gentleman wrote to me to tell me that I didn't know what I was talking about, no Chelo Kebab could be complete without … There followed a list of ingredients for which I would have difficulty in finding the typesetting, let alone a source of supply. What he said, however, is undoubtedly correct. It is difficult enough to make an authentic French meal in England with only twenty miles between. To make any sort of foreign meal means a certain degree of compromise.

Originally the kebab was essentially lamb cooked over an open fire on a metal skewer. The metal conducted heat along the centre of the meat and cooked it from the inside, while the fire cooked it from the outside.

There is no limit to the application of this principle.

Spear on to a metal skewer (or stout wire):

1 Lamb kidney + liver + lamb + tomato + mushroom + onion.
2 Bacon + shelled shrimp + bacon.
3 Lamb + aubergine + onion + green pepper.
4 Bacon wrapped around crabmeat.
5 Bacon + scallops.

There is no limit; use any meat in any variety. Perhaps the classic recipe eaten in the Souks of Marrakesh (sounds great, doesn't it?) is:
6 Lamb kidney fat + lamb liver. (Eat this with lots of wholemeal bread.)

Offal is the most neglected, cheapest and most delicious selection of food on sale today. It is among the highest on the nutrition list. It is simple to prepare and has great variety. Follow these rules:

The Best	Type of Offal	Preparation
Best brains = calf **Best sweetbreads = lamb**	Brains and sweetbreads	Pre-cook* immediately. Remove tough fibres. Refrigerate. Fry gently.
	Kidneys (veal or beef)	Pre-cook.* Rinse. Braise.
Best kidney = lamb	Kidneys (pork or lamb)	Use as meat, but cook pork right through.
Best liver = calf	Liver (beef or calf)	Use as meat; undercook slightly.
Best hearts = sheep	Hearts	Remove tough tissues, stew till tender.
Best tripe = always ox	Tripe	Sold pre-cooked almost always. Stew.
	Tongue and pigs' feet	Needs no special preparation. Braise. Cook slowly.

* Use one pint water to which one tablespoon vinegar and a teaspoon salt has been added. Simmer gently 5–10 minutes.

A QUEUE of BEEF

1. CHOOSE
a bright, lean OXTAIL. It will feed 3. Have it jointed.

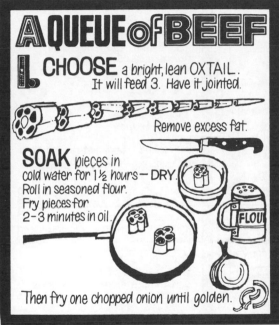

Remove excess fat.

SOAK pieces in cold water for 1½ hours — DRY. Roll in seasoned flour. Fry pieces for 2-3 minutes in oil.

Then fry one chopped onion until golden.

2. HEAVE
tail + onion into a casserole with well fitting lid.

ADD:
6 oz. dry white wine.
[o.k., then: red wine]

bay.
parsley.
one clove of crushed garlic.

ADD ENOUGH WATER TO COVER (BUT DON'T DROWN IT)

COVER IT

COOK it in oven Reg 2 (270°F) until tender. (About 3 hours).

3. SKIM FAT
Easiest way is to drain liquid— cool it (You can use ice to speed this).

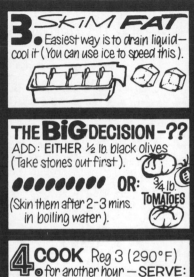

THE BIG DECISION -??
ADD: EITHER ½ lb. black olives (Take stones out first).

OR: ¾ lb. TOMATOES
(Skin them after 2-3 mins. in boiling water).

4. COOK
Reg 3 (290°F) for another hour —SERVE:
TOMATO VERSION: with mashed 'spud'
OLIVE VERSION: with plain rice.

THE Crépinette

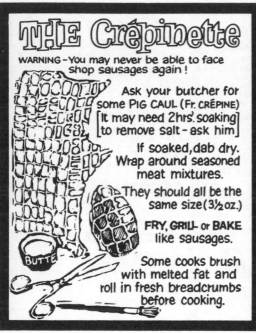

Ask your butcher for some PIG CAUL (Fr. CRÉPINE) [It may need 2 hrs. soaking to remove salt – ask him]

If soaked, dab dry. Wrap around seasoned meat mixtures.

They should all be the same size (3½ oz.)

FRY, GRILL or BAKE like sausages.

Some cooks brush with melted fat and roll in fresh breadcrumbs before cooking.

You will probably have your own theories about filling.

Here are some of mine:

1. Never use cooked meat.
2. Have at least a little fat on the meat.
3. Add just a little fresh breadcrumbs (soaked).
4. Add dash of brandy, sherry or wine if you have it.

Don't forget that the butcher will grind the meat for you.

De Ighton
Equal quantities veal and pork. Add beaten egg, lemon rind, nutmeg, trace of sage and seasoning.

DE PORC
Minced pork and chopped parsley – dash of brandy

De volaille
Chopped raw chicken and a little fat pork, goose liver & truffles.

D'agneau à la Liègeoise
Minced raw lamb, chopped lightly-fried onion and some crushed juniper berries.

Crêpinettes are often served with piquant or rich savoury sauces and creamed potatoes.

They are delicious cold....

When I first published this Crépinette recipe, letters arrived telling me that very few butchers sell pig's caul. Various retail associations said: 'There's no demand for it.' Pigs in England either have no caul, or it is thrown away, and in any case, they don't care. However, if you nag your butcher, he might be able to supply some. I suggest you put in a regular order for a small amount once a week, for Crépinette is not merely a convenient way of making sausages, but a fatty tissue that occurs exactly where it is most needed, i.e. between the meat and the pan. Also, like most kinds of meat fat, it contains a great deal of flavour, and this flavour impregnates the Crépinettes and gives them, whatever their meat content, a distinctive taste.

In Italy it is not unusual to add small amounts of grated cheese to sausage mixtures.

Sausages without skins are little more than divided sections of meat loaf. Use the Crépinette recipe and spread the mixture to a depth of one inch, then carefully cut it into fingers approximately the size of a chipolata sausage. Such sausages will break up more readily than sausages with skins to hold them together. Therefore, they are best cooked in the oven. The length of cooking depends upon the type of meat you use, but twenty minutes at Regulo 7 (420° F.) is a medium cooking time.

Generally speaking, the cook will find game best at the start of its season, and of course old birds are tougher than young ones. Test the spur at the back of the leg – the softer it is the better. Hare, pigeon and venison are the cheapest game buys. Others items tend to be expensive. A good rule is to roast if possible, for this brings out the best flavour; casserole if you think it might be tough.

* For more complete information see Foods in Season section.

	FEEDS	BEST AT*	REMARKS
Grouse	2	Sept./Oct.	Good for a terrine. Suffers in cold storage – non-refrigerated ones are second to none.
Blackcock Grey Hen Black Grouse		Sept./Oct.	A little larger than grouse.
Capercaillie	4		Perhaps the most delicious game bird.
Golden Plover	1		Cooked whole (not drawn).
Pheasant (Cock) Pheasant (Hen)	4 2	Oct./Nov.	Perhaps the most common in the shops.
Partridge	2	Oct.	Soon will disappear altogether.
Snipe Woodcock	1	Oct./Nov.	Roasted undrawn and served on toast.
Teal Widgeon Wild Duck	2 2 3		Most delicate flavour. Slightly fishy in taste. Slow roasting is good.
Pigeon	1	Any time	Roast only if you are sure it is tender.
Hare	6	Autumn	Can be roasted, jugged or made into a terrine. If in doubt, marinade and casserole.
Venison		Autumn	Must be hung. Tends to go dry. Marinade it – strips of fat help.

PARTRIDGE

(Perdreau, Perdrix)
Dwindling in numbers every year.
The common grey one is the finest from the cook's point of view.

Should not be hung more than 4 days. They are best young. (legs yellow, bills sharp)

Allow one bird to two persons.

ROAST.

A young grey bird deserves this simplest possible treatment:
Pluck, singe, draw and truss (or buy prepared).
Wipe inside and out. Dust with salt & pepper.
Dot with butter.
Roast 30 min. Reg 7 450°F.
Remove bacon.
Another sprinkle of flour then another 5 min. in oven.
Drain fat, add a little stock to pan to make gravy.

streaky bacon (OR PORK FAT)

SEND TO TABLE WITH A GARNISH OF Watercress AND LEMON slices

serve with BREAD SAUCE

¼ pint milk + ¼ pint white stock. In it put
3 cloves ♦♦♦
chopped onion
3 peppercorns
A trace of garlic + nutmeg
Simmer about 30 min.
STRAIN. Add fresh white bread crumbs, knob butter and a little cream.

Casserole:

Line a casserole with streaky bacon.
Put birds on top then add stock made by simmering giblets for 45 min.

Add:
sliced carrot
sliced onion
squeeze of lemon

bed of lightly cooked drained pressed cabbage
BACON

GARLIC IS OPTIONAL · SO IS SOME RED WINE REDUCED OVER A FIERCE FLAME

Cover casserole. Cook Reg 6. 400°F. about 45 min.

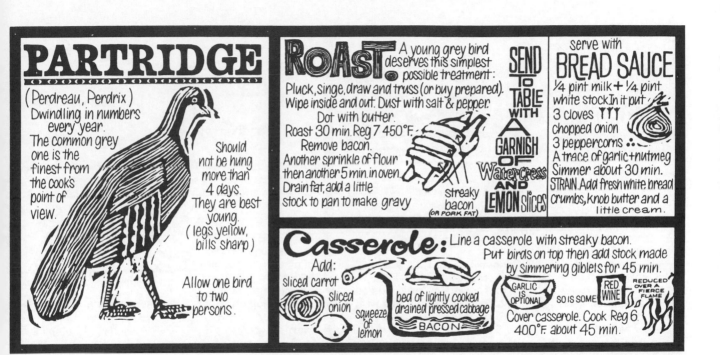

STEAK & KIDNEY PUD

USE SAME RECIPE FOR O FRUIT PUD.
...BUT LESS TIME...
Tie firmly

SUET CRUST

10 oz. S.R. flour
5oz butchers suet-
(chop very finely, removing crisp fibre as you go)
Add enough water to make a dry, stiff dough. <u>Some experts</u> mix a teaspoonful of treacle into the water.

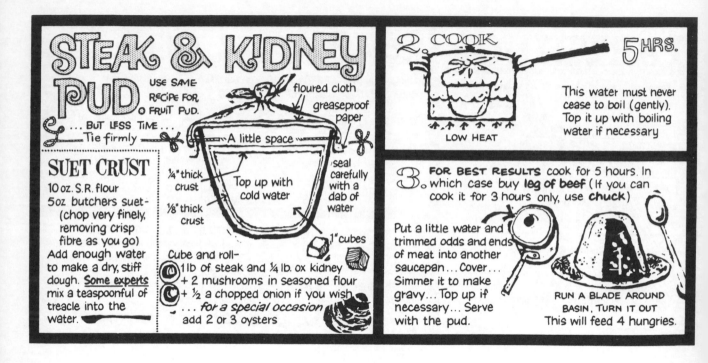

floured cloth
greaseproof paper

A little space

¼" thick crust

Top up with cold water

⅛" thick crust

seal carefully with a dab of water

1" cubes

Cube and roll-
1 lb of steak and ¼ lb. ox kidney
+ 2 mushrooms in seasoned flour
+ ½ a chopped onion if you wish
... *for a special occasion* add 2 or 3 oysters

2. COOK

5 HRS.

LOW HEAT

This water must never cease to boil (gently). Top it up with boiling water if necessary

3.

FOR BEST RESULTS cook for 5 hours. In which case buy **leg of beef** (If you can cook it for 3 hours only, use **chuck**)

Put a little water and trimmed odds and ends of meat into another saucepan... Cover... Simmer it to make gravy... Top up if necessary... Serve with the pud.

RUN A BLADE AROUND BASIN, TURN IT OUT
This will feed 4 hungries.

This same suet-crust recipe can be varied to make a rabbit, a chicken, an apple, plum or rhubarb pudding, in which case it will need 2–2½ hours.

Another way of making a pudding is to roll the suet crust flat. Sprinkle with jam, marmalade, currants, mincemeat, chopped cherries, chopped figs, chopped dates or chopped ginger – or any combinations of those that appeal to you. You need to sprinkle sugar over it. Roll it up like a Swiss roll, trapping as much air inside as you can, for this is what makes it light. Wrap the roll in a generous piece of floured cloth and tie it.

Don't tie it too tightly, for it must have space to expand.

This is the shape in which a bacon pudding is prepared. Dice the lean bacon and sprinkle it thickly over the crust – a little diced ham improves the flavour. Roll it, tie the cloth, etc., drop it into fast-boiling water.

Keep it boiling for about an hour for a three-inch-diameter roll.

Suet crust rolled into little balls (about one inch across), floured and dropped into fast-boiling water (not into a fast-boiling stew) become big dumplings. Have a large pan of water, put the lid on it, and don't lift it to see how they are going. Don't forget that they swell, so don't overcrowd them. A quarter of an hour will see them cooked.

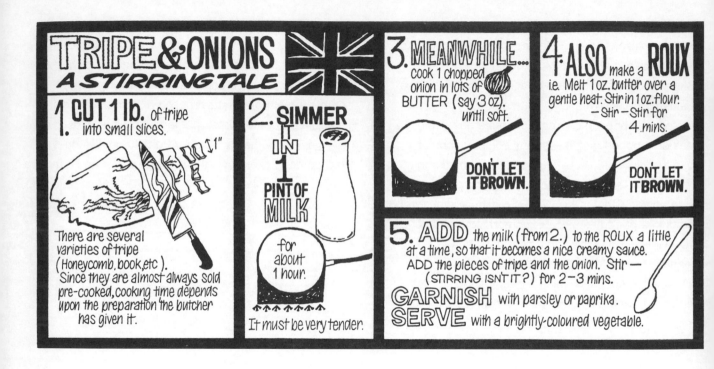

TRIPE & ONIONS
A STIRRING TALE

1. CUT 1 lb. of tripe into small slices.

There are several varieties of tripe (Honeycomb, book, etc). Since they are almost always sold pre-cooked, cooking time depends upon the preparation the butcher has given it.

2. SIMMER IT IN 1 PINT OF MILK for about 1 hour.

It must be very tender.

3. MEANWHILE... cook 1 chopped onion in lots of BUTTER (say 3 oz). until soft.

DON'T LET IT BROWN.

4. ALSO make a **ROUX** i.e. Melt 1 oz. butter over a gentle heat. Stir in 1 oz. flour. — Stir — Stir for 4 mins.

DON'T LET IT BROWN.

5. ADD the milk (from 2.) to the ROUX a little at a time, so that it becomes a nice creamy sauce. ADD the pieces of tripe and the onion. Stir — (STIRRING ISN'T IT?) for 2–3 mins.

GARNISH with parsley or paprika.
SERVE with a brightly-coloured vegetable.

Tripe is 'the large stomach of ruminating animals'. If you are a tripe-fancier you are in good company along with Rabelais, William the Conqueror and Homer. It is just as well that most tripe is sold pre-cooked because preparing the stuff is quite a complicated business. Since salt is often added during this pre-cooking you should add more with caution. In the north of England tripe is sometimes served cold with an oil-and-vinegar dressing. Whichever way you prepare it, make sure it is cut into small pieces before it is served, for a lot of prejudice stems from grappling with huge sheets of it on a small plate.

Because it is rich in gelatine, tripe is a good ingredient for a stew or stock that you want to have a rich thick texture. Like pigs' feet and pieces of pork skin it can be discarded at the end of the cooking period.

Tripe is a popular dish in northern France and it is not unusual to find the drinks of that region – cider and Calvados – used in the cooking. In France tripe is never – in my experience – served in white sauce. It is usually 'étuvé' (cooked in a very low oven) for about 10 hours, and has carrots, onions, leeks and parsley, and, if possible, a basis of good stock. There is a great mystique surrounding this dish, but the only secret of **Tripes à la mode de Caen** is the long slow cooking.

To drink with *Tripes à la mode de Caen* what can beat cider?

Boiled LEG OF Mutton

WITH CAPER SAUCE

TO FEED OVER A DOZEN

Once one of the most famous of English recipes, now so unpopular as to be almost extinct. TRY IT!

1. BUY a LEG OF MUTTON (about 10 lb.)

Cover with water.

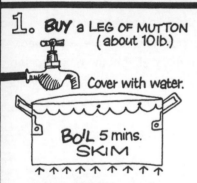

BOIL 5 mins. SKIM

SIMMER for 1½ hours. Add 1 teaspoon salt.

SIMMER until tender... about another 2-2½ hours.

2. Drain joint.

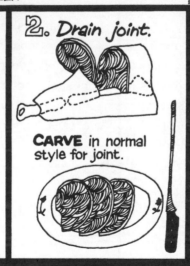

CARVE in normal style for joint.

The Caper Sauce

Melt 2 tablespoons butter.

Stir in 3 tablespoons flour

ADD
½ pint cooking liquid (from mutton), salt and pepper.

COOK 5 mins. Slowly add 3 tablespoons melted butter.

LOW HEAT

Stir all the time over low heat.

FINISH with a squeeze of lemon and a cupful of capers.

The idea that mutton is inferior to lamb is both an incorrect and a recent notion. Mutton is from an animal that is over one year old, and nowadays mostly under two years old. Many Victorian gourmets, however, demanded three- or four-year-old mutton because it had a stronger flavour. Lamb they thought a very bland item.

Even now there are plenty of mutton-fanciers around. They claim that it's not only revivifying, wholesome and highly digestible, but also that it's an aphrodisiac!

This recipe for boiled mutton produces a particularly good cold joint. Decorate the sliced meat with generous amounts of bottled capers and serve with your favourite chutneys and pickles.

Any butcher will agree to sell you half a leg joint if you prefer it. Opinions vary as to whether the lower (knuckle) end or the wide (fillet) is best. The cooking time will vary according to the shape of the joint.

The traditional English accompaniment would be a purée of turnips. For a final touch poach sliced marrow bones and mix the marrow into the purée as you would butter. If you use this same recipe to prepare boiled leg of pork the correct English accompaniment is pease pudding (purée of lentils).

OSSO BUCO

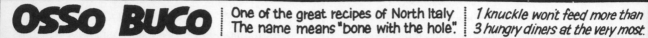

One of the great recipes of North Italy
The name means "bone with the hole".

1 knuckle won't feed more than
3 hungry diners at the very most.

1 TELL your butcher to slice a veal knuckle

1½"

right through the bone.

THE MEAT portions are uneven.

THE MARROW is the choice part — guard it!

2

1 carrot   1 onion

piece celery   chop vegetables small

4 oz. butter

(celery seed will almost do)

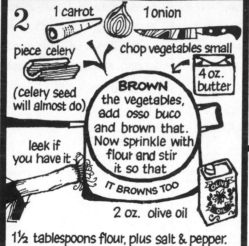

BROWN the vegetables, add osso buco and brown that. Now sprinkle with flour and stir it so that

IT BROWNS TOO

leek if you have it

OLIVE OIL

2 oz. olive oil

1½ tablespoons flour, plus salt & pepper.

3 ADD 1 glass dry white wine, stir around. Add same amount of stock, plus a tin of Italian peeled tomatoes, and 2 tablespoons tomato purée.

COVER

Simmer 2 hours

4 Remove vegetables if you wish.

SERVE osso bucos carefully to preserve marrow in its right place. GARNISH with chopped parsley and a trace of lemon juice in the sauce.

Accompany with plain rice or plain noodles.

210

The English are not great veal eaters, and the cook is best advised to go for Dutch veal, because most English veal comes from what the trade calls 'bobby calves', or calves slaughtered very soon after birth. This meat is rubbery and tasteless.

Veal at its best is superb. The feet and knuckle are rich in gelatine and so are used for stocks and aspics. The liver is the finest (although this does not apply to bobby-calves' liver, which is full of pipes), the kidney is wonderful braised in dry white wine, the sweetbreads are a delicacy. Used as a roasting joint veal must be larded or covered with strips of pork fat (bacon is too strong in flavour). French butchers (and really fine butchers in England too) will cover a roasting joint of veal with pig caul to provide a thin fatty protection. Veal is never 'hung'. Breast of veal is quite unlike the rather dreary breast of lamb, but it should be boned, stuffed and rolled in the same way. A large knuckle makes a succulent roast. Escalopes are very thin slices from the fillet. They must be *cut* thin: no amount of hammering will help a thick slice. It will merely revert to size while being cooked. **Jarret de Veau à la Provençale** is almost identical to Osso buco.

SHARP AND SWEET TONGUE

Some cooks may prefer to use other types of tongue (veal, lamb etc.) The procedure is the same.

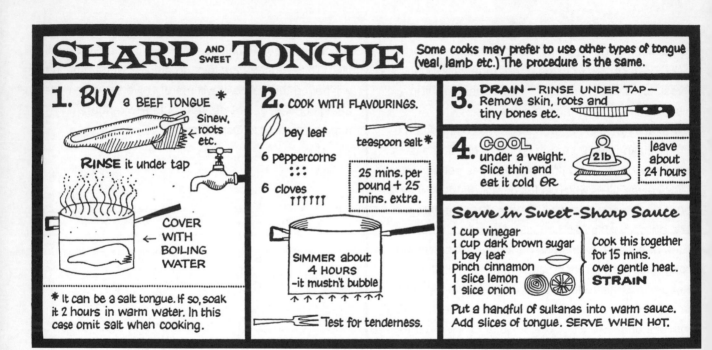

1. BUY a BEEF TONGUE *

Sinew, roots etc.

RINSE it under tap

COVER WITH BOILING WATER

* It can be a salt tongue. If so, soak it 2 hours in warm water. In this case omit salt when cooking.

2. COOK WITH FLAVOURINGS.

bay leaf

6 peppercorns

6 cloves

teaspoon salt *

25 mins. per pound + 25 mins. extra.

SIMMER about 4 HOURS -it mustn't bubble

Test for tenderness.

3. **DRAIN** – RINSE UNDER TAP – Remove skin, roots and tiny bones etc.

4. **COOL** under a weight. Slice thin and eat it cold OR

2 lb

leave about 24 hours

Serve in Sweet-Sharp Sauce

1 cup vinegar
1 cup dark brown sugar
1 bay leaf
pinch cinnamon
1 slice lemon
1 slice onion

Cook this together for 15 mins. over gentle heat. **STRAIN**

Put a handful of sultanas into warm sauce. Add slices of tongue. SERVE WHEN HOT.

Tongue can be stewed, smoked, salted, poached, pickled, baked or fried. It is as fine cold as it is hot. It has a bland flavour which gives you a chance to use all types of sauce with it. Salt-tongue strips are wonderful in a terrine, ground tongue is great in stuffing. Tongue can be warmed up without much loss of flavour and yet so much of the tongue one sees is straight out of a tin. That circular chunk in the grocer's is out of a bigger tin.

So next time you have a party serve cold tongue. Salted tongue is perhaps best if you are serving it cold. Decorate with fine slices of cooked mushroom, carrot, etc., to make patterns. Glaze the surface with a clear jelly, slice it carefully and scatter capers and slices of pickled cucumber. Perhaps alternate the slices with some freshly cooked ham. Have mustard available, and some horseradish.

Small tongues, veal or lamb, can be casseroled in a low oven with onion fried brown and a little good stock. (Add chopped tomato if you like.)

With cold tongue and pickle, or with Sharp and Sweet tongue, I would serve pale ale, chilled.

SERVE ANY OF THESE LAMB DISHES ON HOT PLATE. LAMB IS NOT PLEASANT TO EAT IF ONLY WARM. AIM TO HAVE MEAT MOIST AND SLIGHTLY PINK.

Remove excess fat.

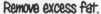

1″ 1″

BONE & ROLL LAMB CHOPS

Secure with a toothpick.

Rasher streaky bacon

GRILL 12–15 minutes.

2″

Cut gash as far as bone to make pocket.

STUFF WITH THIS KIND OF MIXTURE { breadcrumbs minced onion melted butter beaten egg garlic fresh mint.

DIP WHOLE thing into beaten egg then into soft crumbs. **BAKE** 30–40 mins. 450° (REG 8).

If there isn't much fat add strips of pork fat to protect while roasting. Allow 2 chops per person.

SALVAGE LEAN MEAT FROM THIS PART FOR A STEW. THROW FAT AWAY.

ROAST 300° Reg 1½ 25 mins. per lb.

Have butcher cut along here.

MAKE A PASTE by crushing 2 cloves garlic, 1 teaspoon of Rosemary + salt & pepper, adding OLIVE OIL. Spread this all over joint before cooking.

The whole back (2 loin joints) left together is called a—

SADDLE OF LAMB

but it is too **big** for most domestic ovens.

bone. A meaty chop from other end of loin is called a CHUMP CHOP.

When you are buying lamb the meat should be darker than beef, even slightly brown. Although New Zealand lamb is excellent it has to be frozen and this results in the fat going whiter. If you want home-killed lamb watch for fat that is a creamy colour.

The chump chop is to lamb what rump steak is to beef. There are only two or three chump chops on each side of a carcass and they are always expensive.

If you don't know how many guests are eating, ask the butcher to separate the loin into chops. Between each chop put a stuffing (e.g. ground lamb, beaten egg, breadcrumbs and rosemary) and assemble the loin when you know the numbers. Wrap tinfoil around the bottom to hold the mock joint together. Easy to serve, too.

Best end of lamb can be used just like loin. It has a better flavour, although it's less meaty. Avoid meat that is littered with bone splinters. A good butcher trims away gristle and saws bone neatly. Signs of skilful butchery usually indicate a knowledgeable butcher selling good meat.

Drink a claret with it.

CORNED BEEF AND THE NEW ENGLAND BOILED DINNER

1. CHOOSE a nice piece of beef.
(e.g. Silverside or Brisket) Ask your butcher to salt it. (i.e. corn it)

3½ lb.

When it is ready it should be securely tied. Rinse, then wipe with a damp cloth. Cover with cold water, bring slowly to boil. BOIL 5 mins. SKIM.

2. SIMMER
[IT MUST NOT BOIL OR BUBBLE] **FOR 4 HOURS**

COVER

GOOD BUT NOT ESSENTIAL – CHOPPED ONION BAY LEAF MARJORAM – A PIECE OF SALT PORK.

N.B. You may have a very tough piece of meat. When tender it is ready.

3. INTO THE STOCK PUT

2 parsnips
4 carrots
3 small turnips } PEEL & QUARTER
5 small onions
4 potatoes

SIMMER UNTIL NEARLY TENDER.

4. THEN ADD
a cabbage in BIG chunks

BUT REMOVE CORE.
COOK 10-15 minutes.

5. SERVE MEAT & Vegetables [NOT STOCK]

Glaze the vegetables with a piece of butter to improve appearance.

ACCOMPANY WITH horseradish sauce mustard.

DRINK: beer.

ALTERNATIVE

AFTER **2.** LET BEEF COOL IN STOCK, THEN PUT A WEIGHT ON IT OVERNIGHT. SERVE COLD. SOME COOKS REMOVE THE LAYERS OF FAT BEFORE PRESSING IT.

2lb

When you cook the recipe here you may find it difficult to equate it with that strange stuff that you have prised out of tins from time to time.

Corned Beef and Cabbage is a variation on the New England Dinner. All you do different is to leave out all the vegetables except the cabbage and the onion. Serve after discarding the onion.

Corned Beef Hash is usually made from tinned corn beef, but there's no reason for not doing it with the real thing. Here's how. Combine equal amounts of cold corned beef and cold cooked potato. Add a little chopped onion (some cooks use it raw, some cooked), moisten with a little cream, and give it a shake of salt and pepper. (Some recipes use ginger and allspice, too.) Now melt some butter in a good-quality frying pan and put the hash into it. It should be over a very low heat so that after 20 minutes a thin crust has formed on the bottom. Now you can fold it in half so that the appetizing crust is visible, and serve it with tomato sauce, or you can make hollows in the top of the hash with the bowl of a spoon and drop raw eggs into the hollows. Pop the pan under the grill to cook the eggs. This **Corned Beef Hash with Eggs** is a top-favourite American supper dish. Drink tomato juice with it.

PorK Loaf

A useful standby: Vary the flavourings with herbs and spices of your choice.

Cut down work by telling the butcher to grind the pork. If he complains, shop elsewhere.

1. GRIND THIS VERY Fine {

1 lb. HAM
1 lb. PORK (not too fatty)
1 ONION
1 teaspoon SAGE.

SAGE

2. ADD

salt, pepper,
4 oz. cream
1 beaten egg white.

Stir Together.

3. ARRANGE

Mix

strips of HAM FAT *
around the loaf of meat

* Ask for some when you buy the ham.

4. TIE (not too tightly)

into a cloth.
SIMMER in water 2½ hours.

N.B. Better to add a wineglass of vinegar to water.

5. DRAIN PRESS SLICE →

DON'T LET IT STICK TO POT

2 lb.

12 HOURS

This is a standard item of American cooking. The cooking process is an interesting variation of the terrine (baked with or without a water-jacket) and the galantine (where the forcemeat is put inside a fowl before being poached and pressed). When served, however, these various American meat loaves are used as a main or meat course, while the terrine, or pâté, is a first-course dish, and usually a luxury dish.

A more common meat loaf in America would be two pounds of ground chuck steak mixed with half a cupful of breadcrumbs (or porridge oats) that have been well soaked in milk, a couple of beaten eggs, a well-chopped onion, and some of your favourite herbs. This would be cooked in a tin (e.g. a loaf tin) for about an hour at Regulo 4 (350° F.). Sometimes such a meat loaf would have the top painted with a dressing for the last half of the cooking period. Mustard, brown sugar and tabasco sauce mixed with a little water would be a typical 'paint'.

Meat loaves can be adapted to almost anything. It's not unusual to find pork and beef mixed. Nor is it unusual to have layers of mushroom, potato or even spaghetti in them.

Ris de Veau A LA CRÈME

A Michelin ✿ from the CENTRAL RESTAURANT, Chaunay, Vienne, France.

1. BUY ¾ lb of Veal throat sweetbread (from a young animal is best).
BLANCH it. i.e.,

Put into cold water.

BRING TO BOIL

SIMMER 5 MINS — **DRAIN** — **COOL**: then remove any membrane. **CUT** into 1" slices. →

2. FRY sweetbread slices golden in lots of butter. Stand them aside.

CUT 3 slices of bread and fry them very crisp in the remaining butter.

3. PUT the slices of sweetbread on the crisp bread.

STAND in warm place.

HOT PLATES HELP

4. FRY 6 oz. of sliced mushrooms + finely chopped shallot in same pan.

DON'T BROWN THEM

By now you'll need more butter.

5 ADD some grated nutmeg, (this is the secret of this recipe — about a salt spoonful should do it)
✝ salt and pepper
✝ 4 tablespoons of double cream.
SIMMER FOR 4 MINS.
Stir it or the cream will curdle.

Pour it over slices — SERVE.

This is a rare old delicacy, and because fewer people are eating it it's getting a little cheaper. It's just loaded with vitamin A and has a light earthy taste that deserves something better than drenching in dark wine sauce as so often happens in restaurants.

The recipe in the strip is very rich and can be served in small portions. Perhaps you will prefer to roll the pieces in egg and breadcrumbs and then fry or grill them. Another method is to spear the pieces on to skewers alternately with pieces of best-quality bacon. Brush with butter then grill gently. Sometimes the sweetbread pieces are wrapped in slices of bacon, fixed with a toothpick, then baked gently.

You can use the recipe in the strip but put the result into warm vol-au-vent cases. Whatever way you decide to cook them sweetbreads should always be blanched first, as shown in the strip.

It takes a lot of nerve to try to compress the story of bacon into one cook strip, so naturally I failed. I didn't mention streaky bacon for a start. Like most cuts of meat of its sort it is much more flavourful than the large areas of completely lean. Streaky can be thick sliced and slow cooked, or sliced paper-thin and cooked as crisp as a potato chip.

Rashers of bacon can be grilled or fried; either way the lean part should be protected from the heat, i.e. when frying, let each lean part rest upon the next rasher's fat part. The fat needs more cooking. Removing the rind with scissors will prevent it curling up. Rinds can be put into a stockpot, or fried until very crisp and puffed up. They can then be served as appetizers, or to accompany soup. They are a little like pork crackling, which is not surprising.

Green bacon is bacon which has been brine-cured, but not smoked. It is rather mild in flavour, but some people, especially in the north of England, prefer it. Most bacon is smoked after it is cured. The smoking process makes it a little drier, and imparts the smoky flavour (often that of oak wood).

If you are boiling green bacon it is best to cut down the pre-soaking time. There are fancy types of bacon on the market now. Like most foodstuffs, their flavours are growing sweeter all the time. Try some of the famous old ones as well as the new ones with slick names.

The curing of bacon is much milder nowadays, and it is sometimes hard to tell a slice of gammon from a slice of ham.

Whether cooked or uncooked, gammon or ham, it is better kept in a cool draughty place than put into a refrigerator. Protect it with a wrapping of muslin, and be sure it doesn't get even slightly damp. Damp is the great enemy.

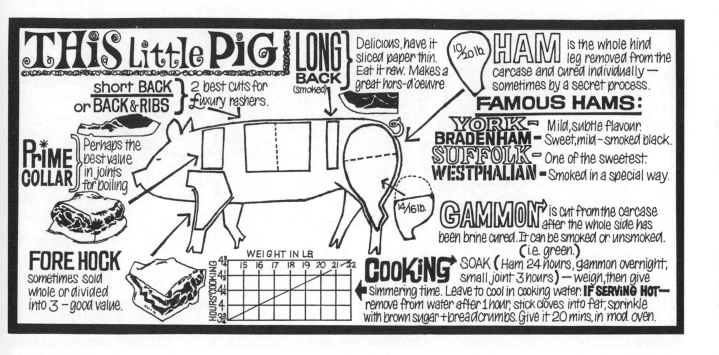

THiS Little PiG

LONG BACK (smoked)

Delicious, have it sliced paper thin. Eat it raw. Makes a great hors-d'oeuvre

short BACK or BACK & RIBS } 2 best cuts for luxury rashers.

HAM is the whole hind leg removed from the carcase and cured individually — sometimes by a secret process.

10/20 lb

FAMOUS HAMS:

YORK — Mild, subtle flavour.
BRADENHAM — Sweet, mild — smoked black.
SUFFOLK — One of the sweetest.
WESTPHALIAN — Smoked in a special way.

PriME COLLAR | Perhaps the best value in joints for boiling

GAMMON is cut from the carcase after the whole side has been brine cured. It can be smoked or unsmoked. (i.e. green.)

14/16 lb.

COOKiNG → SOAK (Ham 24 hours, gammon overnight, small joint 3 hours) — weigh, then give simmering time. Leave to cool in cooking water. **IF SERVING HOT** — remove from water after 1 hour, stick cloves into fat, sprinkle with brown sugar + breadcrumbs. Give it 20 mins. in mod. oven.

FORE HOCK sometimes sold whole or divided into 3 — good value.

WEIGHT IN LB

HOURS COOKING
4¾ 4½ 4¼ 4 ¾ ½ 3¾
15 16 17 18 19 20 21 22

223

A CURRY MEAL
FOR 6 DINERS

BEEF VINDALOO

1 Tablespoon ground coriander,
½ Teaspoon ground cumin,
1 Teaspoon ground turmeric,
½ Teaspoon ground mustard seed,
½ Teaspoon ground chillies,
1 Salt spoonful ground black pepper,
A pinch of ground ginger.

1. MIX TO PASTE WITH VINEGAR

VINEGA

2. FRY for 3 mins. Then add paste (as above) for 3 more mins

1 large onion
3 cloves garlic
2 green chillies
ALL FINELY SLICED.

3. Chop 1 lb. leg of beef. Add water only if it gets too dry. (Look at it every half-an-hour.)

REG 3 (330°F) for 2½ hours
COVER CLOSELY

CHICKEN KORMA

1. JOINT a chicken (the butcher will do it) then marinade the pieces in YOGHOURT
+ 1 teaspoon ground TURMERIC
+ 1 clove GARLIC.

YOGHU

2. ADD: (To chicken + marinade)
1 teaspoon finely sliced fresh ginger. (Canned will do).
5 cloves
5 whole cardamoms
1 stick cinnamon
1 sliced (lightly fried) onion + clove garlic.

COVER

3. COOK Reg 3 (330°F) 45 mins.

ON THE TABLE PUT—

a big bowl of plainly cooked rice,

dessicated coconut;

raw onion + raw tomato, chopped,

some bananas,

a bowl of dhal [dilute a can of pease pudding if you want to cheat],

puppadums (even Indians buy these ready made – do the same)

some chutneys & pickles.

Use a good quality fat (ghee if possible). DON'T LET ONIONS FRY BROWN!!

India is a vast sub-continent; it houses (or often fails to) people of many different languages, cultures, religions and races. There are many taboos about beef and even more about pork.* Some communities eat no meat at all because of religious conviction, others because they can't afford it. Indian food is most complex. This is a curry meal, I will claim no more for it, except that it won't disgrace you whether your guests are punkah wallahs or pukka sahibs.

To complete the atmosphere buy a tin of ghee. It will keep for months under refrigeration and can be used as a very fine type of cooking fat. Cook the powders in the Beef Vindaloo carefully before adding the meat, for this is an important part of the process. *Do not add flour or use cooked meat.*

The Chicken Korma is a milder dish so that you can please even those guests who dislike the idea of curry.

The Kormas (or Quormahs) are Moglai or Muslim dishes. They are usually marinaded in sour curds, for which yoghourt is an excellent substitute. The Vindaloos are hot curries from Southern India, but with the long cooking I have suggested, you might well find that, for the first time, you are enjoying your curries hot. Try it at least once before cutting down on the green chillies.

* Tenacious ethnic groups, decimated by pork tapeworm, have renounced pork on religious grounds. Nowadays in a temperate climate, properly cooked and with supervised production and sale, pork is a safe and delicious part of a normal diet.

LOW-CALORIE LUNCH for 4

1. Ask butcher to grind ¼ lb. of liver (ox-liver will do) + 1 lb. of beef

1 beaten egg

pinch of nutmeg

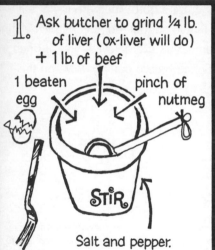

STIR

Salt and pepper.

2. SHAPE

3. GRILL fiercely.
SERVE THEM very underdone with...

4. RAW CABBAGE

Half a medium head - shredded.

Add yoghourt, salt and pepper.

5. TOMATO SALAD

¾ lb. roughly chopped tomatoes

½ finely-chopped onion
1 teaspoon oil
1 teaspoon vinegar.

Finish with dessert apple, milk (*skimmed if possible*).

226

Here's a wild little invention of mine. It's the only culinary invention I have ever made, apart from discovering that it's best to sprinkle the salt on the bread and butter when eating a soft-boiled egg.

The most difficult part of this recipe is bullying the butcher into dirtying his meat-grinder with liver. He'll do it, but he will grumble. Tell him you want both liver and beef ground and then he will put the beef through second, to drive the remnants of the liver through. Perhaps you have an electric grinder, and then you can grumble quietly to yourself.

Using yoghourt as a dressing is very simple and delicious. It goes just as well over chopped cucumber, raw chopped mushrooms, celery or fennel.

These same 'burgers can be eaten inside a soft bun, and in this case put a thick slice of raw Spanish onion on the meat. Mustard and horseradish sauce are welcome.

Drink Shloer apple juice to keep up the healthy mood.

There is a sharp division between the fashionable and the unfashionable in the fish shop. A shrewd shopper will take advantage of this. As far as the smaller varieties go, the expensive items are:

Smelts	(or Sparlings: French Éperian). Can be all sizes but the small (4-inch) ones are best Perhaps more delicate in flavour than any other fish. Rinse, then fry in butter.
Whitebait	See opposite.
Oysters	Natives (Whitstable, Burnham, Colchester) graded by size. Biggest are most expensive. Portuguese are a different species: green in colour, and less expensive. A squeeze of lemon is not essential. Eat freshly opened oysters with a Muscadet wine – great.
Scallops	Expensive, but go a long way. Ask fishmonger to remove the tiny brown fibre. Delicious fried with bacon.

N.B. *All the items on page 240 are expensive except shrimps.*

Lower-priced small varieties are:

Cockles	Known in France as the poor man's oyster. Generally sold cooked in England. Eat with a sprinkle of vinegar or use in a fish stew, etc. Most mussel recipes apply. May be in brine: if so rinse.
Shrimps	Too often found only under a nasty pink synthetic mayonnaise. If they are good, serve them plain; if they aren't – don't buy them.
Whelks	Not very digestible. Boil, or buy cooked; serve with vinegar or vinaigrette, and a simple salad.
Winkles	As whelks.
Mussels	See notes above on cockles. Can be bought shelled, but since the water inside the shell is the important factor these are not completely successful, except as an ingredient.

small FRY

A quick look into the ocean
(FISHY DRAWINGS ARE TO SCALE)

GENERALLY SOLD COOKED. Can be eaten raw or cooked (as mussels).

COCKLES

MUSSELS Small, imported, sand-free ones are best. If they have to be opened before cooking (to get them clean) don't bother to buy them.

MARINIERE Put 2 qts. of cleaned (but not opened) mussels + ½ bot. dry white wine + handful chopped parsley + wineglass olive oil + crushed garlic + a little fresh pepper into a big pot. COVER. Bring to boil; lower heat. Soon all shells will open. Eat mussels; drink sauce.

WHITEBAIT
Variously described as young smelt, young herring or young sardine. Now available all year round (Although best in late spring)

Crisp WHITEBAIT
FLOUR sparsely. Shake excess flour away. Drop into deep boiling fat **SERVE** Crisp; ACCOMPANY with brown bread & butter + lemon.

PACIFIC PRAWN (grey brown)

LARGE, rather coarse in texture.

Pacific Salad
Put wedge of lemon + teaspoon fennel in a saucepan of simmering water. Add prawns for 3 mins. **COOL. SHELL.** SERVE with home-made mayonnaise. **GARNISH** with hard-boiled egg + anchovy

MEDITERRANEAN PRAWN (orange)
These are more expensive than Pacific.

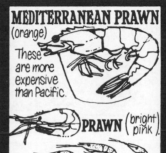

PRAWN (bright pink).

SHRIMP varying size (brown/pink).

Sour Cream Sauté
SAUTÉ ½ onion in generous butter till golden. Add 1 lb. cooked shrimp + ½ lb. sliced mushrooms. COOK 5 mins. Add plenty (up to ¾ pint) sour cream. Let it heat but **NOT Boil.** SEASON. Add wine – glassful of sherry. **SERVE.**

OYSTER (Portuguese).

OYSTER NATIVE
(Whitstable) Observe R-in-month rule.

Open them yourself. (Watch the fishmonger do it!) Eat with brown bread & butter. OTHERWISE lightly fry in butter or add to scrambled egg or even to a steak-and-kidney pudding!

Red Mullet

In French cooking the Gurnet and the Red Mullet are called **ROUGET.**

Sometimes called **BÉCASSE DE MER** (sea woodcock) because all the inside is eaten. Its liver is particularly liked *!*

ROUGET FLAMBÉ AU FENOUIL

You must have some fresh fennel on stalks (it is worth a little trouble). Lay fish on fennel, dot with butter – GRILL gently until it is cooked on both sides. Pour a glass of warm Armagnac over, then apply match.

Eat it when the fire is out !

COLD Poach gently in fish stock and white wine. *COOL.* Sprinkle with olive oil and lemon juice. *Serve very cold.*

ROUGET A LA NIÇOISE

1. **CHOP.** and simmer tomatoes. Add tarragon (fresh if possible).

Strain into a fire-proof dish.

2. Dust fish with flour and seasoning.

Brown quickly in oil

3. Lay fish upon tomato purée. Garnish with strips of anchovy (and chopped olive if you like). Sprinkle with breadcrumbs and drips of oil.

COOK 10 mins. Reg 5 (380°F). Serve with lemon slices.

The recipe using fennel twigs is a wonderfully flavoured dish, as well as being a spectacular party piece. You do not have to have red mullet, you can have its poor cousin, grey mullet, or bream, or bass, in fact any of these medium-sized fish. Put a few twigs of fennel inside the fish, and perhaps a few fennel seeds. The flavour of the fennel should be quite distinct, or it hovers too discreetly in the background, which may well be disliked by diners who think its presence inadvertent. This recipe is suitable for use on a barbecue range, for like meat-barbecue recipes, the smoky carbon-like flavour is a most important part of the finished result. Just before putting the red mullet under the grill in the recipe shown opposite, you can, if you wish, paint the fish with melted butter. You will find that the burning performance at the end of the cooking is quite spectacular. Stand back, for the dried fennel will be highly inflammable, and the smoke pungent. Have a plate ready to which to transfer the fish, or you will be serving it from a bed of charred ash.

The second recipe – **Rouget à la Niçoise** – has even wider application as far as varieties of fish are concerned. As well as the fish that resemble red mullet (grey mullet is a bargain in England), even the oilier fishes like mackerel can be used in this recipe.

TROUT

BUY ONE ½ LB. FISH PER PERSON.

A delicate fresh-water fish of the same group as salmon. Flavour and colour vary with water in which it lives. Dark pink flesh is called SALMON TROUT. River trout (seldom sold in shops) are better than tank bred ones. **FRESHNESS IS ALL-IMPORTANT.**

TRUITES A LA MEUNIÈRE

1 Dip into milk then into flour.

2 **COOK** for about 10 min. in 2-3 oz. of hot butter. **BEWARE STICKING**

3 **REMOVE FISH** — add 2 oz. more butter and juice of 1 lemon. (Some cooks use cream instead of this butter) STIR THIS AROUND PAN — pour over fish. If you use olive oil instead of butter this becomes **A LA VAUCLUSIENNE. N.B.** HOT PLATES!

TROUT
AU BLEU

CLEAN but don't scrape or wipe fish. Sprinkle a tablespoon of vinegar over it, then plunge into water + vinegar (one part vinegar to 7 water) **COOK 5-10 min.** according to size — **DRAIN SERVE** on hot plates with melted butter

ACCOMPANY with tiny potatoes (so make them tiny) rolled in melted butter then in finely chopped parsley.

Many trout-eaters prefer their fish served with

HORSERADISH SAUCE.

Peel and grate finely a root of horseradish. Put 4 tablespoons of it in a dish.

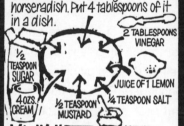

2 TABLESPOONS VINEGAR

½ TEASPOON SUGAR

JUICE OF 1 LEMON

4-OZS. CREAM

½ TEASPOON MUSTARD

¼ TEASPOON SALT

Mix Well

TASTE. Add more mustard if you prefer it hot. (Some have 5 times the above amount)

Either of these can be used in place of cream.

SOUR CREAM YOGHOURT

Trout au bleu is a recipe for poaching fish and can be applied to any fish. Vary it as you wish. For instance, make a **court-bouillon** by boiling up one carrot, one onion, some parsley, thyme, 6 peppercorns, knob of butter, salt, 2 bay leaves, ½ pint of good-quality white vinegar and 2 quarts of water. Poach the fish of your choice very gently in this court-bouillon. It will take about 10 minutes according to size. Remove carefully; serve.

A la Meunière, as shown opposite, can also be used with any type of fish; so can **Truite en Papillote.** Clean trout, then brush inside and out with melted butter and seasoning. Now get two pieces of paper (greased heavy paper) and do a thorough wrapping-up job, tucking in the envelope ends. 20–25 minutes at Regulo 6 (400° F.) should see it cooked. It can be served in the paper so that each diner has the task (or pleasure) of opening his own packet of trout.

You will find that almost any fish, from fillet of sole to a cod steak, will respond well to being cooked in a papillote. You can open the envelope and finish under the grill. Many cooks cheat by using tinfoil. I do sometimes.

SOLE BERCY

A recipe noteworthy for its unusual use of RED wine with fish.

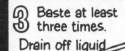

Dover soles weighing less than ½ lb. are called SLIP SOLES. They are more flavourful than larger ones. Allow one per person.

Your fishmonger will clean the fish. DON'T FILLET IT. Whiting may be cooked in the same way for MERLAN À LA BERCY. Other suitable substitutes. Lemon Sole, Dab. Witch Sole, Megrim.

1 Chop up some SHALLOTS (or ONION) and fry lightly in butter.

Sauté ¼ lb. of mushrooms in butter

2 Into a buttered fireproof dish put:

A surround of mushrooms.

A bed of onion

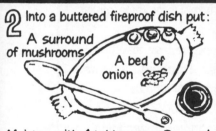

Moisten with 4 tablespoons Burgundy. Place fish on top. Season. Cook Regulo 4 (355°F) 25 min.

3 Baste at least three times.

Drain off liquid

and reduce it by ½ over fierce flame.

Add a knob of butter + a little lemon juice.

Coat fish with this sauce and glaze it for a minute or so under a hot grill.

In France the whiting is considered a first-rate culinary fish, while in England it is most often purchased for the cat. Certainly it has great unexplored possibilities, and while having a different flavour from the delicious sole, it is not inferior. Similarly lemon sole, dab, witch sole and megrim are quite excellent and can be used in any recipe that calls for sole. Fish, like meat, gains a great deal of its flavour from the bones during the cooking process; therefore should you decide to have any fish filleted, you would be well advised to take the head and bones away in order to cook them in a little water and reintroduce this lost flavour into the dish.

This seems a good place to mention the two other classic English fish. **Halibut,** which can be anything from 1½ to 200 lb., is said by some to rival the salmon. It is a valuable source of vitamin, and halibut liver oil is obtained from it. Once again I recommend that it should not be filleted, but a steak cut on the bone should be poached in the simplest possible way.

Turbot is the third great English fish. Small ones, less than 4 lb., are known as chicken turbot, although fully grown fish can be anything up to 30 lb. This should be cooked with skin and fins still attached, as, like the bones, they are a valuable flavour ingredient. The traditional English method of serving these two fish is with parsley sauce, in which case the latter must contain a very large quantity of parsley and real cream.

CUTTLEFISH SERVED IN ITS INK

This will feed 4 people.

Big town fishmongers often have cuttlefish if you order them.

This recipe by Joao Barreto, of Albufeira, PORTUGAL, is one of the world's great dishes.

1 BUY 1 doz. cuttlefish (SIZE AS BELOW). Ask the fishmonger to remove the stomach, or do it yourself.

STOMACH is a small (pea size) transparent piece. Remove it by making cut exactly as marked.

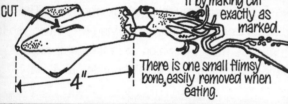

CUT

4"

There is one small flimsy bone, easily removed when eating.

2. Rinse to remove sand or grit.
Some cuttlefish may have no sand in — RINSE THESE VERY LITTLE AS TOO MUCH WASHING CAN REDUCE THE FLAVOUR.

3. HOLD UNDER TAP

Water flowing in here

comes out through the cut you made.

4 BOIL cuttlefish in pan with
1 piece of tiny pimento
10 whole peppercorns
5 cloves garlic
½ bay leaf.

COOK for 1¼ hours (uncovered for final ½ hour) final sauce should be thick black and oily.

8 OZ OLIVE OIL

MEDIUM FLAME

Dessert spoon salt.

Wine-glass water.

5. REMOVE cuttlefish.
Remove peppers etc. with a strainer before serving with plain boiled rice.
DRINK a Red Wine with it.

This is a very popular dish from the Mediterranean coast of Italy to the Atlantic coast of France. It has been going since the Roman Empire. Cuttlefish come in all sizes, from the tiny ones, about one and a half inches long, that are eaten whole as an aperitif, to the sort of thing that threw a scare into Captain Nemo. The flesh of the cuttlefish is quite rubbery, no matter how long you cook it it won't get very tender. This makes it very suitable for stuffing with all manner of mixtures, then sealing with a toothpick and cooking in a thin sauce.

Another method of preparation is to slice the cuttlefish so that the body becomes a series of rings. These are then deep-fried in batter to become crisp.

The recipe opposite depends upon having good-quality fresh cuttlefish, but these are becoming more common in the fancy fishmongers' shops. The resulting dish is thick, black and oily and should be served in small portions. You'll need a very plain vegetable with it – rice is unbeatable, but plain boiled potato will do – and only the simplest dessert to follow. What about fresh fruit?

A red Folinari to drink with it.

EEL ACROSS EUROPE

From Berlin (Aal grün) to Brussels (Anguilles au Vert) one finds variations on this theme.

Eels and elvers (young eels) are sold by weight. Small, tender eels caught in fast-moving water taste best. **THEY _MUST_ BE FRESH**

This recipe from Vught Castle "PALING IN GROEN SAUS" is a Dutch version.

1. Wash and cut up fresh eel. About ⅓ lb. per person.

FILLET it if you ~~wish~~ can.

2"

---

2. 2 CLOVES GARLIC — 4 OZ. DRY WHITE WINE

BAY LEAF

SOME COOKS ADD A LITTLE SAGE AND/OR CHERVIL

PEPPER & SALT

Add water — just cover. Poach gently until tender — (about 15 min.) Save ¼ pint of liquid. Drain and skin the eel pieces.

A VARIATION: After poaching, eels can be drained, skinned, and served with vinaigrette dressing (1 part vinegar to 3 parts olive oil + pepper & salt.) Otherwise continue to 3.

---

3. Make a roux — i.e.

1 oz. butter

+ 1 oz. flour

COOK GENTLY OVER **LOW HEAT** FOR 3 MIN.

---

4. Add about ¼ pint of liquid from eels to roux, stirring until a thick, creamy sauce is free of lumps

Add 4 oz. of thin cream DON'T LET IT BOIL OR IT WILL RUIN.

Add a cupful (or more) of very finely chopped parsley. STIR IT. Pour over eel pieces. **SERVE** hot or cold with brown bread & butter & boiled potatoes. Oh yes! and the rest of the wine.

It is asking for trouble to write a section on eels and not mention *jellied eels*. Few things could be easier to make, since fish of all kinds is more gelatinous than meat. Clean the eel, cut it into one-inch lengths, and poach it gently in water to which has been added a bay leaf, juice of a lemon and a pinch of salt. Let it simmer for 45 minutes, then leave it to set. Could anything be easier? In the south of England jellied-eel fanciers like their jellied eels really jellied, and will often put a veal knuckle to simmer for an hour or two, then use the stock in which it has cooked to poach the eel. Another variation is to make a court-bouillon and cook the eel in this.

French cookery books really go to town with eel. One item in their preparation is well worth trying. They grill the eel sections – the skin crisps and blisters and is easily removed. This process also decreases the fat-content and makes the eel more digestible. Another French recipe has the eel sections filleted and flattened with the side of a heavy knife. Marinade the eel pieces in olive oil and lemon juice for four hours. Then wipe them dry, dip into egg and breadcrumbs and fry gently. This is a very rich dish and should be served in small portions.

	Latin name	French Menu says	Remarks
LOBSTER	Homarus	Homard	Common or garden lobster, more flavourful than Langouste.
CRAYFISH	Astacus	Écrevisse	This is a fresh-water crustacean. It is very small (2–3 oz.).
NORWAY LOBSTER	Nephrops norvegicus	Langoustine	Dublin Bay prawn. Found in North Sea. Slender claws. Often called scampi.* Only tails are eaten.
SPINY LOBSTER ROCK LOBSTER SEA CRAYFISH	Palinurus	Langouste	No great claws. 'Lobster tails' are generally from this.
PRAWNS	Leander	Crevette rose	Called shrimp in U.S.A. Goes pink when cooked.
SHRIMP	Crangon	Crevette grise	Unknown in U.S.A. Pinkish-grey when cooked.

* Strictly speaking only those from the Mediterranean should be called 'scampi'.

Lobster NEWBURG

WASH, SPLIT (or have split) a Lobster. Reserve coral (if any) Leave meat in shell (most decorative) or remove it (most convenient)

EQUALLY CORRECT

COOK IN FISH STOCK
(2 LB. NEEDS 10 MIN)
BEFORE SPLITTING

N.B. A 2 LB. LOBSTER YIELDS 3/4 LB. MEAT

Remove SAC etc.

Season

Brown pieces in GENEROUS BUTTER about 5 min. Remove them.

Add liqueur glass of Cognac + 1/4 pint MADEIRA (or Sherry.)

REDUCE Fiercely BY HALF

Replace Lobster pieces adding mushrooms and truffles.— Simmer 25 min. while preparing CORAL BUTTER.

Mix Lobster Coral with equal amount of butter and 2 yolks. WHISK into the sauce piecemeal. (The yolks will thicken it)

Do NOT LET iT BoiL!

Add 1/2 pint cream.

Serve with **Rice**

241

COQUILLES ST. JACQUES

[MY WAY] Allow at least 2 scallops per person.

1. Wash 12 scallops under the tap.

Remove yellow part — save it. Divide white part into 3 pieces. →
6 SHALLOTS chopped finely. (onion will do)

COOK GENTLY FOR 10 MINS.

¼ lb. sliced mushroom.

2 tablespoons of pork fat. (Make it by frying a piece of pork belly.)

A sprinkle of salt + pepper.

2. REDUCE BY HALF

(by rapid boiling) ¼ bot. dry white wine.

3. ASSEMBLE,

including yellow parts. Also add 2 beaten yolks and 4 oz. cream.
COOK — for 20 mins. over a tiny flame. — SERVE when thick.

A Posh Way To Serve...

Put a generous heap of final mixture on a scallop shell.

COVER with breadcrumbs + grated cheese.
DOT with butter.

Put under the grill until it is nicely brown. SERVE ON SHELL.

OYSTER STEW

Open oysters by levering the hinge.

A beer-can opener can be used.

12 oysters + juice.

½ teaspoon celery seed (or finely chopped leaves).

BRING ALMOST TO THE Boil

DASH OF WORCESTER SAUCE

1 cup milk or ½ milk + ½ cream.

SERVE in warmed bowls, using a pat of butter + a pinch of paprika as decoration.

Coquilles St Jacques, or scallops, are in season from October to March, but at no time of the year is this an inexpensive dish to prepare, which is why some restaurants fake the contents of their shells with cod in white sauce. It is quite all right to have the fishmonger open the shells for you for, unlike oysters, there is no precious liquid inside to spill or waste. However, if you wish to open them yourself they will open easily if put in a warm place, e.g. the plate rack. Be sure the rounded part is downward. The sticky part is not eaten, which will leave you with a large white piece and a soft tongue of coral, which is bright orange. The American types do not have this coral content, which is bad luck because this is the most delicate and delicious part. Whenever possible the coral should be less cooked than the harder white part, whether you grill or poach or fry. Scallops can be prepared in any of those ways, and a traditional English way to serve them is fried with bacon. Incidentally, it's the way my fishmonger eats them for Sunday breakfast.

You should allow at least two per person, and if it's a main course, more. To make them go a long way chop them finely and use as a filling for pastry turnovers, pancakes or vol-au-vents.

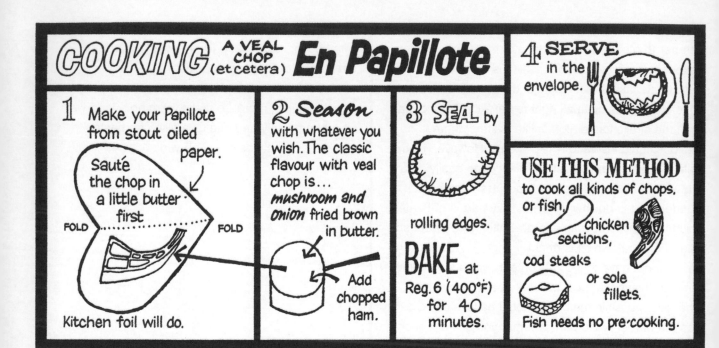

COOKING *A VEAL CHOP (et cetera)* En Papillote

1 Make your Papillote from stout oiled paper.

Sauté the chop in a little butter first

FOLD .... FOLD

Kitchen foil will do.

2 *Season* with whatever you wish. The classic flavour with veal chop is... *mushroom and onion* fried brown in butter.

Add chopped ham.

3 SEAL by

rolling edges.

BAKE at Reg. 6 (400°F) for 40 minutes.

4 SERVE in the envelope.

USE THIS METHOD to cook all kinds of chops, or fish, chicken sections, cod steaks or sole fillets. Fish needs no pre-cooking.

'En papillote' is the French for 'in a cocoon'. This method of cooking is mentioned elsewhere in this book in connection with trout, but it can be applied to a thousand different dishes. Any sort of fish will cook well: turbot, halibut, salmon slices, rolled-up fillets of sole or plaice, or even pieces of haddock or kipper. Because the food is tightly sealed during the cooking period the steam and flavour is all kept in the flesh, and if you use the stout oiled paper it is usual to let each guest cut his own papillote open. If you use tinfoil it is better to remove the foil before serving, but this can be done at the table to let everyone enjoy the smell as each one is cut open.

Fish is a popular 'en papillote' dish because the raw slice can be flavoured and put into its packet, but if you cook meat or chicken this way it is normally cooked for a little while beforehand. There is a certain amount of judgment involved because I can't possibly guess at what rate you will pre-cook it. For the first few times you will find it best to use tinfoil because this can be unwrapped – carefully – then wrapped up again if the contents are not fully cooked. Ideally, however, oiled paper, not unwrapped till it gets to the table, is the only really correct method.

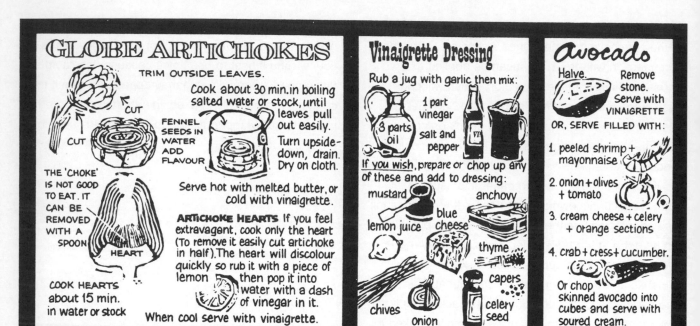

GLOBE ARTICHOKES

TRIM OUTSIDE LEAVES.

CUT

CUT

FENNEL SEEDS IN WATER ADD FLAVOUR

Cook about 30 min. in boiling salted water or stock, until leaves pull out easily.

Turn upside-down, drain. Dry on cloth.

THE 'CHOKE' IS NOT GOOD TO EAT. IT CAN BE REMOVED WITH A SPOON

HEART

Serve hot with melted butter, or cold with vinaigrette.

ARTICHOKE HEARTS If you feel extravagant, cook only the heart (To remove it easily cut artichoke in half). The heart will discolour quickly so rub it with a piece of lemon then pop it into water with a dash of vinegar in it. When cool serve with vinaigrette.

COOK HEARTS about 15 min. in water or stock

Vinaigrette Dressing

Rub a jug with garlic then mix:

1 part vinegar

3 parts oil

salt and pepper

If you wish, prepare or chop up any of these and add to dressing:

mustard

anchovy

lemon juice

blue cheese

thyme

chives

onion

capers

celery seed

avocado

Halve.   Remove stone. Serve with VINAIGRETTE

OR, SERVE FILLED WITH:

1. peeled shrimp + mayonnaise

2. onion + olives + tomato

3. cream cheese + celery + orange sections

4. crab + cress + cucumber.

Or chop skinned avocado into cubes and serve with soured cream.

Those on a diet should be warned that avocadoes are 20 per cent oil and only 2 per cent protein. There are many recipes using the meat of the avocado, which mashes very easily, though I have never found one which compares with a pear served with the simplest possible vinaigrette dressing.

The artichoke can be served in any number of different ways, and since the French cook is very keen on recipes that employ small quantities of meat, the centre of the artichoke is often replaced by various meat mixtures, after which they are braised. Many cooks will feel, as I do, that there is far too much work involved in eating a globe artichoke leaf by leaf, and will therefore serve the heart only in one form or another.

Vinaigrette Dressing. Many cold cooked vegetables which are fried the following day would be far more appetizing served with a small jug of vinaigrette dressing. This same vinaigrette dressing can be used to make a raw tomato salad, about which there are as many theories as there are varieties of tomato. Some cooks will prefer to dip the tomatoes in boiling water in order first to remove the skins; others will insist that the skins are the best part. A lot, I feel, depends upon the type of tomato and its place of growth. My own particular heresy is the addition of generous amounts of finely chopped raw Spanish onion.

3 or 4 WAYS WITH SPUDS

For flavour and nutrition they should whenever poss. be peeled **AFTER** cooking.

1. Mealy floury varieties. Good for baking, mashing and some good for chips.

2. Firm yellow waxy ones. Best for potato salad and for covered baking (Anna or Dauphinoise). For soufflé potatoes this type is essential.

POMMES DE TERRE DAUPHINOISE

Butter a straight-sided dish or pan, with a good lid.

Peel, slice, rinse, dry 1 lb. potatoes ← 1/8"

Grate 3 oz. Gruyère

SMALL PIECES BUTTER
GRATED GRUYÈRE
POTATO SLICES
SMALL PIECES BUTTER
GRATED GRUYÈRE
POTATO SLICES

season each layer.

POUR INTO DISH 4 oz. cream (milk + butter or 4 oz. oil will do) COVER. Cook 65 min. Reg 6 (375°F) Longer won't spoil it.

If you omit the cheese and halfway through cooking turn the potato cake upside down, replace lid and finish cooking, you'll have, **POMMES DE TERRE ANNA.**

Hot Pot Salad

Sliced hot cooked potato + 1 small finely-chopped onion.

2 TABLESPOONS SUGAR. GENEROUS SALT & PEPPER

½ CUP VINEGAR

SOME VERY CRISP STREAKY BACON

SERVE while still warm.

POTATO PANCAKES

Peel 3 medium-size potatoes. Grate them carefully [OR USE A BLENDER IF YOU HAVE ONE]

SQUEEZE DRY IN CLOTH AND EMPTY INTO BOWL

½ cup FLOUR

2 EGGS

1 TEASPOON SALT

2 CUPS MILK OR ENOUGH TO MAKE A THICK BATTER.

DROP a spoonful into a hot greased (not buttered) pan. When cooked brown on one side, turn over. They will take 5-10 min. according to thickness.

The cook should be concerned with two basic types of potato. There is the waxy yellow kind – Record, Bintje and Conference – which holds together, responds beautifully to certain frying and without which 'Pommes de terre soufflées' is doomed to failure. The other, very white, soft, floury – King Edward, Majestic and Redskin – mashes excellently but breaks up easily. The yellow ones go to the factories which make potato crisps. We are told that the housewife only wants very white floury 'gravy soakers'.

The nearest thing to a yellow waxy potato available in Great Britain is the Dr McIntosh. The best to use for chips, etc., at present is Majestic.

For those less fortunate, here is the classic mashed-potato recipe. **Pommes de Terre Duchesse.** Boil 1 lb. of potatoes until they are tender, then drain them. Add 2 oz. of melted butter, a dust of nutmeg and 3 beaten egg yolks. You will need to add a little salt and pepper too. Serve as it is, or roll in egg and breadcrumbs, and fry. You will have **Potato Croquettes.** The Duchesse recipe is used when piping potato to decorate, and as a top for meat dishes (Shepherd's Pie), or it can be mixed with pounded fish and Béchamel sauce (or a thousand other things) to make croquettes.

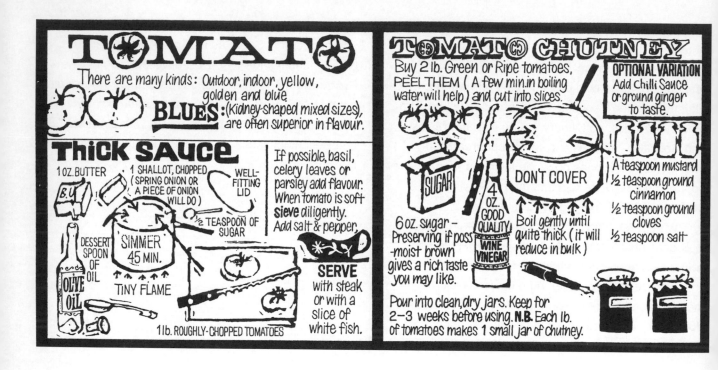

TOMATO

There are many kinds: Outdoor, indoor, yellow, golden and blue.

BLUES : (Kidney-shaped mixed sizes), are often superior in flavour.

Thick Sauce

1 OZ. BUTTER

1 SHALLOT, CHOPPED (SPRING ONION OR A PIECE OF ONION WILL DO)

WELL-FITTING LID

½ TEASPOON OF SUGAR

DESSERT SPOON OF OIL

OLIVE OIL

SIMMER 45 MIN.

TINY FLAME

1 lb. ROUGHLY-CHOPPED TOMATOES

If possible, basil, celery leaves or parsley add flavour. When tomato is soft **sieve** diligently. Add salt & pepper.

SERVE with steak or with a slice of white fish.

TOMATO CHUTNEY

Buy 2 lb. Green or Ripe tomatoes, PEEL THEM (A few min. in boiling water will help) and cut into slices.

SUGAR

4 OZ. GOOD QUALITY WINE VINEGAR

DON'T COVER

6 oz. sugar – Preserving if poss -moist brown gives a rich taste you may like.

Boil gently until quite thick (it will reduce in bulk)

Pour into clean, dry jars. Keep for 2–3 weeks before using. **N.B.** Each lb. of tomatoes makes 1 small jar of chutney.

OPTIONAL VARIATION Add Chilli Sauce or ground ginger to taste.

A teaspoon mustard
½ teaspoon ground cinnamon
½ teaspoon ground cloves
½ teaspoon salt

In Britain the growers of tomatoes have concentrated upon producing a bright-coloured, well-complexioned fruit of even size and weight, and no flavour whatsoever. In Italy and France the tomatoes are hideously uneven in shape and often marred with scars and blemishes. On the other hand, they have a wonderful flavour.

The tomato is about the most versatile item in the vegetable rack and never gives the cook trouble. But it is as well to remember that when you are adding tomatoes to a dish which will be spoilt by excess moisture, you must go to the extra trouble of removing the moist interior and using only the outside flesh.

The French cook uses the tomato as a container for stuffings. Stuff them with mushrooms, meat, ham, fish, shrimp, using a little cooked rice or soft breadcrumbs to give body. These *tomates farcies* can be served hot (as an entrée for a dinner party, or as a supper dish) or cold (you can glaze them with a little aspic jelly if you want to). With certain fillings (tuna fish and sliced olives) they can even be served raw. The tomato can either be left whole or scooped out.

Tomatoes can be sliced and lightly fried in butter (careful now, or they will fall to pieces) and served with the merest pinch of sugar over them, or halved and baked in a low oven.

Here are two very starchy items, liked perhaps because they transgress so many diets. Most American recipes would have the beans much sweeter than this recipe – at least twice as much sweetening. There are many types of beans, and recipes usually take the one that grows close to where the recipe originated; of course, they are interchangeable. Cook any sort of beans in any bean recipe. You can cook them (simmering) in plenty of water, then drain and use as follows:

Beans with Cheese. Mix cooked beans with crispy fried, streaky bacon pieces, fried onion, skinned tomatoes, then add grated cheese just before serving. (This recipe can have a shot of tabasco in if you like it.)

Beans and Sour Cream. Fried onion and fried mushrooms are cooked in plenty of butter. Add a sprinkle of flour and stir over a low heat while the flour cooks (three minutes). Stir this into cooked beans, then add plenty of sour cream. Keep it over low heat until the cooked flour thickens it all up. Serve.

Tinned baked beans are sometimes used to make 'real' baked beans, but still they aren't the same. Phoney world, isn't it? Add tinned baked beans to a little molasses (for this recipe golden syrup will do), some Worcestershire sauce and a little mustard.

Although fine potatoes will be even better baked, you can bake pretty terrible ones with good results. Eyes are the things to watch out for. No guest will like seeing the inside of a poor spud. That's why it's a good idea to scoop them out yourself and refill before serving. If you scatter mixed fine breadcrumbs and grated cheese over the final result, you can grill them to give a brown crisp top. Another serving idea is to sprinkle crushed crispy (streaky) bacon on top of each.

BOSTON BAKED BEANS

1. WASH ANY BEANS (Red kidney beans are good). Soak overnight.

2. Add tiny piece **PORK FAT**

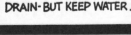

SIMMER ½ hour

DRAIN - BUT KEEP WATER.

3. BURY PORK IN BEANS.

Stir into a little of the cooking water
{ ½ teaspoon mustard
½ teaspoon salt
½ cup treacle }

...THEN POUR

A big pot that will fit into your oven ← beans
½ lb. salt pork belly.

ADD rest of cook water until beans are covered. Fit lid. Cook 300°F (Reg 1½) for 6-8 hours. **SERVE.**

NOTE. When cooking beans see that they don't dry up and burn.

For final hour remove lid and haul pork to surface. Rind (if any) should be crackling when beans are served.

Some cooks add more strips of pork over top.

Baked Potatoes

1. Scrub medium-size potatoes clean— Dry— Cut a cross in top.

Put them on a tray in oven (easier to remove).

Prod side for tenderness.

Brush with butter to make them shiny!

Metal skewer or nail conducts heat to centre.

About an hour at 350° (Reg 4) should be O.K., but any heat is O.K.

2. **WHEN** cooked, scoop out centre and mix it with:-
{ pepper and salt,
melted butter,
sour cream (or cream cheese if you prefer it). }

Replace in skins — **SERVE.**

KNOW YOUR ONIONS

Try the onion stuffed with garlic – CIPOLLE CON AGLIO – for a breath of Italy

GOLDEN ONIONS
GLASIERTE ZWIEBELN

Skin, then boil, small onions...

20 - 30 mins. in boiling water.

DRAIN, then *

finish them in frying pan with...

15 MINUTES

...1 tablespoon honey,
1 tablespoon brown sugar
1 tablespoon butter } melted together.
SERVE.

*OR after this douse them in SOUR CREAM plus salt and pepper.
SERVE.

GRILLED

Butter

¼

Sprinkle with salt and pepper.

GRILL about 7 mins. per side.
SERVE.

DEEP FRIED

¼"

SEPARATE RINGS, dip into milk, DRAIN – dip into flour.

FLOUR

FRY in deep fat about 5 mins.

Use as a garnish or eat them as they are.

FARCIS

Skin and boil for 20-30 mins.
DRAIN. COOL.
Hollow out.
(Use apple corer or sharp knife)

Fill with any of these.
Top with crumbs.

❶ butter + chopped garlic
❷ cheese, crumbs + mushroom
❸ ham, crumbs + seasoning
❹ cooked chicken + egg

PAINT outside with butter.

BAKE 350° (Reg 4) ½ hr.
Serve

Baste often.

Stock and butter in bottom of tray.

Onions belong to the lily family and they grow almost everywhere. In England you can buy onions from Holland, France, Spain, Portugal, Italy and Egypt as well as home-grown ones. As a general rule onions from northern Europe are more pungent and juicy than those from the south. The Spanish onion – although not always from Spain – is a clean mild onion, very suitable for eating raw. The ones that men on bicycles bring are Breton onions. Polish onions are good for keeping, if that is important to you, although none keep very well. They should be stored in a cool place with room between for air to circulate. Bedfordshire onions are best for pickling (Silverskins). English onions are always strong. Spring onions are the thinning of the crop and are especially good for salads. It's possible to have white, yellow, rose, orange and red onions – anyone for a bouquet of onions?

If you want tiny onions you can simply remove the outer layers from large ones. Use the outer layers in cooking. When onions are cooked a chemical change takes place: they no longer make the eyes water, and they taste quite different. Frying onions caramelizes the sugar, and if fried long enough they will go brown. To speed this you can add a trace of sugar. When a recipe says fried onions it does not necessarily mean brown ones; e.g. no curry recipe should have the onions fried brown. Raw onion is underrated in Europe. No hamburger is complete without a slice of raw onion on the top. Use raw onion also in tomato salad, beetroot salad, celery salad. Gardeners might like to try 'Bedfordshire Champion'.

BÉARNAISE

ONE OF THE GREAT (IF NOT *THE* GREATEST) SAUCES OF FRENCH COOKING...

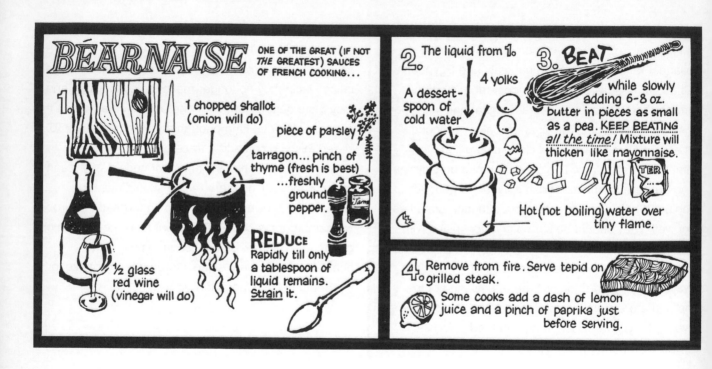

1. 1 chopped shallot (onion will do)

piece of parsley

tarragon... pinch of thyme (fresh is best) ...freshly ground pepper.

½ glass red wine (vinegar will do)

REDUCE Rapidly till only a tablespoon of liquid remains. <u>Strain</u> it.

2. The liquid from **1.**

A dessert-spoon of cold water

4 yolks

3. BEAT while slowly adding 6-8 oz. butter in pieces as small as a pea. <u>KEEP BEATING all the time!</u> Mixture will thicken like mayonnaise.

Hot (not boiling) water over tiny flame.

4. Remove from fire. Serve tepid on grilled steak.

Some cooks add a dash of lemon juice and a pinch of paprika just before serving.

Many cooks have a 'thing' against making French sauces. It is true that there are one or two difficult ones, but they are not the ones that have acquired a terrible reputation. Béarnaise, for example, is widely regarded as one of the most difficult sauces, while really it is merely one of the greatest.

The reduction of the wine, in section one, is sometimes regarded as unnecessary because in section two a dessertspoon of water is being added again. But the rapid reduction is not done in order to decrease the bulk, but because changes take place chemically when wine is subjected to this sort of heat. Vinegar will do as well as wine, but it must not be that synthetic stuff, it must be the real thing based upon wine (although cider vinegar will do). It will be impossible to distinguish whether wine or wine vinegar has been used when tasting the finished product.

This recipe can only go wrong if you get too enthusiastic adding the butter. Slowly does it. An expert can get more butter into the mixture than a beginner; remember it's not getting easier as it goes along, so don't speed up as you would making mayonnaise.

If you ignore section 1, and just follow section 2 (using one tablespoonful lemon juice where it says 'liquid from 1'), you will have a Sauce Hollandaise.

Use Sauce Béarnaise on steak, poached fish or grilled chicken. Use Hollandaise on fish, eggs, or delicate vegetables.

Steak with or without Béarnaise sauce is great with a Nuits St Georges wine.

MAYONNAISE

1. Utensils and ingredients must be **WARM**. Into a basin put:

½ teaspoon mustard
½ teaspoon salt
½ teaspoon sugar (optional)

1 tablespoon vinegar or lemon juice.

2 egg yolks

pinch of white pepper

SUGAR

SALT

2. Use A or B or C

OLIVE OIL

to beat mixture while **SLOWLY** adding one pint of oil. A & B. Add the oil drip by drip. C. Add it in a trickle. **OLIVE OIL** GIVES BEST FLAVOUR. OTHER OILS ARE BLANDER. End with 2 tablespoons of hot water while still beating.

3. **Serve** on cold salmon or white fish, on cold vegetable or hard-boiled eggs. USE it to make **RUSSIAN SALAD** or POTATO SALAD (don't forget the raw onions).

AioLi

A famous (or infamous) SOUTHERN FRENCH dressing for hot or cold fish. Put 8 crushed GARLIC cloves into the first mixture then it's a repeat operation.

Some people prefer it to be very thick (indeed almost like butter), others prefer it to be more of a sauce. It can be made thicker by increasing the quantity of egg yolks that starts the process, but you may find that this gives a too eggy taste to the finished mayonnaise. One of the great dangers in the preparation is that the mayonnaise will separate. The usual cure for this is to begin the whole business over again, dripping the separated mayonnaise on to the egg yolk as you had dripped the olive oil. In many cases, however, you will find that a dessertspoonful of very hot water dropped into the separated mayonnaise and a furious beating will restore the separated mixture to an emulsion.

The crux of any mayonnaise must be the quality of the oil used. The finest, first-pressing oils are very often obtainable from wine merchants. If you buy in bulk, the cost of these very high-quality oils will be no more than that of the less good ones bought in small bottles. However, many cooks prefer their mayonnaise to be without the characteristic olive taste. In this case, a good-quality peanut oil can be used, or you can use parts of olive oil and peanut oil, until the mixture is to your taste. There are a great number of variations on mayonnaise. (*See* Remoulade and Tartare in Cooking Terms section.)

It is unwise to put mayonnaise into a refrigerator, for extreme cold will cause it to separate. It is best kept in a cool place.

Coffee Soufflé

New laid Eggs make the best ones!

1. Cook together over a low heat, 1½ oz flour + 1½ oz butter for 3 min.

2. Add ¼ pint sweet creamy coffee stirring as you do it. Remove from heat.

3. Add 4 beaten yolks.

The Tricky Bit:

4. Fold this mixture into 5 stiffly beaten whites.
— Gently Now!

5. Tip into a buttered soufflé dish. Sprinkle chopped hazelnuts and sugar on top. COOK Reg 6. (400°F) 30 min.

Variations

HAZELNUT: Steep chopped roasted hazelnuts + a vanilla pod in ¼ pint scalded milk. Remove pod before use.

CECILIA: As Hazelnut but put sponge biscuits soaked in Chartreuse in bottom of dish.

Chocolate: Melt PLAIN chocolate in the ¼ pint of milk.

Soufflé au Thé: Infuse tea in the milk

Soufflé Rothschild: Steep vanilla pod in milk. Put chopped candied fruit (soaked in Brandy) in mix. Add candied cherries to top before serving.

MY Special Soufflé

Make three separate soufflés — cook them together.

1. HAZELNUT
2. Chocolate
3. Coffee

A FINAL WORD

Eggs at room temperature. Egg beater spotlessly clean.

some like a soufflé underdone (runny) — if it is well done serve cream to make it moist.

Be an Optimist—FIX A HIGH PAPER COLLAR

If you find the inside is too moist for your taste (I like them like this, as the middle provides its own sauce – if you like it dry, serve cream with it) your soufflé needs a longer cooking time. If the soufflé starts to sink too soon (i.e. almost as you bring it out of the oven) it has probably been in too hot an oven.

You need a proper soufflé dish, or at least a dish with straight sides so that the mix can rise straight up.

The soufflés I have shown opposite are sweet, but there is a vast range of savoury recipes. Ham is great: pound it and mix with a good Béchamel sauce. Cheese can be substituted for the ham, or can be mixed with the ham. The flavours of ham and cheese enhance each other in almost any dish.

Cooked fresh salmon can be mixed with the Béchamel to make a salmon soufflé. Tinned salmon is far too watery; if carefully drained, it will be O.K., but it is tricky.

Duck, turkey or chicken soufflé is one of the best ways to use up cooked poultry. Remove skin, pound carefully, adding sauce a spoonful at a time. Some cooks also pound the liver of the duck with a trace of orange juice and mix this with the flesh meat.

THE PROFITEROLE MOTIVE

PROFITEROLES AU CHOCOLAT

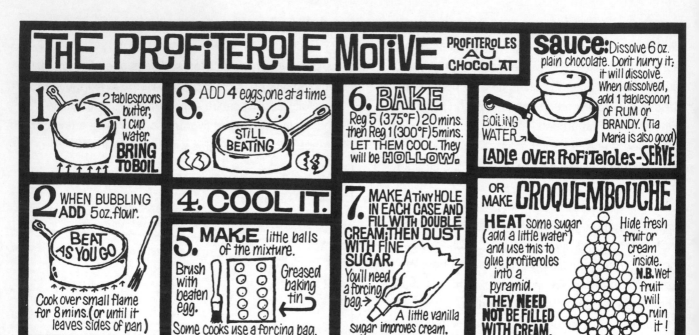

sauce: Dissolve 6 oz. plain chocolate. Don't hurry it: it will dissolve. When dissolved, add 1 tablespoon of RUM or BRANDY. (Tia Maria is also good)

BOILING WATER→

LADLE OVER PROFITEROLES - SERVE

1. 2 tablespoons butter, 1 cup water. **BRING TO BOIL**

3. ADD 4 eggs, one at a time. STILL BEATING

6. BAKE Reg 5 (375°F) 20 mins. then Reg 1 (300°F) 5 mins. LET THEM COOL. They will be HOLLOW.

2 WHEN BUBBLING **ADD** 5 oz. flour. BEAT AS YOU GO. Cook over small flame for 8 mins. (or until it leaves sides of pan)

4. COOL IT.

5. MAKE little balls of the mixture. Brush with beaten egg. Greased baking tin. Some cooks use a forcing bag.

7. MAKE A TINY HOLE IN EACH CASE AND FILL WITH DOUBLE CREAM; THEN DUST WITH FINE SUGAR. You'll need a forcing bag.→ A little vanilla sugar improves cream.

OR MAKE **CROQUEMBOUCHE** **HEAT** some sugar (add a little water) and use this to glue profiteroles into a pyramid. **THEY NEED NOT BE FILLED WITH CREAM.** Hide fresh fruit or cream inside. **N.B.** Wet fruit will ruin it!

Ramequins: Make and bake balls as shown opposite (say about the size of an apricot). Brush with egg and roll in finely chopped cheese (Gruyère or similar). Bake ten minutes in a hot oven. Make a hole and fill with a creamy cheese sauce, put them in a warm place so that they can be eaten while still warm. These are served as hot hors d'œuvres.

For Petits Fours try **Carolines.** These are just tiny éclairs (about the size of your little finger) filled with thick cream.

Or try **Salambos.** Make small choux pastry balls. Fill the inside with thick cream. Paint the top with melted sugar (heat it with a little water) so that you can stick lots of chopped pistachio nuts on top.

Tyrolians are covered with chopped almonds in the same way, then put back in the oven so that the almonds scorch a little bit. Then you fill them with almond cream.

Almond cream is very easy to make in a blender. If you don't have one, you must pound the ingredients by hand (using e.g. pestle and mortar).

Put three ounces almonds and three ounces sugar together and crush them with care. Add two yolks still beating, then a shot of rum, still pounding away. When it is a thick cream, use it, if it hasn't all disappeared in the tasting.

Since the ROMANS mixed egg & honey (ova mellita)

OMELETTES

have been the pancake's rich relations

Have a good thick pan, or scrambled eggs (and emotions) will result.

1. HEAT the dry pan over a low flame for 2 mins. Turn flame high. Now with speed and skill moisten pan with butter – before it burns add:

The Mix (for a one-man omelette) 2 eggs + ½ shellful of water

salt and pepper

Mix until yolks and white combine but don't beat it.

After use wipe pan with paper – don't wash.

2. Use a wooden spoon to drag cooked egg to centre so that

uncooked mix runs to edge.

TIP PAN AS YOU DO IT

3. Before omelette is dry fill, fold and tip.

Shine top with melted butter

FLAVOURINGS CAN BE IN THE MIX OR USED AS FILLING.

More than 2 big spoons of filling will burst it !

USE THE REST AS A GARNISH ALONGSIDE LIKE THIS

Au Bacon (or Jambon) Add diced cooked bacon or ham

Chasseur Sautéed chicken liver and mushroom

Au Crevettes Peeled shrimp

A Mais Cooked sweetcorn + cream

Aux Tomates Peel, seed and dice tomato

A la Suisse grated Emmenthal + cream

AUX ROGNONS Diced calf or lamb kidney sautéed in

Aux Fine Herbes lots of parsley chervil butter, tarragon, chives, or as many of them as you can find

and sweet (Add 1 teaspoon sugar to the mix)

Aux Confitures A little home-made jam

Aux Liqueurs Flambée Pour a glass of warm liqueur (cognac whisky etc) over and set it alight
... OR JUST EAT IT AS IT IS !

Omelette-making isn't an art or a craft – it is a knack. If you have never made an omelette before, don't be disappointed if the first time is a little unsuccessful, for, like sex and smoking, it is worth persevering with. Try again.

These are the basic rules of omelette-making:

1 Heat a good-quality (i.e. thick) omelette pan.
2 Have eggs mixed and ready. Have filling warm.
3 Work quickly.
4 Fold and serve while the centre is still moist.

A Spanish omelette is served flat with filling spread upon it, and is (unlike any other sort) crispy underneath if correctly served. In the U.S.A. this is known as a Western omelette and generally has a ham topping (you can heap a lot on because you don't have the problem of folding it).

Omelettes d'entremets (sweet omelettes, sometimes called Polish or German omelettes) should have a good spoonful of thick cream and of sugar added to the egg mixture. They should have a filling of best-quality jam (there are many variations, of course) and after folding the omelette should be sprinkled with sugar. At this stage, for a really impressive result, hold a red-hot poker (or piece of wire) against the top of the omelette to brand it with a criss-cross pattern. Drench it with warm brandy, set it alight.

CROISSANTS

They are a lot of bother and they are very fattening and they are quite expensive to make and they take a long time to prepare.......... THEY TASTE GREAT !!!

1. DISSOLVE a knob (as big as a walnut) of fresh yeast. (YOU BUY IT AT A REAL BAKERS) in a tablespoon of warm water.

YEAST.

1 PINT HOT (NOT BOILED) MILK.

1 TABLESPOON LARD.

1 TABLESPOON SUGAR.

½ TABLESPOON SALT.

2. ADD flour to the milk until it is 'KNEADABLE'

Flour

3. KNEAD FOLD PUNCH FOLD for **4** minutes.

4. STAND covered in warm place (e.g. airing cupboard) until bulk doubles THEN CHILL IT FOR 1 HOUR.

5. ROLL OUT— ←¼"

Then spread it with 4 tablespoons butter — just like buttering bread.

Then fold into 3 like this.

6. Roll it, BUTTER IT FOLD IT — 3 MORE TIMES Swinging it around each time before rolling.

CHILL **2** HOURS

7. MAKE CRESCENTS THEN CHILL 30 MINS.

8. BRUSH with milk or cream — BAKE 30 mins. at 400° (Reg 6) SERVE with coffee. SPREAD with butter.

You might easily find that the most difficult part of this recipe is finding the fresh yeast. Everyone tells me that dried yeast is just as good. I have found the dried variety to be not so reliable, so if it's your first go at croissants, try to get fresh yeast. The recipe here is simple and can be prepared up to stage 7, then cooked fresh as you want them.

Croissants are served only at breakfast. French people never have a mid-morning snack. Accompany with best-quality butter, home-made apricot jam, and lots of white coffee.

Crescents (croissants) are said to date from 1686, when the Turks were besieging Budapest. The bakers heard noises in the night, and so the Turks were discovered mining under the walls. The Turkish symbol was fashioned as a pastry to celebrate the bakers' alertness. Crescents are sometimes made from puff pastry – use the flaky pastry recipe on pages 272–3 – in which case you can put a dab of jam on the wide end of the wedge before rolling them up (stage 7). This is an Austrian recipe. Sprinkle the cooked crescent with fine sugar.

Beignets

There are **2** basic types,: the 'stirred in' (e.g. the sweet corn) and the 'coated' (e.g. scallops).

SCALLOPS

Remove yellow part (coral). Heat in butter. Use as garnish. Slice white part into 3 dip each slice in batter.

Basic Batter

Try a thin and thick batter until you get it the way you like it.

3 raw egg yolks

Tablespoon olive oil

MIX together then **ADD**:-
3 tablespoons flour (a little at a time) and water until it is LIKE THICK CREAM

JUST before using batter, stir in gently

3 stiff egg whites.

SWEET BEIGNETS- Use nut oil instead of olive. ALSO add a tablespoon BRANDY.

SWEET CORN

Stir whole corn kernels into the batter. Drop spoonful into well greased pan

Cook both sides.

STIRRED IN

1. Chopped cooked chicken.
2. Cheese (stir grated cheese) in). Beware sticking to pan.
3. Cooked peas with chopped ham.
4. Chopped shellfish.

COATED

1. Banana - dip into lemon juice before coating.
2. Cooked vegetables (e.g. cauliflower, asparagus, broccoli, carrots etc.).
3. Apple rings.
4. Raw veg. (e.g. celery, mushroom caps, cucumber); don't overcook.

Beignets and fritters are exactly the same thing, but the French are rather more exact in defining what they mean. There are five distinct varieties of beignet, including some made with yeast rather like the croissant recipe, and another made of pastry. The two types described opposite will enable you to deal with either soft or hard categories of food, and I have called them 'stirred in' and 'coated' to make it easier to define.

There is almost nothing which can't be made into a beignet, from aubergine (slice it, peel it, marinade in oil and lemon juice for an hour, coat it, cook it) to potatoes (grate a raw potato, pat dry, season with salt, pepper and nutmeg, stir into batter as opposite).

Ground meat needs batter round it if you deep-fry it. If you don't have it the shrinking meat will release all the delicious meat juices into fat. These will become nasty burnt specks. The beignet batter is particularly suitable for ground meat because it is very puffy, and will contain the moisture well.

This batter is also an especially good one to use for fried fish. It will give you a large puffed-up result, which is why restaurants like to use it. Meat or fish beignets are best cooked in deep fat.

Bread reacts well to beignet batter. For instance, make a cream-cheese or mozzarella sandwich. Any cheese with a low melting point will do. Dip the whole closed sandwich into the batter and fry gently so that the outside is dark brown, and the cheese inside fully melted. Garnish with anchovy fillets before serving.

SHORT PASTRY

I don't want to get into any fights about this – if you know a better recipe, STAY WITH IT.

keep all utensils cold. Handle lightly. Some cooks will keep pastry overnight in cold between stage 3 and stage 4.

1. MIX:

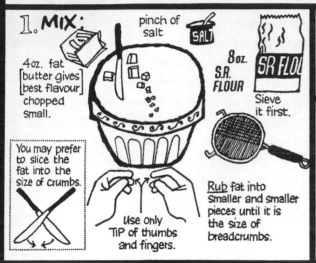

pinch of salt

4oz. fat [butter gives best flavour] chopped small.

8oz. S.R. FLOUR

Sieve it first.

You may prefer to slice the fat into the size of crumbs.

Use only TiP of thumbs and fingers.

Rub fat into smaller and smaller pieces until it is the size of breadcrumbs.

2. ADD

2 beaten yolks

–gently but thoroughly.

3.

You may need <u>no</u> cold water to make a firm pastry that holds together. **BEWARE** of too much water, add it just a sprinkle at a time. When it needs just a little more, it has enough!

4.

Roll pastry out.

Use it to line tin.

Making a Pastry-Case

Prick case, then put dry beans or crusts in it (to prevent its rising).

BAKE this empty case until it's just firm but still unbrowned, Reg 4 (350°F) 15 mins. Remove beans (or etc.), brush bottom with egg white. Return to oven 5 mins.

If you intend to use a sweet filling you can add 1½ oz. fine sugar to the first mixture.

This is one of the basic types of pastry. Short of the primitive types of flour-and-water mixture, like Chappatis (Indian cookery), this is one of the very simplest.

The notion behind this recipe is the combining of fat and flour into crumbs so that air expands in the tiny cavities formed by the crumbs. Since the air here isn't so tightly trapped the pastry doesn't rise as high as flaky pastry does. Heavy hands tend to knock the air out of the pastry instead of knocking it in – subtle difference. All I can say to reassure you is that if you understand the principle involved you are probably handling it right.

Because the action of expanding air is involved it is best to keep everything as cool as possible. Furthermore, cold fat is more manageable. The optional beaten yolks make the pastry rather tougher and less likely to soak up the subsequent filling. Similarly, egg white on the surface also proofs the pastry against moist fillings.

This recipe mixes 8 ounces of flour with 4 ounces of fat. The amount of fat could be reduced to 2 ounces to make a stronger, drier crust. Or it could be increased to 5 or even 6 ounces to make a very rich, fatty – very short – crust.

FLAKY PASTRY

Some cooks rest the dough overnight between Stage 1 and 2. The procedure is designed to get EVEN layers of air inside the pastry. The air gets hot in the oven and the whole thing becomes layers. Beginners – bypass Stage 4.

1. Rub fat into flour until it is size of breadcrumbs, using only **TIPS** of thumbs and fingers.

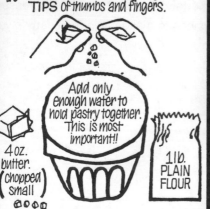

Add only enough water to hold pastry together. This is most important!!

4 oz. butter. (chopped) small

1 lb. PLAIN FLOUR

2. ROLL out into an even strip. Dot it with 3 oz. (cold) butter.

The butter should be of same hardness as the dough

Don't bring pieces right to the edge.

←⅓—×—⅓—×—⅓→

Fold it like this.

Pinch edges to trap air and fat inside.

SPRINKLE FAT WITH A TRACE OF FLOUR

↑

Turn pastry at right angles.

3. Repeat stage 2. If fat pops through, shake flour on it.

4. OPTIONAL Repeat Stage 2. Careful now – it gets tricky about here.

5. ROLL to ½" thick layer. Top a pie with it, using scraps to make decoration. (Re-rolling will spoil it.) Brush with a beaten egg.

6. BAKE golden about 20–30 mins. at Reg. 7 (420°F). Too long in the oven will spoil the pastry, so the contents (e.g. steak, chicken, etc.) should be pre-cooked to within ½ hour of perfection.

The origins of pastry-making go as far back as the Greeks. There are experts who classify pastry-making into ten distinct separate categories. One of these is puff pastry, and flaky pastry is a less rich, more everyday version of that. It still remains a rich, light miracle, delicate to the touch and sometimes adding up to seven hundred layers of pastry.

Remember while making it that you are trying to build thin layers of cold air into the dough and fat. Some cooks keep the pastry (board, pin and ingredients, too) in a refrigerator between rolling. Some roll out on a sheet of marble. This preoccupation with coldness not only keeps the fat at a manageable solidity, but also gets those air layers really cold.

When the pastry is in the oven each of those trapped pockets of air warms up, the air expands the only way it can: upward. This gives you that intricate texture which the French pâtissier calls **mille-feuilles** (a thousand leaves).

There are two ways to make this pastry: the 'Continental method' which wraps like an envelope, and the 'English' or dabbing method shown here, which, although less professional, is a little easier – that's why I use it.

3 FRENCH TARTS

THESE RECIPES ARE THE FILLINGS. BAKE AN EMPTY PASTRY CASE (SO IT IS WHITE NOT BROWN) AND ADD THE FILLINGS. THEY WILL TAKE ABOUT ½ HOUR AT REG 3½ (350°F). TEST MIXTURE WITH SKEWER UNTIL IT IS SET. **EAT HOT OR COLD.**

TARTE A L'OIGNON

1. SLICE about 1½ lb. onion.

2. COOK in butter, bacon fat or pork fat. (Ask butcher for it).

about ½ hour

↑ GENTLE FLAME ↑

3. Remove from heat. Add 3 beaten eggs (new laid if pos.) and 3oz. grated cheese (Gruyère is best).

4. ADD: 3 tablespoons double cream.

Note: You can add ½ doz. stoned black olives.

QUICHE LORRAINE

1. BEAT 3 eggs.

2. SEASON with freshly ground pepper and a trace of salt.

3. ADD ½ pint of **cream** (single or double).

SALT

½ pt. CREAM

4. POUR this over chunks of ham (not tinned), cut thick.

Quiche

1. BEAT 2 eggs.

2. ADD: 4 oz. of grated cheese. (Almost any kind will do although Gruyère is the authentic one.)

3. SEASON with ground pepper, salt and nutmeg.

4. ADD ¼ pint milk + ¼ pint double cream.

¼ pt. MILK

¼ pt. CREAM

5. STIR WELL

These three fillings can be put into pastry cases made from either short or flaky pastry. They can be eaten hot or cold, and are equally suited for a dinner-party entrée or a TV snack. Please note that after the filling is put into the crust the result needs cooking as described at the top of the strip.

Pies, as you know, are tarts with pastry closing across the top. The recipes here can be used as pie recipes and here are some more.

Cevennes Pie. Boil some chestnuts until they are cooked. Mash them and add equal parts of apple and raw ground pork. Stir one beaten egg into it. Season it. Put the top on. Cooking time will depend on the depth of the filling. Try one hour. Cut the top to inspect it if in doubt.

Lorraine Pie. Marinate pork and veal (very small pieces) in Madeira and cognac overnight. Drain meat and add chopped onion and seasoning, including a sprinkle of nutmeg and some parsley. When the pie is nearly cooked (try one hour, inspect if in doubt), stir some of the marinade into two beaten eggs and funnel that into the top of the pie.

Vosges Pie. This is just like Lorraine Pie except that you use only pork, and instead of mixing the beaten egg with marinade you mix it with cream.

If you want to make a pie with cooked leftover chicken, game or meat, chop it all quite small then stir into it beaten egg + cognac. This is then usually called a **Pie de Campagne,** which, as you see, doesn't mean a thing.

Crème Caramel

1 Scald (almost boil) one pint of Jersey milk — ½ milk + ½ cream is even better. (A vanilla pod steeped in the milk improves the flavour)

Pour the milk **SLOWLY** on to 4 eggs + 2oz. sugar that have been well beaten. (A hand whisk will do) ..... STRAIN.

2 CARAMELISE 3½ oz. sugar. It should go dark brown but not black.

medium flame

Watch out-it's **HOT!**

Coat bottom and sides of buttered dish while caramel is liquid. Pour custard in.

3 COOK in water jacket.

Water must not boil (or bubbles appear inside custard!)

RAISE DISH AWAY FROM JACKET

Cook Reg 3 (330°F) about 45 min. **TURN OUT.** Eat hot or cold.

Crème à la Viennoise, moulée

Cook caramel golden only & dissolve in the hot milk.

For other flavours mix chocolate or coffee into milk, or make a vanilla flavour without caramel.

The same recipe (omitting the business with the burnt sugar) cooked very gently (in a double boiler is best) on top of the stove, gives you a sauce: **Egg Custard (Crème à l'anglaise).** In this case, a tiny teaspoonful of cornflour will make perfection easy. Do not regard this adding of flour as cheating. It will save you anxious moments and it is done by the finest chefs. Packets of custard powder should have no place in the kitchen of cooks like you.

Crème Brûlée (burnt cream) is the ultimate of the enriched Crème Caramel, and what is more (appropriately enough for an English dish with a French name), it is a Crème Caramel upside down.

Beat four egg yolks into six ounces of double cream, and add a dessertspoonful of fine sugar (vanilla-flavoured sugar is even better). Put the mix into small individual containers (if you have them), then cook as Crème Caramel. Cooking time will vary according to size. Test with a needle. When the Crème Brûlée is firm, sprinkle the top *lightly* with fine sugar and pop it under the grill. Note: the sugar must not go black: honey-colour is just right. Serve the Crème Brûlée chilled.

MOUSSE

NO LONGER AN EXACT TERM. HERE ARE THE 2 BASIC FRENCH STYLES AND A TYPICAL HOME PRODUCT. (HURRAH!)

1. FRUIT MOUSSE

Make a purée of 1 lb. fruit and 10 oz. sugar. (Soft fruit needs little or no cooking, just sprinkle sugar over fruit — let it dissolve)

ADD A LITTLE LEMON JUICE

sieve it

COOL, then fold gently into 1 pint of thick whipped cream.

CHILL about 8 hrs.

2. CREAM MOUSSE

BEAT 3 yolks + 3 oz. sugar and a good pinch of corn flour

YOU CAN FLAVOUR THE MILK WITH COFFEE, CHOCOLATE OR FLAVOURING SYRUP

Add ½ pint scalded (almost boiling) milk. KEEP BEATING.

THEN: Scald (DO NOT BOIL)

COOL. Fold in 1 pint of thick whipped cream. **CHILL** 8 hrs.

3. LEMON MOUSSE

ANGLO-US. STYLE

Beat 2 tablespoons sugar + 2 yolks till creamy

Add: GRATED LEMON RIND AND JUICE.

Then stir in about ¼ oz. gelatine (dissolved in hot water).

Wait until this mixture begins to jellify. Then fold in 2 stiffly beaten egg whites — CHILL 2 hrs.

N.B. Keep gelatine to ABSOLUTE MINIMUM for best results.

In France a mousse is a part of an ice cream, and certainly has no relationship to the rubbery substance that English and American cook-books would have us make.

Two simple French mousses shown in the grid are great party pieces, and need not be surrounded by other flavouring matters, but can be served exactly as they are. Should you prefer the one more common to our kitchens, use a very small amount of gelatine indeed. You will perhaps have noticed that **Chocolate Mousse** is a favourite recipe in our cookery books. This is because the chocolate itself, when the mousse gets cold, will act as a solidifying agent, and thus these recipes for chocolate mousse seldom mention gelatine. However, chocolate is only one of an enormous number of flavours to which the mousse lends itself. A ham or salmon mousse is a most welcome feature of summer-evening dining. Even tinned salmon can be made into a most exciting supper dish in this way.

A mousse can be made with poultry, game, foie gras, fish, shellfish or many other ingredients. In each case, the ingredient should be puréed. Cream, a little aspic jelly or a sauce may be added, according to the consistency of the ingredients.

CHEESECAKE:

Everyone has a theory about cheesecake: SOCRATES, LUCULLUS and APICIUS included.

An Ancient Greek Recipe uses cheese, honey, sesame, tops it with fruit.

1. THE CRUST:

3 oz. melted butter
1 yolk
FLOUR

Mix adding a little water if needed. Rest in cold place 1 hr. **ROLL LINE BAKING TIN**

½ lb. sifted flour
2 oz. sugar
2 drips vanilla flavour or 2 tablespoons sherry (SHERRY IS BETTER)

QUICK CRUST

CORN FLAKES

CRUSH:
2 cups of cornflakes (or crackers, Zwieback etc.) mix with:
3 oz. sugar
3 oz melted butter

PRESS HARD. Use as a base only.

2. FILLING:

BEAT 20-30 oz. of CREAM CHEESE
3 tablespoons S.R. flour.
ELECTRIC BEATER HELPS
AT LEAST 3 oz. of DOUBLE CREAM (whipped)

STIR BETWEEN ADDING EACH ITEM

S.R. FLOUR
CREAM CHEESE

CREAM 5 eggs together + 2 yolks and 10 oz. sugar

Grated rind of an orange and a lemon. Add the juice if you like a sharp taste.

3. BAKE

Reg. 9 (445°F) for 12 min, then Reg. 4 (355°F) for an hour. Test with needle; it should come out clean. Leave in oven (heat off) another hour. CHILL. **N.B.** Don't jar or knock until it is cold.

ITALIAN

Use Ricotta instead of cream cheese. Add candied fruit and almonds to mix.

TOP WITH FRUIT

when cold. Use cornflour + juice to glaze. Dark fruit looks best.

There are more theories about cheesecake than there are people who cook it. I remember asking an accomplished cook what she knew about cheesecake, just before writing this piece. 'I just love to eat it,' she said.

People just love to eat cheesecake, and when they have finished devouring yours voraciously, they will tell you that there was not quite enough lemon or perhaps a little too much cheese. Generally speaking, people come down heavily on the side of cheese or lemon.

Don't be disappointed if the centre of your cheesecake sags. This tends to happen with even very experienced cheesecake-makers. Perhaps this was the reason that a coating of fruit was first invented.

BUTTERSCOTCH PEARS

1. CHOOSE RIPE PEARS WITH A STALK

PEEL THEM BUT LEAVE WHOLE

2. HEAT (until they combine):

juice of 2 lemons

1 oz. butter

½ lb. brown sugar

3. STAND pears in this sauce, (cover if possible). Simmer very slowly until tender (about ¼ hr.).

Remove pears, BOIL sauce until it is **thick** and treacle-like. **TURN HEAT LOW**

4. BASTE pears with this coating, using a spoon. Keep low heat going. **TAKE CARE !!!** It is **HOT** — see why you need the stalks. When they are thoroughly coated (it will take 5 min.) put them onto a serving dish. Pour sauce over.

Serve **HOT** or very **COLD**. Great with sour cream! you'll need —

No one would want to deny that fresh, dessert-quality fruit deserves to be brought to the table in a fruit basket, and that's about all the preparation it needs. However, there are times of the year when the fruit available needs a little help – not much, perhaps, but a little. This is why the syrup was invented.

The very simplest syrup is merely 2 lb. of sugar in half a pint of boiling water. Stir it while it dissolves (it is best left overnight). Pop a vanilla pod into it and after three weeks you will have vanilla syrup.

Any number of fruits can be treated with this kind of syrup: for instance, peeled bananas poached for five minutes in syrup with a final dash of Kirsch gives you a **Compote de bananes.** Peeled pears (leave them whole or quarter them) simmered in syrup gives you **Compote de poires,** etc. etc.

To flavour the syrup you can use orange or lemon peel, instant coffee, cinnamon, cloves or vanilla pods. Use the flavourings with discretion and when in doubt use just the simple unflavoured syrup. Any suitable liqueur can be added at the end. Compotes can be just one type of fruit or mixtures of suitable ones. They should always be served cold, the syrup in which they have been cooked being served with them. In France bottled syrups of many flavours are sold. If you find them in your local shop, buy them; they are very useful.

ENGLISH TRIFLE

Take it to the table before serving, as it looks like hell on the plates.

A PLEASANT VARIATION IS TO USE CHOC. CUSTARD + COFFEE CUSTARD + BANANAS (SLICED). IN THIS CASE USE TIA MARIA OR CRÈME DE CACAO ON THE FRUIT.

1. CHOOSE an impressive-looking large dish—

of any SHAPE or SiZE.

2. LINE IT

— with plain cake or sponge. Sprinkle cake with lots of sherry. (But it should hold its shape — not go SOGGY.)

SHERRY

3. HAVE REMAINING INGREDIENTS COLD BEFORE ASSEMBLY.

DECORATE with cherries angelica almonds

Repeat at least once— changing type of fruit.

TOP with blobs of thick cream (Use a forcing-bag for a really ambitious job.)

EGG CUSTARD (with a trace of Cornflour)
JELLY (not too firm)
FRESH FRUIT + BRANDY
APRICOT JAM (best poss.)
CAKE + SHERRY.

THE FRUIT should be poached in syrup before use. (Use tinned or frozen for a less than perfect result.)

284

When I was an assistant pastry chef my boss once said to me, 'There's only one essential ingredient in trifle: first-class sherry.' He was a man much given to exaggeration, but the point is a good one. Don't go to all the trouble involved in making a trifle if you are going to use leftover stale cake, odds and ends, and tickle it up with cooking sherry.

Many cooks make the custard and jelly firmer than they otherwise would. Some cooks put jelly and sherry into the sponge. This is to prevent the whole thing collapsing as you serve it. This is especially important in a restaurant because the trifle must remain on the sweet trolley, and look appetizing for an hour or so.

You may prefer to switch alcohols and use any of the fancy liqueurs, like the Tia Maria I have suggested in the strip. Some people sprinkle a little rum, Kirsch or brandy on each portion as it's served. As you see from all these variations, it's a very personal business. Develop your own personal style. My mother's trifles are famous far and wide. They are a long labour of love, and usually end up so vast that only the bread-mixing bowl can hold them.

APPLE PANDOWDY
AND SOME VARIANTS

TRADITIONAL SAUCE : **HARD SAUCE**
CREAM BUTTER & BROWN SUGAR
TOGETHER - THEN DRIP BRANDY INTO IT -
STILL BEATING ! SERVE CHILLED.

---

1. BUY some

apples. Don't buy big, horrible, acid, green ones marked

COOKING for this recipe*

peel them and slice

*And don't buy them for any other recipe either!

---

2. MELT about 6oz.

butter.

Don't BROWN it

CUT slices of nice bread into fingers.

Dip them quickly in butter.

---

3. LINE a dish

with the bread fingers

ANY SHAPE DISH WILL DO IF IT IS OVENPROOF

Top is bread

apple	
apple	
apple	

Add apples and some brown sugar in layers.

AMOUNT OF SUGAR depends upon how sweet apples are and how sweet you want them.

---

4. VARIATIONS

Sprinkle apple with:

1. CRUSHED (heads) of cloves (do it with fingers)
2. Lemon/orange juice
3. Sultanas
4. Cinnamon powder

5.

YOU can either let top bread go crisp (in this case be prepared to funnel a **LITTLE** water in it if it gets too dry) **or** COVER

Bake Reg 4 (350°F) 1 hr.

This could be described as a transatlantic Apple Charlotte. Everything I say about Bread and Butter Pudding, pages 300–1, applies here. This is a very good-tempered dish, it can be delayed (as long as it doesn't go dry), warmed up and even served cold. A French recipe very like this purées the apples first, mashing them with lots of butter and apricot jam and a generous slug of rum. This is spread over the fingers of bread just as in the American recipe. French desserts of this sort are always served drier than their Anglo-Saxon equivalent. It would therefore be accompanied with a light sauce – thinned down top-quality jam – or thin cream. The American cook would be far more likely to serve it with a portion of ice cream, an addition always marked by the words 'à la mode' on the menu.

Apple Pandowdy is sometimes made by cooking butter, apples and molasses briefly, turning it into the dish and topping it with biscuit dough. This goes into a moderate oven for half an hour and can, if you wish, be served upside down, apple covering pastry. Biscuits in America are rather like English scones. Make them by adding three teaspoons of baking powder and a sprinkle of salt to half a pound of flour. Rub in 3 ounces of fat (lard and butter mixed) and enough milk to make a stiff paste. Roll it so it's about half an inch thick. Now cut it into biscuits – 15 minutes at Regulo 7 (430° F.) – or use it as above.

MILK PUDDING *de luxe*

THIS WILL FEED SIX PEOPLE

1 SPRINKLE ¼ lb. any of these: MACARONI, VERMICELLI, TAPIOCA, SEMOLINA, SAGO into 1 pint boiling milk

2 ADD 2 oz. sugar and 3 oz. butter.

3 STIR to remove lumps.... **COOK** at Reg. 1½ (300°F) for 25 mins.

4 TIP IT OUT and mix 2 beaten yolks and 2 oz. butter into it, then ...

5 GENTLY mix in 2 stiffly beaten egg whites

NB *Clean mixer!*

6 PUT final mixture into a buttered dish, which must stand in water.

hot water supports (e.g. skewers)

Give it 1 hour in the oven Reg. 3½ (350°F)

Serve ... (with cream?)

I included this recipe because it is the great French way of making 'pouding au riz', but the French version of this dish is much more dry and solid than our own, so it is usually served with a sauce of some kind. This can be home-made jam warmed with a dash of brandy in it, or a creamy custard (Crème à l'anglaise, *see* pages 276–7).

Some French cooks add half a bar of plain chocolate to the pudding at stage one; in this case the finished pudding can be garnished with shavings of chocolate. Serve with thin cream.

LEMON MERINGUE PIE
You'll need a cooked pastry case

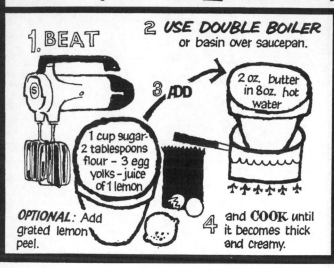

1. BEAT

2 USE DOUBLE BOILER or basin over saucepan.

3 ADD 2 oz. butter in 8 oz. hot water

1 cup sugar - 2 tablespoons flour - 3 egg yolks - juice of 1 lemon

OPTIONAL: Add grated lemon peel.

4 and **COOK** until it becomes thick and creamy.

5. BEAT 3 or 4 egg whites.

New-laid if possible.

MANY COOKS add 3 or 4 tablespoons of castor sugar to stiff egg whites for a final beating.

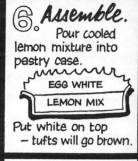

6. Assemble. Pour cooled lemon mixture into pastry case.

EGG WHITE
LEMON MIX

Put white on top – tufts will go brown.

7. Bake 15 mins. at Reg 6. (400°F) until meringue is crisp and dry. *SERVE COLD.*

There is a whole range of these American dessert pies: banana, butterscotch, coconut, chocolate and anything you can invent based upon the same blancmange-style filling. As an alternative to the meringue you can top any of the fillings mentioned with a thick layer of heavy whipped cream. Two tablespoons of castor sugar, beaten into half a pint of cream, will make it very thick. Don't put this thick cream on it until the pie is quite cold. It is usual to refrigerate it again after adding cream so it's very cold when served. These are then chilled cream pies, e.g. banana cream pie.

Fresh eggs will give you a better result than ordinary shop eggs. Everyone has a theory about beating eggs; French cooks often use a copper bowl, which apparently helps. Others swear by adding a quarter of a teaspoonful of cream of tartar while beating them.

BAKED ALASKA

THIS SOMETIMES APPEARS ON FRENCH MENUS AS AN OMELETTE. ANOTHER VARIATION HAS HARD FROZEN ICE-CREAM WRAPPED INTO AN ORDINARY SWEET OMELETTE. **SPEED IS THE SECRET!**

1. YOU NEED THE HOTTEST OVEN YOU CAN GET

Turn it to the highest setting and leave it 20 mins. until the whole thing is about to go into orbit!!!

2.

Ask your shop to freeze a block of ice cream <u>as hard as it will go</u>.

Well drained fruit.

Sponge cake.

SOAK a board (bread board?) in cold water before use.

ICE CREAM	DRAINED FRUIT
VANILLA	CRUSHED PINEAPPLE + MINT + TRACE OF CREME DE MENTHE.
COFFEE	FIGS (OR TIN OF MARRONS).
CHOCOLATE	MASHED BANANA.

3. BEAT 4 egg-whites very stiff and make thick layer, leaving little tufts that will go brown.

Ice cream
Fruit
Sponge

4. COOK it so that it is golden outside; ice-cold within. Try 3 mins. exactly.

Until the mass production of ice cream made it an everyday dish, ice cream was a prima donna of the kitchen. Even today a cook who makes his own ice cream feels justly proud of the feat. The Chinese are said to have thought it up, with the Indians, Persians and Arabs adapting it to their own tastes. Ice cream was brought into France by an Italian in the late seventeenth century, and finally the North American, with the invention of the electric refrigerator, has made ice cream the caviare of U.S. cuisine.

Only in certain places in Italy is the U.S. expert equalled in invention, technique and artistry. Peppermint-flavoured ice cream, with slivers of chocolate, is one of my fondest memories of New York City in summer-time. So it was right that the U.S.A. should give birth to Baked Alaska, never mind about Omelette à la Norvégienne (the French counterpart).

Take a hot oven, ice cream, eggs and whisk and tell everyone to synchronize their watches.

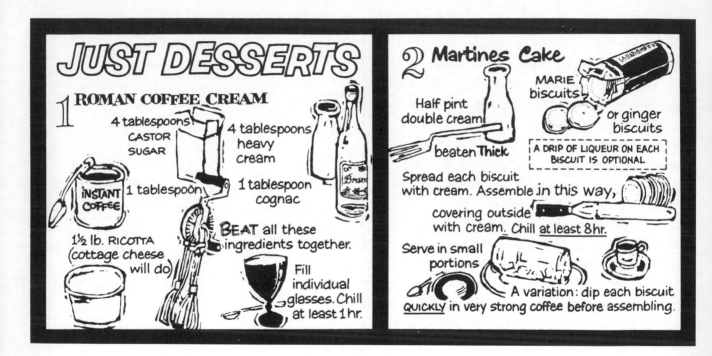

JUST DESSERTS

1 ROMAN COFFEE CREAM

4 tablespoons CASTOR SUGAR

4 tablespoons heavy cream

INSTANT COFFEE

1 tablespoon

1 tablespoon cognac

1½ lb. RICOTTA (cottage cheese will do)

BEAT all these ingredients together.

Fill individual glasses. Chill at least 1 hr.

2 Martines Cake

Half pint double cream, beaten Thick

MARIE biscuits

or ginger biscuits

A DRIP OF LIQUEUR ON EACH BISCUIT IS OPTIONAL

Spread each biscuit with cream. Assemble in this way, covering outside with cream. Chill at least 8hr.

Serve in small portions

A variation: dip each biscuit QUICKLY in very strong coffee before assembling.

Dinner parties, and in fact all catering for small or large numbers, will benefit by the occasional simply made dish which can be made well in advance and has merely to be brought to the table at the right time. Both these desserts are of this kind, and Martines Cake in particular can lend itself to so many different variations that one could serve it on several occasions to the same guests. Although in France the Marie biscuit is almost invariably the one used, I have tasted this made with oatmeal biscuits and found it to be equally delicious. It is most important that the fat content of the cream is given ample time to saturate the biscuits, and when the cake is served, the biscuits should have completely lost their identity. If not, the next time you must give it even longer.

MRS. DASHFIELD'S (WINNER BBC T.V. COOKERY CLUB)
Christmas Pudding
A really wonderful recipe that will tempt even the most diet-conscious

½ lb. S.R. FLOUR

grated rind + juice of an orange and lemon

6 well-beaten eggs

½ lb. fresh bread-crumbs

½ lb. chopped beef suet

½ lb. currants

¾ lb. sultanas

¾ lb. stoned raisins

½ lb. brown sugar

* foot sugar is even better.

1 teaspoon salt
1 teaspoon mixed spice

½ pint Old Ale or a wine-glass Brandy.

STIR. ALL THE INGREDIENTS TOGETHER
MIXTURE MUST BE STIFF BUT NOT DRY —
Add moisture (milk) if really necessary.

This makes 4 medium-sized puddings

THESE INGREDIENTS MUST BE CHOPPED SMALL:
¼ lb. candied peel
¼ glace cherries
6 oz. almonds blanched
1 small carrot
1 small apple

2. COVER
2 in. space
floured cloth
greased paper.
Tie tightly
COOK.

DON'T LET IT BOIL DRY. ADD BOILING WATER
BOIL GENTLY 8 HOURS

3. COOL. Replace paper and cloth with clean ones. Store in a cool place. Boil for another 3 hours immediately before serving with.....

RUM BUTTER (SERVE IT VERY COLD)
BEAT 3 oz. butter with 3 oz. icing-sugar

A warm basin makes it easier

SLOWLY add 3 tablespoons of Rum.

SOME COOKS add 2 beaten eggs at the beginning and 4 oz. of whipped (thick) cream at the end.

IF YOU DON'T LIKE RUM BUTTER, POUR WARM BRANDY ETC. OVER THE PUD. THEN SET FIRE TO IT.

Although Christmas puddings are made only at Christmas, dried fruit is a useful kitchen item at any time. Here are a few notes about it.

Dried Fruit	Mostly sun-dried	Use as it is	Needs brief rinse before use Store in the dry
Evaporated Fruit	Mostly sun-dried	Needs soaking	Won't keep for ever
Glacé Fruit	Treated in boiling syrup	Can be eaten or soaked and simmered to make a compote	
Crystallized Fruit	As glacé, but double boiled		
Currants	Tiny seedless grapes	Plump blue/black	Vostizza are best
Raisins	Can be bought stoned	Honey-brown	Valencia are best
Sultanas	Small seedless grapes but sometimes marked 'seedless raisins'	Yellow	Australian and Californian are both good

BANANAS

Cooked bananas can be served as a vegetable with chicken or ham. Use fruit yellow with freckles.

Never put bananas in a refrigerator. Ice cream is great with most cooked banana recipes.

Banana Boat Special

A piquant dessert recipe.

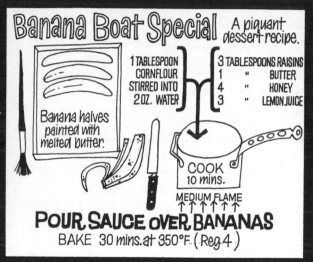

1 TABLESPOON CORNFLOUR STIRRED INTO 2 OZ. WATER

3 TABLESPOONS RAISINS
1 " BUTTER
4 " HONEY
3 " LEMON JUICE

Banana halves painted with melted butter.

COOK 10 mins.

MEDIUM FLAME

POUR SAUCE OVER BANANAS
BAKE 30 mins. at 350°F. (Reg. 4)

Sauté

Quarter —

Sprinkle with FLOUR

sauté brown in a little butter.

SERVE sprinkled with Sugar
OR with heated RUM,

— in which case — light it !!

SERVED UNCOOKED

1. Mashed with sugar and cream.
2. Beaten with milk, a trace of vanilla, an egg and some ice cream to make a de luxe milk shake.
3. Whole, sprinkled with lemon juice and sugar.

Bananas have a high nutritional value; they contain vitamins A, B and C. Canary ones are excellent. Bananas must never be put into a refrigerator, and should not be peeled until immediately before being eaten, or they will discolour (although a sprinkle of lemon juice will discourage that tendency). Bananas which have gone dark at room temperature are good – even better – to eat. They can be cooked – still in their skins – in a low oven. The outer skin will go black but the inside will be hot and piquant.

Bananas blend well with other fruit. Banana and pineapple is a good mixture, especially in a French recipe in which the pieces are sprinkled with plenty of white sugar and kirsch, then have lots of thick cream stirred into them. The pieces should be well coated before serving.

There is a Hindu theory that the banana is the original forbidden fruit.

BREAD BUTTERED BOTH SIDES

Bread-and-butter pudding - a neglected favourite.

1. BUTTER some bread on both sides.

Remove crusts.

Currant bread or brown bread is great!

LINE a suitable oven dish.

2. ARRANGE layers, finishing on bread

BREAD
SULTANAS
BREAD
SULTANAS
BREAD

(Add a dust of cinnamon if you like)

3. POUR ONTO IT -

beaten {
1 pint milk
4 oz. cream
3 eggs
pinch nutmeg
4 oz. brown sugar.
}

IV. Let it stand

for 30 mins. until bread is soaked through.

5. COVER (tin foil will do)

COOK 30 mins.
UNCOVER -
COOK 30 mins.
} At 325°F (Reg 3)

Final Result should have a crisp brown 'toasty' top. (Finish under grill if you like) BEWARE burnt sultanas. Ugh!

The bread on sale today – squashy, bleached chalk-white, deprived of its nutritional germ, then synthetically brought up to par with chemicals, sliced and wrapped in aromatic paper – is as far a cry from real bread as a baker is from a bread-seller. If you think I am exaggerating, taste bread fresh from the oven, made from wholemeal flour and smelling of real live yeast.

If you can't get real bread then this is a good thing to do with the best you can find. Prejudice against bread puddings starts in the schools and nurseries; that's because they didn't use cream, and not always eggs either. Stack the whole thing with plenty of sultanas, lavish more cream if you fancy it; angelica won't hurt, nor glacé cherries. Don't stint with the best of the ingredients, because, as I was saying, the bread won't be worth a damn.

CHEESE

LABEL: 50% E.S. (Extrait Sec) means the cheese is ½ water. 50% de matières grasses means ½ remainder is fat content.

There are three basic kinds
1. Fresh (cream cheese, petit suisse etc.)
2. Fermented (Camembert etc.)
3. Cooked (gruyère, port salut, etc.)

Wensleydale (U.K.)

A clean, sour-tasting cheese from Yorkshire. Must be eaten soon after cutting.

EDAM (Holland)

As clean, honest and forthright as it's native land.

Brie (France)

A soft cheese. Tricky to keep, mild in flavour... similar process to Camembert. Best in autumn.

Tome de Savoie (France)

A mild but quite flavourful cheese if you don't mind eating all the grape pips.

Mozzarella (Italy)

A buffalo-milk cheese. Sold individually. It has a low melting-point so is useful in cooking. Neapolitans eat it with olive oil and fresh pepper.

STILTON (U.K.)

The classic English cheese sometimes served with a scoop. Often preferred distinctly overripe.

GRUYÈRE (Switzerland)

A sweet cheese smaller and more flavourful than Emmental, which it closely resembles.

Port Salut (France)

A creamy whole-milk cheese made to a secret formula by Trappist monasteries. There is also a Danish version.

Petit Suisse (France)

A soft cream cheese upon which the French gourmet is apt to sprinkle sugar. Tastes like sour cream. Can be served with fruit (fresh).

Gorgonzola (Italy)

A popular blue, it is rather strong. Its manufacture is complex - best in Spring and summer.

Taste a new cheese two or three times a week. There are over 500 well-known, distinctive kinds of cheese, so you will be able to go on for quite a time.

Cheese originally was a way of preserving milk, but soon the many ways of doing this, coupled with local ingenuity and local climate, herbs and flavourings, produced extraordinary varieties.

Have cheese before the dessert, with a loaf that you have saved specially, preferably of a different type from the bread eaten so far with the meal.

Fresh celery can accompany the cheese course, and Burgundy or one of the bolder clarets is an essential part of cheese enjoyment.

Do not forgive the guest who prods or pummels your Camembert.

Rely upon a good grocer to sell you only excellent produce, and tell him how soon you intend to serve it.

Camembert, like Brie, should have a yellowish-orange crust and there should be no black streaks. The cheese must be pale yellow, smooth, and there should be no holes in the texture. Whatever anyone says to the contrary, it must not be runny.

The goat cheeses are very strong in taste; serve only one of these with other milder cheeses, unless you are sure of your guests.

Cheese is a classic food, and a taste for it can and should be developed by perseverance and experiment. A small lunch of bread, cheese and wine has a historic perfection.

The summer of 1529 was wet. The relentless heavy rain was an important factor in our lives for it helped to defeat the 350,000 besieging Turks who, until then, looked like overwhelming not only Vienna, but all points west! When they withdrew the Turks left behind them tiny brown beans. The Austrians boiled them but found them not worth eating. The gravy on the other hand was not unpleasant – coffee had come to Europe.

Nowadays coffee is grown right across the world. The rugged Robusta plant has helped the economy of many newly independent nations. There is always a good market for Robusta coffees, for although they are less delicate in flavour they are quite good enough for the dark-roast treatment that the French and Belgians like so much.

As well as the very dark 'Continental Roast' many coffees are available in light or dark roast. If you wish to develop a palate for various coffees you should compare unblended coffees which have been light-roasted. The lighter the roast the greater the amount of coffee to water; that's why coffee bars serve very dark roast. Try: Tanganyika, Kenya, Mocha and Blue Mountain – they are classics. Most blending is done to economize. Here are some good combinations: Costa Rica with Tanganyika (Chagga); Mocha mixed with Mysore; Kenya mixed with any West African coffee.

Coffee deteriorates quickly after it is ground. The moral is, have a grinder (electric if possible), grind coffee immediately before use. The finer the coffee is ground, the lighter the roasting, so when using Turkish coffee (ground to powder) you'll need a light roast. Mocha is usually chosen. The coffee in this case is not strained – it remains as sludge in the bottom of the cup.

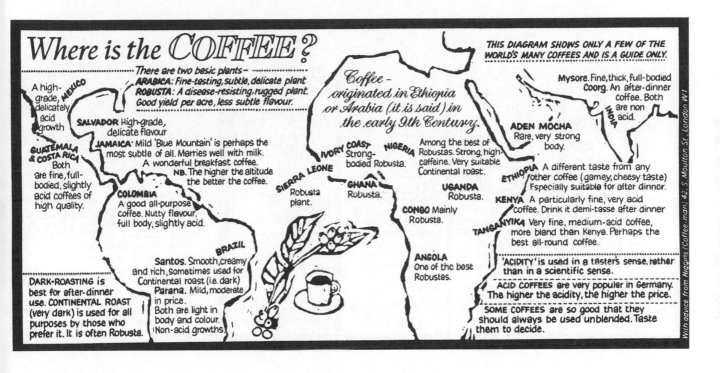

Where is the COFFEE?

There are two basic plants —
ARABICA: Fine-tasting, subtle, delicate plant
ROBUSTA: A disease-resisting, rugged plant. Good yield per acre, less subtle flavour.

Coffee — originated in Ethiopia or Arabia (it is said) in the early 9th Century.

THIS DIAGRAM SHOWS ONLY A FEW OF THE WORLD'S MANY COFFEES AND IS A GUIDE ONLY.

MEXICO A high-grade, delicately acid growth.

SALVADOR High-grade, delicate flavour

JAMAICA Mild 'Blue Mountain' is perhaps the most subtle of all. Marries well with milk. A wonderful breakfast coffee.
NB. The higher the altitude the better the coffee.

GUATEMALA & COSTA RICA Both are fine, full-bodied, slightly acid coffees of high quality.

COLOMBIA A good all-purpose coffee. Nutty flavour, full body, slightly acid.

BRAZIL Santos. Smooth, creamy and rich, sometimes used for Continental roast (i.e. dark) Parana. Mild, moderate in price. Both are light in body and colour. Non-acid growths.

DARK-ROASTING is best for after-dinner use. CONTINENTAL ROAST (very dark) is used for all purposes by those who prefer it. It is often Robusta.

IVORY COAST Strong-bodied Robusta.

NIGERIA Among the best of Robustas. Strong, high-caffeine. Very suitable Continental roast.

SIERRA LEONE Robusta plant.

GHANA Robusta.

UGANDA Robusta.

CONGO Mainly Robusta.

ANGOLA One of the best Robustas.

MYSORE. Fine, thick, full-bodied **Coorg.** An after-dinner coffee. Both are non acid.

INDIA

ADEN MOCHA Rare, very strong body.

ETHIOPIA A different taste from any other coffee (gamey, cheesy taste) Especially suitable for after dinner.

KENYA A particularly fine, very acid coffee. Drink it demi-tasse after dinner

TANGANYIKA Very fine, medium-acid coffee, more bland than Kenya. Perhaps the best all-round coffee.

'ACIDITY' is used in a taster's sense, rather than in a scientific sense.

ACID COFFEES are very popular in Germany. The higher the acidity, the higher the price.

SOME COFFEES are so good that they should always be used unblended. Taste them to decide.

With advice from Higgins (Coffee-man) 42, S. Moulton St. London W1

How is the *COFFEE* ? *A FEW POSSIBILITIES*

SIMPLE
One pint of fresh boiling water goes into a warm pot containing four heaped dessert-spoons of coffee. Stand one min.— Skim froth. Stand four min. Strain it. (Pot shown has built-in strainer). Drink . . . .

FRENCH DRIP
Coffee (medium grind) in same proportion. Put into upper section. Boiling water poured into it. Perhaps the finest and clearest way, but it may get cold, so stand pot in warm water. The grind must be exactly right.

TURKISH
Combine two table-spoons pulverized coffee (e.g. light-roast mocha) and four tablespoons sugar. Add two cups water. Heat until it rises in a froth. Remove from heat. Repeat twice... Serve with Turkish delight.

ESPRESSO
Usually demands finely ground coffee (dark roast). Follow instructions.

VACUUM
When water boils top half is added. Reduce heat; water rises to meet coffee. The heat must be exactly right. Built-in heat source saves many harsh words.

CAFÉ DIABLE Mix peel of ¼ lemon and ¼ orange, 4 cubes sugar, 6 cloves, 1 cinnamon stick and 1 cup of warm cognac. Set light to it. Slowly add 2 cups espresso coffee.

CAFFÈ BORGIA Espresso coffee and hot chocolate in equal parts. Drop thick cream on it. Sprinkle grated orange peel.

CAPPUCCINO Equal parts *hot* milk and espresso coffee. Beat milk if you like it frothy. (You don't, do you?)

1. A coffee-grinder will enable you to make more flavourful coffee.
2. Don't economize in use of it.
3. Fresh water (empty kettle - refill).
4. Better keep coffee hot for hours (in water jacket) than reheat it.
5. Never boil the milk or the coffee.
6. Keep the utensils clean.

Water is obviously the vital factor in coffee-making. Use fresh water. Don't use water from the hot-water system, nor water left in a kettle that has already been heated once. The gadgets that fix on to a tap in order to increase the aeration of the tap-water are excellent improvers of coffee. Some experts say that metal coffee pots make inferior coffee to earthenware or glass pots. I think it's more likely that metal pots are not so thoroughly cleaned before use.

Freshly drawn water, freshly ground coffee and a spotlessly clean pot will give fine coffee, so don't put boiled milk into it. Cold milk is better than boiled milk, but warm milk is better than either.

If you put cream into the coffee it is best to sugar and stir it first. The coffee can then be sipped through the layer of cream. If you add a measure of whisky to the coffee before adding the cream you have a most interesting drink that a smart P.R. man named Irish Coffee, specifying at the same time that the whisky must be his alone.

Coffee is a luxury drink. In many parts of the world it fetches extremely high prices. Treat it like a luxury. Make it carefully, serve it hot and don't waste it by making weak brews.

Instant coffee, although not worth drinking, should be kept in the flavouring cupboard. Use it when making coffee-flavoured sauce, cake, mousse, caramel, frosting or cream.

CIGARS ARE THE END

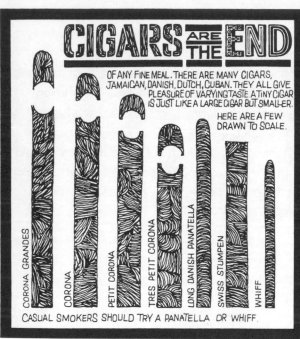

OF ANY FINE MEAL. THERE ARE MANY CIGARS, JAMAICAN, DANISH, DUTCH, CUBAN. THEY ALL GIVE PLEASURE OF VARYING TASTE. A TINY CIGAR IS JUST LIKE A LARGE CIGAR BUT SMALLER.

HERE ARE A FEW DRAWN TO SCALE.

CORONA GRANDES
CORONA
PETIT CORONA
TRES PETIT CORONA
LONG DANISH PANATELLA
SWISS STUMPEN
WHIFF

CASUAL SMOKERS SHOULD TRY A PANATELLA OR WHIFF.

CROSS SECTION:
Various layers may come from different parts of the world.

WRAPPER: Gives bouquet. Green or yellow spots do not affect quality, nor does colour show strength. Often made from Sumatran.

BINDER: Gives the burning quality.

FILLER: This is the important part, the 'meat' of the cigar.

END: will show evenness of rolling (important for drawing.)

SELECTING:

People roll cigars to see if they crackle. THEY ALL DO. Better to select a good cigar merchant.

NEVER ➔ PIERCE IT
CUT IT
very sharp knife

Rotate cigar while holding it firmly.

LIGHTING
HOLD MATCH AWAY

Draw until entire end is well alight.

COLD DEAD ONES taste bitter if relit. If you must relight, remove dead ash first.

BIG BAND *Controversy*
TRY THIS SIMPLE TEST. Smoke half a cigar with band **ON**. Remove band. Does it taste different?

Larousse tells us that professional tasters have to renounce smoking.

Smoking during a meal should be discouraged, but the aroma of cigar smoke at the end of a meal, blending with the aroma of good brandy, gives the host or hostess a fine feeling of complacency.

Good drawing depends upon careful, even filling. Buy cigars which are regular in size, shape and colour, for these are likely to have been best filled.

Uneven burning can usually be traced to wrong preparation. Never pierce the end, because this is an inadequate 'flue' and will give several different troubles at once (e.g. heat and tobacco oil in the mouth), so make a large vent in the end.

Provide a cigar cutter if you can. Don't put the open end in the mouth and light the closed end, for although this gives a good draught, it may come unwrapped.

England is the only place where there is a nonsensical tradition of removing the band. Do as you wish, but don't be upstage about smokers who leave the band on.

1 Never stub a cigar out; it will go out quickly enough.
2 If your cigar goes out before you are finished, relight it immediately. Once it gets cold, it will taste bitter if relit.
3 Don't leave cigar butts in the dining-room overnight. They leave a musty aroma.
4 Lighted candles in a room where cigars are being smoked reduce the smoke and the musty aroma the next day.

Remember that a tiny cigar can be just as good in quality as a large one (or better), and have a few small or slim ones for guests who don't normally smoke cigars.

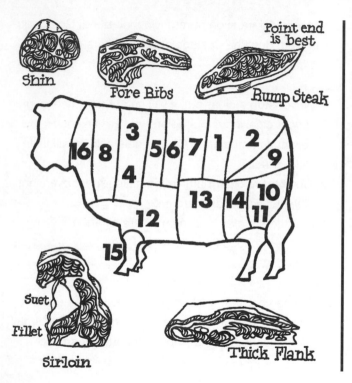

Shin

Fore Ribs

Point end is best

Rump Steak

Suet

Fillet

Sirloin

Thick Flank

BEEF

Sirloin (1) is the king of all joints. Notice how the one shown has the fillet attached to it. The fillet is often served alone. A slice across that Sirloin would be a T-bone steak. Back Ribs (3), Top Ribs (4), Ribs (5), Fore Rib (6) and Wing Rib (7) are all prime-quality roasting cuts from which a steak may be cut. Butchers usually bone these joints and roll them up. Buy them still on the bone to lessen the risk of getting the wrong one or a large chunk of inferior meat artfully inserted into the roll. Meat cooked on the bone gives the best flavour. Rump Steak (2) is never roasted. It is very flavourful but not as soft as fillet. Chuck (8) is top-quality braising beef. A home-killed Chuck steak can even be grilled if well hung. Aitchbone (9) and Topside (10) are good value for braising. Silverside (11), Brisket (12) and Flank (13) are suitable for salting. Choose one and ask the butcher to salt it. Don't buy from his brine-tub, because unsold pieces are often consigned there as a last resort. Top Rump (14) is suitable for stewing or careful braising. Clod (16) is for pies and stews. Shin or Leg (15) is the cheapest and toughest but will give you better flavour than any other cut if you give it at least four hours' cooking. This is the cut for Steak and kidney pudding and also for superb stock or beef tea for invalids. All beef must be well hung or it will be tough.

VEAL

Veal means different things in different countries. In southern Europe it can mean a calf three years old. In England it can be a fourteen-day-old 'bobby'. The latter are particularly nasty. Most prime-quality veal comes from Holland, where calves are slaughtered between

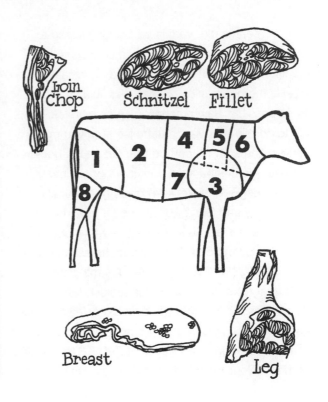

four and six months old. Veal is particularly suited to braising recipes because the covered pot keeps the meat moist. The slice of Fillet (1) called an escalope or Schnitzel is the prime slice of veal. It should be sliced as thin as possible. Few butchers in Britain are skilled enough to do this – or very much else – so you might try yourself. The Loin (2) can be roasted on the bone, or off the bone – leave the kidney inside – or cut into chops. The Best End of Neck (4) gives good cutlets. Middle Neck (5) and Scrag (6) are usually used for stews, terrines or stock, but you might get a piece big enough to braise out of it. The cheapest roasting joint is the Shoulder (3), but if you are careful a rolled and stuffed Breast (7) can be roasted in a slow oven. In some countries the Knuckle (8) is also roasted because it gives those sticky, well-done segments. If you try it, put some strips of pork fat over to protect it. The knuckle gives a rich flavour to stocks and stews or can be cut

up for pies and terrines. All veal stock will go to a jelly, but a calf's foot is sometimes used expressly for this.

LAMB

Don't bother to learn to *recognize* the cuts, but do decide what you want and ask for it by name. Take into account whether meat is frozen, chilled or home-killed. Some cuts of home-killed mutton will be as good as lamb. Mutton is meat from an animal over one year old. It is stronger in flavour than lamb and, providing it is well hung, can be magnificent. The Leg (1) is the prime roasting joint. A mutton leg is often marinaded for a day. The Loin (2) is a roasting joint. Chump chops are cut from the leg end of it. The Shoulder (3) is good for roast but tricky to carve. The Best End of Neck (4) is for cutlets, (5) is Middle and Scrag, used for casseroles and stew. The Breast (6) can be boned,

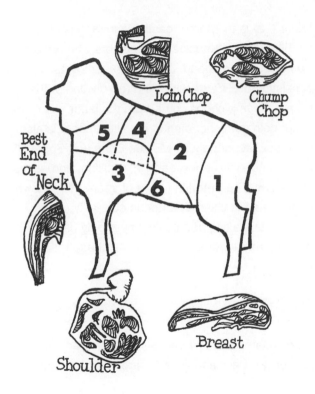

Loin Chop

Chump Chop

Best
End
of
Neck

5 4 3 2 6 1

Shoulder

Breast

stuffed and rolled. Butchers will do this for you but they usually leave far too much fat on it. Remove all the fat you can see and stuff it with a meaty stuffing – rosemary goes well with lamb – for the cheapest cut of all.

For cubes of meat on a skewer Shoulder of mutton or Neck of lamb is the usual choice, although some cooks prefer the much more expensive fillet end of the leg. A thick slice of the fillet end is sometimes grilled, but it goes dry very easily. Tiny sucking lambs – 5–6 weeks old – are often used in French cooking (for instance the leg cooked in pastry). They are called 'Pauillac' lambs.

PORK

Any cut of pork can be roasted and any part can be salted – although the loin almost never is. The Whole

leg (1 + 2) is the prime roasting joint and is often sold as Fillet (1) and Knuckle (2). Butchers who remove the skin are up to no good. Loin is a superb roasting joint consisting of Fore (4) and Hind (3), divided at the kidney. Chump chops come from the latter as in lamb. Tenderloin corresponding to the fillet in beef is also often sold separately. The Blade Bone and Spare Rib (5) give good value for roasting, braising, barbecues and stews. The American style of spare rib – shown dotted – is the classic barbecue cut. Belly (7) is suitable for salting and boiling, but I only use it for dripping and terrines. Hand (6) is a cheap roasting joint.

BACON

Whole Gammon (1), Long Back, Short Back and Oyster (2), Back and Ribs (3) are all super cuts. Top

Back (4), Prime Collar (5), and End Collar (6) are good value as boiling joints. The Fore Hock (7) can be boned and rolled, or split as shown. Streaky Bacon (8 and 11) for rashers; Prime Streaky is best. Flank (10) is for boiling, so is the small lean Gammon Slipper (9). All 'green' bacon – with light rind – is milder than smoked bacon.

ACKNOWLEDGMENTS

Among the people who have been kind to me about the cook strips I must thank Ray Hawkey, Clive Irving and George Seddon, mentors and masters all; the *Observer* – an exemplary employer, changing my words only when I have threatened to topple the Government; John Marshall and Tony Colbert, who have endlessly helped me at the last-minute newspaper needs; Bill Harmer and Howard Lacey (lettering experts); and last but perhaps most important, my readers in England and overseas.

This bound edition presented problems of its own, and without Tom Maschler of Cape, who published it; Isabel Ross who watched over it carefully; the designer, two artists – Roy Castle and Ruth Antonsen – who did the drawings of blender, refrigerator and vegetables; without the person who stocked it, the one who bought it as well as those that borrow it, it would still be something I will do 'one of these days'.

INDEX

317